MEMORY IN PLACE

Locating Colonial Histories and Commemoration

MEMORY IN PLACE

Locating Colonial Histories
and Commemoration

EDITED BY CAMEO DALLEY
AND ASHLEY BARNWELL

ANU PRESS

ANU PRESS

Published by ANU Press
The Australian National University
Canberra ACT 2600, Australia
Email: anupress@anu.edu.au

Available to download for free at press.anu.edu.au

ISBN (print): 9781760466077
ISBN (online): 9781760466084

WorldCat (print): 1393519433
WorldCat (online): 1393505284

DOI: 10.22459/MP.2023

This title is published under a Creative Commons Attribution-NonCommercial-NoDerivatives 4.0 International (CC BY-NC-ND 4.0) licence.

The full licence terms are available at creativecommons.org/licenses/by-nc-nd/4.0/legalcode

Cover design and layout by ANU Press

Cover artwork: Tony Albert, *Rebirth After the Fire*, 2022, acrylic and vintage appropriated fabric on canvas, 300 x 200 cm. Photography: Aaron Anderson.

This book is published under the aegis of the Humanities and Creative Arts editorial board of ANU Press.

This edition © 2023 ANU Press

WARNING: Readers are notified that this publication may contain names or images of deceased persons.

Contents

List of illustrations — vii
Acronyms — xi
Contributors — xiii
Acknowledgements — xix

Memory at scale: Interdisciplinary engagements with Australian histories — 1
   Cameo Dalley and Ashley Barnwell

Part I: History in the landscape archive

1. Matriarch: Reclaiming the mermaid — 27
   Julia Hurst and Karen Maber
2. Spirit of place: The critical case for site visits in the construction of Indigenous Australian histories — 35
   Barry Judd and Katherine Ellinghaus
3. Memory-lines: Ethnographies of colonial violence in Central Australia — 55
   Jason Gibson, Jennifer Green and Joel Perrurle Liddle
4. Tommy Burns and the challenge of truth-telling on the pastoral frontier in the Gulf Country of northern Australia — 85
   Richard Martin and Fred Pascoe
5. Searching for Retribution Camp — 105
   Billy Griffiths
6. The South Australian frontier and its legacies: Remembering and representing the Mount Bryan murders — 117
   Skye Krichauff

Part II: Remembering and forgetting in heritage spaces

7. A stone in the park of empire: Reclaiming First Nations space through burial — 143
   Alexandra Roginski

8. Place as archive: The heritage of children's homes and the legacies of colonial violence   167
   Sarah Hayes, Steven Cooke, Edwina Kay and Antony Catrice
9. Engaging communities in archives and museums   199
   Imelda Miller, Olivia Robinson and Cameo Dalley
10. History by committee: Representing the 'facts' of settler colonialism in a local historical society museum   219
    Cameo Dalley and Ashley Barnwell
11. Displaying frontier violence at the Australian War Memorial   247
    Thomas J. Rogers
12. Blue sky mining and *Sweet Country*: Is it too soon to commemorate colonial violence?   265
    Chris Healy

Afterword: Re-membering history at our current juncture   289
Yin Paradies

Index   297

List of illustrations

Figure 2.1. The importance of place. Lorna and Kat at the Alice Springs Old Lutheran Church Living History Collection, 7 May 2021.   41

Figure 2.2. Intimacy and distance at Rodinga Siding, May 2020.   43

Figure 2.3. Being here matters. Walking back from Lorna showing me where Albrecht used to camp at Titjikala, May 2020.   45

Figures 2.4 and 2.5. Relationality and the servitude of forging ethical research relationships.   48

Figure 3.1. Map of the Central Australian region, showing key places mentioned in text.   57

Figure 3.2. At the Coniston memorial site: Lesley Stafford, Jason Gibson and Huckitta Lynch, 2008.   62

Figure 3.3. The memorial at Athimpelengkwe (Baxters Well) in 2008.   64

Figure 3.4. The late Tommy Thompson Kngwarraye speaking at the Coniston Memorial event, 2003.   65

Figure 3.5. Ruins at Itarlentye (Blackfellows Bones Bore).   67

Figure 3.6. Ken Tilmouth and child at Amwely, Alcoota Station, July 1995.   69

Figure 4.1. Fred Pascoe (far right) with Carpentaria Land Council Chairperson Murrandoo Yanner and Kurtjar Elders Joseph Rainbow (the named applicant on the Kurtjar native title claim) and Warren Beasley (a Kurtjar speaker and senior knowledge holder) during a break in the hearing of the Kurtjar people's native title claim at Delta Downs, 29 August 2019.   91

Figure 4.2. The south-east Gulf Country, showing Normanton and Delta Downs Station.   92

Figure 4.3. Members of the Kurtjar people examine the area near Tommy Burns's grave at Dorunda, 21 June 2016. From left: Cedric Burns, Irene Burns, Joseph Rainbow, Lance Rapson.   95

Figure 5.1. Retribution Camp boab.   105

Figure 5.2. The author at Retribution Camp boab. 106

Figure 7.1. Signage in the Domain parkland. 145

Figure 7.2. Kings Domain Resting Place. 145

Figure 8.1. Cricket stumps painted on an exterior brick wall at the former Kildonan/Allambie Children's Home. 168

Figure 8.2. Left: Plan of the Allambie site, 1962, showing location of main buildings. Right: Aerial photograph of the current Deakin University campus. 170

Figure 8.3a. Print by Hal Thorpe of a 'gypsy' caravan, gifted to the Children's Health Bureau by Dr Apderham in October 1934. 180

Figure 8.3b. Label on the back of Figure 8.3a. 180

Figure 8.4. Floral paintings. 181

Figure 8.5. 'Space Age' poster. 182

Figure 8.6. Wicker basket full of brightly coloured key tags and keys. 183

Figure 8.7. Child-sized plastic chair. 184

Figure 8.8. Plinth in laundry. 184

Figure 8.9a. Laundry chutes. 185

Figure 8.9b. Laundry chutes. 185

Figure 8.10a. Laundry trolleys. 186

Figure 8.10b. Laundry trolleys. 186

Figure 8.11. Laundry shelving. 187

Figure 8.12. Graffito on laundry floor. 187

Figure 8.13. Plastic teddy bears. 189

Figure 8.14. 'CASSIA HEATH' graffito. 189

Figure 8.15. Bundle of children's pyjamas. 190

Figure 8.16. Child's sweatshirt. 191

Figure 9.1. South Sea Islander woman planting sugar cane in a field. 208

Figure 9.2. Australian South Sea Islander community looking at the petition of 1904, when South Sea Islanders were campaigning for exemptions from the deportation. 210

Figure 9.3. 'White Gloves Experience' at the opening of *Plantation Voices: Contemporary Conversations with Australian South Sea Islanders*, State Library of Queensland, 16 February 2019. 214

LIST OF ILLUSTRATIONS

Figure 9.4. Olivia Robinson, Cameo Dalley and Imelda Miller at the State Library of Queensland, 2021.	217
Figure 10.1. Wyndham Historical Society Museum.	225
Figure 10.2. Displays in the front room at the Wyndham Historical Society Museum.	227
Figure 10.3. Objects on display in the middle room at the Wyndham Historical Society Museum.	228
Figure 12.1. Hepburn Memorial.	266
Figure 12.2. Plaque commemorating Western Australians who have died from asbestos-related diseases.	271
Figure 12.3. Mine tailings, Wittenoom, Western Australia.	274
Figure 12.4. Invitation to the 2020 Tunnerminnerwait and Maulboyheenner Commemoration Committee.	277

Acronyms

ADSA	Asbestos Diseases Society of Australia
ARC	Australian Research Council
AWM	Australian War Memorial
DECRA	Discovery Early Career Researcher Award
NAIDOC	National Aborigines and Islanders Day Observance Committee
PKKP	Puutu Kunti Kurrama and Pinikura
PROV	Public Record Office Victoria
QPAC	Queensland Performing Arts Complex
QSA	Queensland State Archives
RSL	Returned Servicemen's League
VALS	Victorian Aboriginal Legal Service

Contributors

Ashley Barnwell is a senior lecturer in sociology at the University of Melbourne. She is interested in sociological aspects of emotions, memory and narrative, and the role of life writing, archives and literature in sociological research. She is an ARC DECRA fellow working on the project 'Family Secrets, National Silences: Intergenerational Memory in Settler Colonial Australia'. This project aims to investigate the inherited family secrets, stories and memories that inform Australians' understandings of colonial history. Ashley publishes across sociology, history and literary studies, and is co-author of the book *Reckoning with the Past* (with Joseph Cummins).

Antony Catrice is the university archivist at Deakin University and manages a substantial archive that includes material on Kildonan and Allambie. He also has honorary positions working on private archives, and has previously published and presented on topics such as archival science, pre cinema technologies and built heritage.

Steven Cooke is an associate professor of cultural heritage and museum studies at the School of Humanities and Social Science, Alfred Deakin Institute for Citizenship and Globalisation, Deakin University. He is a cultural and historical geographer, and an expert on issues related to heritage, memory and identity, particularly the spatialities of difficult histories. Steven spent five years in higher education in the UK, first as a research fellow at the University of Stirling, then as a lecturer in historical and cultural geography at the University of Hull. In 2002, he moved to Australia and worked in high-level management positions in some of Victoria's most significant places, including the Melbourne Maritime Museum – home of *Polly Woodside* and the Shrine of Remembrance. He was appointed to the International Holocaust Remembrance Alliance by the Australian Government's Department of Foreign Affairs and Trade in 2015, where he sits on the Memorials and Museums Working Group.

Cameo Dalley is a settler descendant and anthropologist. Her multidisciplinary research has explored Indigenous identities, belonging in contemporary Australia, native title, pastoral economies and contemporary agribusiness. She maintains research relationships with Lardil, Yangkaal and Kaiadilt peoples in the Wellesley Islands, Gulf of Carpentaria, and groups in the Kimberley region of Western Australia. Her first book *What Now: Everyday Endurance and Social Intensity in an Australian Aboriginal Community* (2021) was published by Berghahn. She has held academic appointments at The Australian National University, Deakin University and the University of Melbourne, where she is a senior lecturer in the Indigenous studies program. She is a board member of the *Journal of Australian Studies* and the director of the Women in Native Title Anthropology Project, funded by the Attorney-General's Department.

Katherine Ellinghaus is an associate professor of history at La Trobe University, where she teaches Australian and Indigenous history. She is the author of *Taking Assimilation to Heart: Marriages of White Women and Indigenous Men in the United States and Australia, 1887–1937* (University of Nebraska Press, 2006) and *Blood Will Tell: Native Americans and Assimilation Policy* (University of Nebraska Press, 2017). She writes and researches in the areas of settler-colonial history, transnational and comparative history, assimilation policies, and the social and cultural history of the United States and Australia.

Jason Gibson has worked extensively with Aboriginal custodians throughout Australia on history, museum and heritage-related projects for close to two decades. His book *Ceremony Men: Making Ethnography and the Return of the Strehlow Collection* (SUNY Press, 2020) was awarded the Council of Museum Anthropology book prize and the Australian Historical Associations' WK Hancock Prize. Jason is an ARC DECRA fellow and lecturer in cultural heritage and museum studies at Deakin University. His research examines the afterlives of returned/repatriated Aboriginal cultural collections, the history of Australian Aboriginal anthropology and the sociocultural histories of Arandic peoples in Central Australia.

Jennifer Green is an honorary fellow in the School of Languages and Linguistics at the University of Melbourne. For over four decades, Green has worked with Indigenous people in central and northern Australia documenting spoken and signed languages, cultural history, art, social organisation and connections to Country. She has been engaged as a researcher on both land claims and native title claims in the Central

Australian region. Her doctoral research pioneered methods for the recording and analysis of sand stories and other forms of multimodal verbal art. Green has also participated in projects investigating archival practices and linguistic research ethics.

Billy Griffiths is a historian and DECRA fellow at the Alfred Deakin Institute, Deakin University. His latest book, *Deep Time Dreaming: Uncovering Ancient Australia* (Black Inc., 2018), won the Felicia A Holton Book Award, the Ernest Scott Prize, the John Mulvaney Book Award, the Douglas Stewart Prize for Non-Fiction and the 2019 Book of the Year at the NSW Premier's Literary Awards. He is the recipient of the 2020 Max Crawford Medal from the Australian Academy of the Humanities and serves as the deputy chair of *Australian Book Review*.

Sarah Hayes is a senior research fellow in the People, Place, Heritage stream at the Alfred Deakin Institute for Citizenship and Globalisation, Deakin University. As an urban archaeologist, her primary focus is on the role possessions play in quality of life and social mobility, and in turn opportunity, inequality and wastefulness. She also conducts research into the material culture of children's institutions. She is an ARC DECRA recipient and honorary associate at Museums Victoria.

Chris Healy teaches cultural studies at the University of Melbourne. His publications include *Forgetting Aborigines* (2008), *Assembling Culture* (co-edited with Tony Bennett, 2011) and *Reading the Country: 30 Years On* (co-edited with Philip Morrissey, 2018). Along with Romaine Moreton and Therese Davis, in 2019 he produced the major knowledge-sharing website, AIF-TV Research (aiftv-research.net/), which is concerned with Australian Indigenous film and television. He is currently completing a book called *Travelling Television*, and he working with Belinda Smaill and Therese Davis on the ARCH Discovery Project, 'Remaking the Australian Environment through Documentary Film and Television'.

Julia Hurst is deputy director of the Australian Centre at the University of Melbourne and a lecturer in Aboriginal and Torres Strait Islander history. She completed a PhD at The Australian National University in Aboriginal history. Her Indigenous heritage crosses Dharawal and Darug land. Her research explores fundamental questions of Australian Aboriginal identity in twenty-first-century Australia. She has a Masters of Urban Planning and a Bachelor of Arts, and has presented her research in local and international forums. She has worked across academia, the arts and corporate sectors.

Barry Judd is pro vice-chancellor (Indigenous) and director of the Indigenous Studies Program in the School of Culture and Communication at the University of Melbourne. Professor Judd is a member of the Australian Institute for Aboriginal and Torres Strait Islander Studies. He was a foundation chief investigator of the National Indigenous Research and Knowledges Network and a foundation editor of *ab-Original: Journal of Indigenous Studies and First Nations and First Peoples' Cultures*. He holds an MA in public policy and a PhD in Australian Indigenous studies. He has worked in support of Indigenous activity in Australian higher education for over 30 years in both professional staff and academic roles. He is widely published and holds several current ARC research grants.

Edwina Kay is a historical archaeologist and research assistant at the Alfred Deakin Institute for Citizenship and Globalisation, Deakin University. She has a particular interest in the built fabric and spaces of institutions for women and children, and the role these institutions have played in our society.

Skye Krichauff is an ethno-historian and oral historian who is interested in colonial cross-cultural relations, the relationship between history and memory, and how societies live with historical injustices (in particular, how Australians live with the enduring legacies of colonialism). She has worked as a history researcher for an Aboriginal community organisation and as an expert ethno-historian for South Australian Native Title Services. Skye is currently employed as an ARC research fellow on the linkage project 'The South Australian Frontier and its Legacies'. She co-edits *Studies in Oral History* (the journal of the Australian Oral History Association).

Joel Perrurle Liddle is an Arrernte man with family ties to the Mparntwe/Tyuretye, Irlpme and Uremerne traditional estates in Central Australia. His mother's family are non-Indigenous and first arrived in Victoria in 1853. His research focuses on cultural continuity in Central Australia and the role of traditional knowledge acquisition in enhancing identity and mental health outcomes. He examines the utility of archival ethnographic collections and their value in nurturing, maintaining and repatriating traditional knowledges to enhance the health and wellbeing of Indigenous people. Over the last decade, he has worked in a variety of engagement roles throughout remote Australia.

Karen Maber is an artist and Dharug Keeping Place Officer within City of Parramatta's PHIVE civic, cultural and arts hub. She is responsible for the operation of the Dharug Keeping Place, custodial care of Dharug cultural material, community engagement and educational programming. Karen is a Cabrogal woman, born and raised on the coastal waterways of her ancestors in Sydney's south on unceded Dharug land with family ties to Wadi Wadi, Dharawal Country. Her position explores and celebrates the relationships between people, place, spirituality, history and emotion. Her passion for storytelling encourages personal and collective journeys of healing. Karen has a Bachelor of Arts with distinction from the University of New South Wales and has presented her stories both locally and internationally.

Richard Martin is a senior lecturer in anthropology at the University of Queensland. He has published a range of scholarly articles based on anthropological research with Aboriginal people around Australia, as well as the book *The Gulf Country: The Story of People and Place in Outback Queensland* (Allen & Unwin, 2019). He has also given evidence in the Federal Court of Australia in relation to numerous Indigenous native title claims, including in the Kurtjar people's native title claim.

Imelda Miller is the curator, First Nations Cultures, at the Queensland Museum. She works with material culture and archival collections inside and outside of traditional museum environments and spaces to create access to collections for communities. Her collaborative curatorial practice incorporates a combination of cultural practices, community engagement and community-led approaches to research and project development. Primarily interested in material culture in museums and archives, Miller enjoys working with communities to re-image these collections to be inclusive of more hidden narratives. Her Australian South Sea Islander heritage drives her passion in creating awareness about Australian South Sea Islander history, heritage and identity.

Yin Paradies is a Wakaya man and chair in race relations at Deakin University. He conducts research on the health, social and economic effects of racism as well as anti-racism theory, policy and practice. He also teaches and undertakes research in Indigenous knowledges and decolonisation. Yin Paradies is a radical anarchist scholar and ecological activist committed to interrupting the devastating impacts of modern societies. He seeks meaningful mutuality of becoming and embodied kinship with life through transformed ways of knowing, being and doing grounded in wisdom, humility, respect, generosity, down-shifted collective sufficiency, voluntary simplicity, frugality, direct participation and radical localisation.

Fred Pascoe is a Kurtjar man from the Gulf Country. He was a Carpentaria shire councillor from 1997 to 2008, the Carpentaria shire mayor from 2009 to 2016 and the chief executive officer of the Bynoe Community Advancement Cooperative Society Limited from 2005 to 2020. He is currently director of the Morr Morr (Delta Downs) Pastoral Company and chair of the Aboriginal Development Benefit Trust.

Olivia Robinson works in cultural heritage and community engagement across museums and libraries. She is a skilled manager, strategist, curator, creator, researcher and facilitator. Leading collection engagement in 'Queensland Memory' at State Library of Queensland, she enjoys connecting communities with collections through storytelling and embracing diversity in the retelling of history. She is a former Queensland-Smithsonian fellow and has a Bachelor of Arts (history) and a Master of Business (public relations). She is a proud Bidjara woman whose traditional Country is in south-west Queensland.

Thomas J. Rogers is a historian in the Strategic and Defence Studies Centre at The Australian National University. He worked as a historian at the Australian War Memorial for nearly six years. His research interests include colonial Australian and British Empire history, the South African (Boer) War, World War I, Indigenous history and frontier conflict. He is the author of *The Civilisation of Port Phillip: Settler Ideology, Violence, and Rhetorical Possession* (2018), which considers the early years of British settlement in the state of Victoria and the relationships between settler rhetoric and frontier violence.

Alexandra Roginski gained a PhD at The Australian National University in 2019. She is a historian, writer and consultant based in Melbourne, on Wurundjeri Country, whose work focuses on practices and ideas of the body, past and present, including in terms of the repatriation of ancestral remains. She is the author of *Science and Power in the Nineteenth-Century Tasman World: Popular Phrenology in Australia and Aotearoa New Zealand* (Cambridge University Press, 2023) and *The Hanged Man and the Body Thief: Finding Lives in a Museum Mystery* (Monash University Publishing, 2015). She is a visiting fellow at Deakin University and the State Library of New South Wales.

Acknowledgements

The seeds of this book project began in a conference paper presented at the 2019 Oral History Association conference in Brisbane with Sana Nakata. We thank Sana for her support in developing these ideas about scale and interdisciplinarity. Many of the chapters in this edited collection were presented at a workshop that we co-convened and held on Zoom in 2020. We also thank Joan Beaumont, Shino Konishi, Sana Nakata, Timothy Neale, Tim Rowse and Andrea Witcomb for their generous contributions to the workshop and feedback on chapters. Tim Rowse was particularly generous in providing feedback on individual chapters, especially for early career authors. Ben Wilson at ANU Press and Rani Kerin, who copyedited the final manuscript, have been supportive and invaluable. We offer special thanks to the contributors for their persistence through the difficult working conditions of the pandemic and lockdowns. We thank Tony Albert for generously allowing us to use his beautiful artwork, *Rebirth After the Fire*, as the cover image for this book.

Memory at scale: Interdisciplinary engagements with Australian histories

Cameo Dalley and Ashley Barnwell

Tracks and memories
Across the land
Across the country
Hold their place

> Extract from the poem 'Rain Clouds' Arrival' by Charmaine Papertalk Green. Reproduced from *False Claims of Colonial Thieves* by Charmaine Papertalk Green & John Kinsella, Magabala Books (2018).

Memory, scale and voice

The nation-state is often the container for conversations about how to remember and commemorate aspects of Australia's history. In Australian memory studies, much of the research on settler colonialism, Indigenous–settler relations and colonial forgetting focuses on the national level. Cutting through this tendency, chapters in this collection focus on the local level, on places and landscapes where the potency of history and memory come together in lived relations that resonate across generations. While official national and state influences are still a critical concern, many of the essays turn to specific landscapes, biographical accounts or family histories to look at how memory plays out on a more intimate scale. The authors locate us in particular places: a museum, a beach, a tree, a sign, a memorial stone, a digital photograph, the ruin of a children's home. In many of these cases, people grapple with the same challenge that faces the nation: how to remember what has been forgotten, especially violent and traumatic histories. Yet, the specificities of place and personal histories make it difficult to fall back on the generalising and mythologising strategies that underpin settler-national memories. In some places, national memory still looms large, particularly in state-funded institutions, where the work of curators consists of navigating channels for particular pieces of memory to speak beyond the well-worn mythos of white settlement that has so often served as the default in cultural institutions. This can mean taking leave of the usual houses of history – archives, books, universities – and rethinking where it is that histories are told and commemorative practices performed, and by whom.

Recently, in cultural institutions and beyond, there has been renewed emphasis on representing accounts of discordant and/or violent histories, even if these accounts are tense, uncomfortable and/or force a reckoning with elements of history that some would prefer to deny, hide, whitewash or forget. Exhibitions such as the National Gallery of Victoria's *Colony* and *Colony: Frontier Wars* (2018) and the Australian Museum's *Unsettled* (McBride & Smith, 2021) have represented the conflict and violence at Australia's foundations and have made a central place for Indigenous artists and storytellers to tell their own histories and counter the colonial script. Co-curator of *Unsettled*, Mariko Smith (McBride & Smith, 2021, p. 10), positioned the exhibition as a place of truth-telling about Australia's history, noting that 'it is time we stop pretending that meaningful change can happen in a system that is grounded in denial'. This shift is noted in literature on both museums and cultural heritage, where major venues or exhibitions have attempted to address histories of conflict, and where sites of trauma and violence have been studied as places for memorialisation, or sometimes 'dark tourism' and education. As William Logan and Keir Reeves (2008, p. 12) argue in *Places of Pain and Shame: Dealing with 'Difficult Heritage'*, places that have unsettling histories:

> are now being regarded as 'heritage sites', a far cry from the view of heritage that prevailed a generation ago, when we were almost entirely concerned with protecting the great and beautiful creations of the past: reflections of the creative genius of humanity rather than the reverse – the destructive and cruel side of history.

In this volume, many of the chapters explore ethical and practical tensions about how memory operates in places where injustice has occurred, and where there are complex reasons for Indigenous and non-Indigenous people to both remember and/or forget, and to share and/or protect knowledge and memories of the past. These are crucial issues to consider as researchers work with the history of the landscape archive, engage with memories of place, and learn from the knowledge of Traditional Owners in processes of truth-telling and collaboration. Chapters here attend to histories of place and also how relations to place are being reclaimed, practised and transformed in the present.

Memory in Place is further underpinned by a set of methodological considerations. The multidisciplinary nature of the chapters in this collection highlights the ways that different scholarly lenses attend to specific scales and registers. History, anthropology, cultural heritage and museum studies are disciplines that have engaged with questions of national memory and history, but each have embedded within them different kinds of attentiveness to context. This attention to detail and locatedness has focused thinking about history to show its workings and centre issues of both memory and place in ways that can disrupt and inform macro approaches. Nonetheless, our aim is not to simply champion localised perspectives. There are also risks, such as the potential generalising or instrumentalising of specific cases, as well as the difficulty of writing critically about a place or set of relations when a scholar is either not embedded or, conversely, very closely situated in the context that they write about. One example is Myall Creek, New South Wales, the site of an infamous massacre of 28 Wirrayaraay people in 1883. Myall Creek is often used to exemplify historical colonial violence, partly because the details of the event became well known through the trials and hangings of at least some of the colonial perpetrators. However, historian Bronwyn Batten (2009, p. 93) has cautioned against using the site as representative at a national scale, given the 'danger that the general may override the specific'. Batten emphasises:

> It is important that the promotion of the Myall Creek site continues to be carried out with the support of the descendants of the Aboriginal people so they can ensure the local story of their ancestors is not lost at the expense of establishing a national narrative. (p. 94)

Decisions about which stories to tell can also be limited by the pragmatic concerns of specific institutional environments such as museums, archives, libraries and so on. These spaces, which have for so long privileged particular voices and types of evidence, grapple with the expectation of presenting straightforward accounts of history to the public, where ambiguous or fragmentary accounts may be more true to the material at hand. More localised memory practices therefore also present a range of ethical and practical issues (Furniss, 2001; Prowse, 2015).

In this essay, we set out some of the conversations that inform and connect the chapters, which are anchored within Australia's settler-colonial context, and the question of how we remember the profound harms of colonialism. Within this collection the authors look in less conventional places for voices from the past. History is not merely held in archives waiting to be released, and the diversity of disciplinary approaches to rethinking where remembering takes place evokes the everyday presence of memory, including in settings where events are still actively in living memory. It is primarily within this frame – seeing history beyond the archive – that the majority of contributions to this volume are couched. The chapters offer a rich space to further explore questions about how the work of remembering and forgetting can be done at different scales, about what is lost or gained in zooming into history as it is lived and/or displayed in place, and about how different scales of memory work together.

In Australia, it has been the case that projects produced at a macro scale have the potential to capture the greater public's attention in a particular way. The most notable example of this in recent times has been *Colonial Frontier Massacres in Australia, 1788–1930* (referred to as the 'Massacre Project'), undertaken by Australian historian Lyndall Ryan and a team of researchers at the University of Newcastle (Ryan et al., 2018). Professor Ryan and her team's work is referred to in several chapters in this collection. The team's public-facing output has been an interactive map of Australia that represents instances of historical violence against Indigenous people. The map relies heavily on pre-existing, formally recorded instances of violence that are corroborated with archival records. Though drawing broadly from different kinds of records, the map tends to privilege non-Indigenous accounts over those of Indigenous oral history or descendant accounts. The necessity to set parameters for input into the map creates some provoking challenges for thinking about the definitional limits on 'massacre' and experiences of violence more generally. For example, as set by the project team, the minimum threshold for inclusion in the map is evidence for 'the deliberate and unlawful killing of six or more undefended people in one operation'. As with many of the chapters featured in this collection, moving between different sources of information – archival, oral history, written and secondary – enriches but also complicates what might otherwise be perceived as straightforward accounts of history.

This is because, somewhat inevitably, the writer ends up positioned as an arbiter. Nonetheless, the cumulative weight of evidence and information contained in the map has been an incredibly useful tool in communicating to the general public where significant gaps remain in awareness about frontier violence.

The contributors to this collection come to these questions from a range of backgrounds and disciplines, each with their own embedded trajectories of representation and engagement with Indigenous people, resulting in a diversity of perspectives and experiences that offer rich insight. There is a powerful need to bring more fully to light the role that Indigenous people have played in Australia's history and to more accurately account for settler and settler-descendant violence. Yet, conversely, it has been the assumed mantle of this history, by non-Indigenous people as narrators, that has exacerbated the erasure of Indigenous people and their voices. The issue of who narrates history is not straightforward. As memory studies scholars Katharine Hodgkin and Susannah Radstone (2006, p. 1) point out in their edited monograph *Memory, History, Nation*:

> The focus of contestation, then, is very often not conflicting accounts of what actually happened in the past so much as a question of who or what is entitled to speak for that past in the present.

Many such concerns about narration are broadly germane to this area of research, and Indigenous scholars have been at the forefront of highlighting these issues. Evelyn Araluen (2019), Shino Konishi (2019) and Jeanine Leane (2014), for example, have each reflected on the damage wrought by non-Indigenous people attempting to narrate Indigenous experiences of history. As acclaimed novelist and Waanyi Aboriginal scholar Alexis Wright (2016, p. 59) points out, this damage reflects pre-existing power imbalances that affect not only the content of history, but also the *way* in which stories are told:

> When it comes to how stories are being told, supposedly on our behalf, or for our interest or supposed good, it has never been a level playing field. We do not get much of a chance to say what is right or wrong about the stories told on our behalf – which stories are told or how they are told.

What Indigenous scholars have brought to the fore is a distinction between history as a product populated by facts on the one hand, and history as a process in which individuals and groups navigate what might be included and excluded on the other. When history is thought of as a process in which multiple people or groups of people come together to discuss and interpret memories, the mode of storytelling becomes itself part of the negotiation. Among the chapters in this collection – from both Indigenous and non-Indigenous authors – are a range of approaches to grappling with these relationships. This book joins an international conversation about the politics of memory and commemoration in other settler-colonial countries including Canada, New Zealand and North America (Black, 2020; Caldwell & Leroux, 2019; Chazan & Cole, 2020; Manning, 2018; O'Malley & Kidman, 2018; Rosenberg et al., 2010).

Truth-telling and the local

Calls for truth-telling have become de rigeur in the arts and social sciences over the last decade, stimulated by discussions and activities that were driven by Indigenous peoples through the *Uluru Statement from the Heart*. Following a series of 'dialogues' held in cities and regional towns across Australia, a large gathering of delegates from First Nations groups was held at the Aboriginal community of Mutujulu, in the shadow of Uluru, in 2017. The subsequent release of the *Statement* began a remarkably successful tour to secure public and political support. This support reflected the mandate of the *Statement* itself, which was signed by 240 Indigenous people who had been part of the gathering at Mutujulu. The success of the campaign was partly due to its charismatic advocate and leader, Kaurareg Aboriginal and Kalkalgal, Erubamle Torres Strait Islander man Thomas Mayo, who had previously been an Australian Workers' Union representative. Mayo partnered with locally prominent Indigenous people across Australia to tour not only the ideas contained in the *Statement*, but also a physical version of the document, to universities, schools, research organisations and public think tanks. Travelling with the *Statement* communicated the importance of the sense of place encapsulated in the document and the experience of those who were fundamental to its creation; at the same time, it generated a sense of communally held memory of place, which went some way towards particularising the *Statement* as a national document. The then federal government did not contest this aspect of the document; rather, it inaccurately represented it, suggesting that the document contained a proposition for Indigenous people to form a 'third tier of government'. This diverted attention from other aspects of the document, such as its call upon government to take an active role in facilitating historical truth-telling.

While the nation has an important role to play in accounting for dispossession, and for making concrete policy and structural change, the parallel uptake of truth-telling in local settings and communities has been powerful in destabilising generic or reductive understandings of history. The Monument Australia (n.d.) database shows an increasing number of local memorials and monuments commemorating frontier conflict. And, as Jack Latimore (2019) has noted, in the 'last two decades some community-driven memorials to Aboriginal resistance leaders have appeared'. Genevieve Grieves and Amy Spiers (2021) have also documented the practice of creating counter-monuments, often through artistic practice. Similarly, where the Australian Government lags, local councils have taken the lead in making changes to commemoration practices, such as not hosting celebratory Australia Day activities (Busbridge, 2021). Indeed, Mark Chou and Rachel Busbridge (2019) have observed that much more robust discussions about changing the date of Australia Day are happening in local councils, making 'local government a key culture war battleground'. Despite a lack of action by the settler state and a suggestion that Australians are not ready for truth-telling, some settler descendants and families are actively engaging with their own histories, seeking to understand, interrogate and position themselves and their ancestors within violent and oppressive histories (e.g. Dalley, 2021; Krichauff, 2017; McCabe, 2017). Though once seen as a benign exploration into the lives of one's ancestors, the work of family history may increasingly include interaction with traumatic pasts and reckonings with inherited family silences (Barnwell, 2021; Russell, 2002; Travis Penangke & Haskins, 2021). Memorial events centred around particular historic events, such as the Coniston and Myall Creek massacres, have been organised by working committees that include members of both Aboriginal and settler families in the area. In both cases, descendants of victim-survivors have sought to educate the public about the impacts of frontier violence on families in the present, and descendants of perpetrators have offered apologies on behalf of their ancestors. As these select examples of locally based initiatives demonstrate, important memory work is being done in arenas that do not receive the same level of attention as national debates about history. Attention to these levels of history-making is a feature of this collection.

Memory and evidence

Memory and place continue to be defining concepts in the understanding of Australian history and, perhaps most importantly, in accounting for violence that European settlers perpetrated against Aboriginal and Torres Strait Islander peoples. Institutions that depict history still often have complicated relationships with representing memory and place, focusing instead on assembling accounts of history that rely, for the most part, on archival and documentary evidence. Indigenous scholars and practitioners have questioned the ongoing dominance of non-Indigenous storytelling and, as a response, scholars and institutions are increasingly rethinking the kinds of stories that count as history. Memory institutions are also being challenged to review their assumptions about what constitutes historical evidence and why, as well as their complicity in the collection and display of materials that, when not explicitly racist, speak to outdated understandings of what makes up Australian identity and omit critical takes on the notion of collective or national identity. There are traditions to what museums, at various scales, have collected – mostly documents and artefacts – to be stored and displayed inside exhibition rooms. Indigenous archivists have turned the lens back on archives themselves, as Nathan Sentance (2019) writes:

> Archives are meant to hold the memory of Australia, but whose memory? The history these official archives preserve and tell is funded, collected, configured, curated, and often created by the colonial settler state. As such, they reflect the state's values and ideology. This is the power that the archives wield: they can turn ideology into history, opinion into fact. Archives are unreliable witnesses.

Projects looking at the continuing trauma involved in colonial record provision (Harkin, 2018; McKemmish et al., 2011; O'Neill, 2016), the need to revise deficit narratives (Barrowcliffe, 2021), and the exclusion or demotion of oral history (Scott & Brown, 2005) have drawn attention to the re-colonising function of current historiographic conventions.

In response to this important critique, curators are finding ways to bring different forms of history and memory into exhibition spaces, and increasingly scholars are also citing less conventional sources of memory. As Billy Griffiths writes in this volume:

> The process of truth-telling called for in the *Uluru Statement from the Heart* demands that historians make space for other forms of evidence. It calls for a reckoning with the culture of the frontier, not just individual events. It asks Australians to listen to the testimony of survivors.

Richard Martin and Fred Pascoe's contribution to this volume also speaks to history outside the archive, a pursuit they promote and model. As Martin and Pascoe explain:

> Our account of Tommy Burns's life and death differs from this and related histories by rejecting the assertion that 'the whole truth' can be 'uncovered' in the archive and repatriated to Aboriginal people … [o]ur discussion of Fred's story about his great-grandfather Tommy Burns indicates that histories of colonisation cannot begin and end in the archive but must engage in dialogue and negotiation with Aboriginal people.

Jason Gibson, Jennifer Green and Joel Perrurle Liddle likewise learn from histories beyond the archive, tracing spoken language as a living palimpsest of change. In each chapter of this volume the question of what historical evidence is and where it can be found is a core concern.

While the contributions here are interdisciplinary and draw out the sometimes lesser-known conversations about commemoration in disciplines beyond history, we acknowledge the pivotal work done by historians in arguing for memory and oral history to be considered valuable and legitimate as historical evidence (Barker, 2008; Darian-Smith & Hamilton, 1994; Johnson, 2005; Kennedy & Nugent, 2016; Reid & Paisley, 2017). Likewise, scholars from various disciplines have considered the role of photography, literature and performance as sites of memory and history (Aird et al., 2021; Edmonds, 2016; Lydon, 2014; Schlunke, 2013), and work has been done to question whose memories and perspectives are included in remembrance (Curthoys, 2004; Konishi, 2019; Nugent, 2013). Readers can already find detailed histories of Indigenous–settler relations in specific locales, sometimes drawing particularly on Indigenous oral history (Blake, 2001; Davis & Heath, 2021; Haebich, 1992; Schlunke, 2010; Lewis, 2012; Shellam, 2020). Building on this invaluable research, this collection demonstrates how the field of memory studies benefits from further attention to the question of scale, and how different disciplines locate case studies and analysis in their attention to memory and commemorative practices.

History in practice and in the present

The interdisciplinary authors in this collection come from various disciplines, such as archaeology, linguistics, history, anthropology, sociology and cultural studies, and include curatorial and museum practitioners and community members. All are engaged with practices of history-making and remembering in place, but crucially in ways that inform how we address erasures and inequalities in the present. In this light, the concept of commemoration is apt in highlighting the *doing* of history – and the very present complicities in keeping particular accounts of the past in play or otherwise refiguring what is remembered. Edward Casey argues that commemoration entails participation, and that history is changed or preserved through the active practice of remembrance, ritual and repeated actions in place. He links commemoration with 'place memory' and 'body memory', marking commemoration as a material way of remembering and a process by which memory is intensified and renews its purchase going forward (Casey, 2000, p. 253). Pierre Nora's influential conception of 'sites of memory' also emphasises ritual as much as material monuments in public rememberings:

> Memory is attached to 'sites' that are concrete and physical – the burial places, cathedrals, battlefields that embody tangible notions of the past – as well as to 'sites' that are non-material – the celebrations, spectacles and rituals that provide an aura of the past. (Hoelscher & Alderman, 2004, p. 351)

While our direction speaks into existing, canonical discussions within memory studies, another aim of this collection is to step away from this framework, somewhat, and to let thinking about memory be informed by the specific places that form the focus of each chapter, as well as the questions that the people who live in these places reckon with in daily life.

While much of the major theoretical work in memory studies is concentrated around European experiences, foremost the Holocaust and the trauma felt in subsequent generations, there is increasingly a turn towards considering contexts and time frames beyond Europe (DeLugan, 2021; Rothberg, 2009). This collection creates a space for readers to rethink the primarily Europe-focused terms by which such theory has conceived of the relation between memory and place. In some cases, ideas of memory have been tied to a progress narrative in which social change slides on a scale from agrarian to modern life, and the conditions of memory-making become increasingly fragmented and divorced from origins (Connerton, 2009; Halbwachs, 1992; cf. Hobsbawm & Ranger, 1983; Misztal, 2003; Nora, 1989). Some of these ideas may still be useful when translated to a settler-colonial context, but others risk reifying imperial assumptions about place and time, and the nature of history. This has been noted by several scholars working in the Australian context seeking to develop less Eurocentric notions of remembrance and to ground memory in specific engagements with place (Collins et al., 2020; Grieves & Spiers, 2021). In this collection, the essays start with specific places and provide a space to think and theorise from there. This is not to say that the authors do not already write from disciplinary histories and traditions that carry many of these same assumptions. Rather the places and the memories in focus call for modes of responding and listening from the authors that have the potential to particularise and refigure existing ideas in memory studies as well as begin to generate more place-specific conceptions of memory. In 'Recovering a Narrative of Place: Stories in the Time of Climate Change', Tony Birch (2018) speaks to the importance of listening to and telling stories of place that can, in turn, teach us how to care for the Country that we live on – a direction that is pressing in the present and future, as discussed by Yin Paradies in the afterword to this volume.

Part I: History in the landscape archive

In the first section of this collection, authors contemplate the power of memory and history vested in place. In various locations – from a Sydney beach, to Melbourne's gardens, to mid-north South Australia, to the remote Kimberley region – contributors describe how the landscape holds onto or reveals physical evidence of displacement, violence, culture and survival. This includes 'natural' environments so constructed, but also built heritage. That landscapes themselves carry evidence and memories was a highly contentious aspect of the History Wars, being that denialists pointed to the lack of physical evidence for such events. Yet the destruction of evidence, both physical and documentary, has been one of the ways that settler colonialism has continued its assaults on Indigenous people, including through the silencing of memory and the degradation of Country. Chapters in this section of the collection also focus on the multitude of ways of knowing place, and the interplay between connections to place built over long and shorter durée. Methodologically, the authors give us a sense of how they learn history by being in place and spending time with people who know these places.

Julia Hurst and **Karen Maber**'s contemplative prose in 'Matriarch: Reclaiming the Mermaid' brings us into a matriarchal memory-scape, and to the beach. Based on oral history recordings, Hurst and Maber capture the poetry of everyday speech, recollection and story in a place where feelings can be complex and ambivalent, recalling intergenerational experiences of both practising culture and family and being discriminated against by the settler state. The oral histories partly respond to an 1843 painting by settler PHF Phelps, *Australian Aborigines, Cabramatta Tribe*, which depicts Karen's ancestors and is held in the State Library of New South Wales. Hurst and Maber trace Maber's process of family history research, which creates a dialogue between this colonial artwork and the memories of her family. The poetic form captures the process of intergenerational transmission of memory whereby Maber's mother's memories become her own, woven into the place – the bay – and the practices – shell-work – that are the materiality of memory. This contribution to the volume gives voice to Indigenous women's memory, and to narratives of family, survival and self-knowledge in and through place.

The photo essay by **Barry Judd** and **Katherine Ellinghaus** is centred on Judd's mother, Lorna Wilson's experiences of the mission superintendent FW Albrecht in Central Australia. Using Wilson's experiences as a base, photographs demonstrate how each of the three actors (Judd, Ellinghaus and Wilson) navigate their relationality to one another and the landscape in which their research is situated. The approach advocated for by Judd and Ellinghaus exemplifies what we conceptualise as history as process, whereby non-Indigenous scholars, in particular, are called out from behind 'big city-based archives' to speak with and engage the Indigenous communities who are the focus of study. The photographs included in this essay communicate the process by which the (intended) subject of study becomes reinterpreted, thereby showing that history is more closely aligned to the desires of the participants. Though these kinds of collaborations are relatively new to the discipline of history, they will be much more familiar to those of fieldwork-based disciplines. The essay also brings to the fore the power of expectation in such interactions, where the (relative) generosity of academic research settings may facilitate more open-ended interactions than those in institutions dictated by exhibition timelines and funding mandates.

Also in Central Australia, anthropologist **Jason Gibson** and linguists **Jennifer Green** and **Joel Perrurle Liddle** similarly describe moving through the landscape with Anmatyerr and other Indigenous collaborators, discussing memories of frontier violence, both inherited and personally experienced. They describe how public monuments comprise only the tip of the iceberg when it comes to colonial violence and the entanglements of Indigenous and non-Indigenous coexistence since colonisation. Their chapter shares much in common with that of anthropologist **Richard Martin** and Kurtijar man **Fred Pascoe**, a well-known political leader in Queensland's Gulf Country. Pascoe narrates the now partly mythologised life history of his ancestor Tommy Burns, whose life during the mid-twentieth century was punctuated by colonial violence. Pascoe's telling and retelling of Burns's life story is driven by a desire to affirm Indigenous survival and persistence, or, in his words, 'to have young Kurtjarra fellas feeling optimistic: out of all the trials and tribulations that their ancestors went through, *the fact is we are still here*' (original emphasis). In this chapter, as in the one by Gibson et al., Aboriginal contributors emphasise their own communities as the audience for stories that expand rather than flatten interpretations of historical violence, thereby emphasising resilience against settler history-telling.

In the two chapters following, historians **Billy Griffiths** and **Skye Krichauff** describe geographically distant but similar instances of known historical violence against Indigenous peoples. **Billy Griffiths** discusses the culture of frontier violence and the limitations of archival and physical evidence in accounting for a massacre where as many as 60 Aboriginal people may have been killed. He describes a field visit to the region of Timber Creek, in proximity to the Western Australia/Northern Territory border, where he and historian and archaeologist Darrell Lewis searched for a site known as Kanjamala on Ngaliwurru Aboriginal land, where the massacre likely took place. As Lewis (2012) and a raft of others have demonstrated, in this region, massacres and kidnapping were techniques of pastoral station workers and managers that enabled the continued dispossession of Aboriginal people (Dalley, 2022; Jebb, 2002; Owen, 2016). In his chapter, Griffiths attends to the histories preserved on a particular boab tree in the region where pastoralists and Aboriginal people carved their names. Boab trees are useful, generally, as a metaphor for the longevity of evidence; their gnarled woody trunk seem to offer permanence when inscribed, but, once dead, quickly decompose and subside into the landscape, creating new silences in the historical record.

The question of the longevity of evidence also sits at the heart of **Skye Krichauff**'s chapter about the murder of several Aboriginal people at Mt Bryan, near where she and generations of her family lived on Ngadjuri Country in Hallett, South Australia. Krichauff reflects on the forgetting and remembering that has been central to family and local settler histories of Hallett, both written and oral. In her attention to the role of historians, Krichauff reflects critically on the work of Lyndall Ryan's research team and their focus on massacres perhaps at the expense of events that do not qualify for inclusion on the map, such as the murders at Mt Bryan. Another interpretation would be that Krichauff's and Ryan's projects exist at either ends of a scale, one intimately concerned with local detail and the other unflinchingly focused on the macro. A fruitful question to explore is how these approaches can be brought productively into conversation.

Part II: Remembering and forgetting in heritage spaces

In the second part of this collection, authors focus on heritage spaces broadly conceived, including museums and keeping places. In these spaces, curators and practitioners are engaged not only with the process of telling history, but also in representing these histories to a (generally) broader public. Within formal institutions, the misappropriation of Indigenous people's material culture and human remains into collections makes them doubly complicated places to explore the politics of storytelling in contemporary Australia. This misappropriation has tangible and ongoing impacts on the capacities of institutions to develop meaningful engagements with communities, and to draw them into the process of representation. Authors also address questions about the brittle nature of institutions, regardless of their size.

As museums and other traditional collecting institutions grapple with engaging Indigenous people and communities in more meaningful ways, a space opens up for non-conventional interpretive spaces to come to the fore. One of these is the stone in the park of remembrance described in **Alexandra Roginski**'s chapter, which opens Part II of this collection. Situated in a park in inner city Melbourne, the stone marks the location of the remains of 38 Indigenous people once held at the Melbourne Museum. The remains were interred at the park in 1985, largely as a result of the activism of Gunditjmara man Jim Berg. The practice of collecting

Indigenous human remains was part of a racist colonial fascination with phrenology, and the failure to maintain records about the remains' provenance perpetuates the violence by rendering it difficult to reunite them with Country. In this essay, the nesting of multiple layers of violence, commemoration and activism are described. The park where the stone is located is on Kulin Country, and Roginski details the history of this part of Melbourne. Since the interment, events held by Indigenous activists at the site have refocused sentiment and commemorations of these ancestors, and, in doing so, draw on the stone as a potent source of inspiration to commemorate more recent injustices and activism.

The following essay, by **Sarah Hayes**, **Steven Cooke**, **Edwina Kay** and **Antony Catrice**, discusses the affective meaning of physical traces left at the site of a former children's homes Kildonan and later Allambie, now incorporated into the site of Deakin University's Burwood campus. Though not all children at Kildonan and Allambie were Indigenous, across Australia these homes were part of systemic state practices of the removal of Aboriginal and Torres Strait Islander children from kin, meaning that they are deeply imbricated in the structural racism of the settler colony. Many children, now adults, have traumatic memories of their time in state care, separated from family and sometimes subjected to physical, sexual and emotional abuse. For curators, including essay co-author **Antony Catrice**, now working with the extant physical remains that comprised these homes, such materials are potent holders of recent memory. Photographs of children's clothes and toys illustrate this haunting atmosphere. Given the recency of Allambie's closure in 1990, this essay is a vital inclusion in the collection as a reminder of the ongoing potency of history and its lived realities.

Affect is a similarly present theme in a transcript of an interview between **Cameo Dalley** and curators **Imelda Miller** and **Olivia Robinson**. Miller and Robinson reflect on their careers in large collecting institutions and their relationships to their communities of origin, particularly given that their cultural backgrounds are not well represented in the institutions in which they work. As long-term collaborators, Miller and Robinson reflect on their shared work, including a 2019 exhibition at State Library of Queensland titled *Plantation Voices*, which featured the experiences of South Sea Islanders brought to Australia to work in various agricultural industries, particularly Queensland's cane fields. Perhaps unexpectedly, both Miller and Robinson highlight the educative role of the institutions they work for (Queensland Museum and State Library of Queensland), describing them as necessary for representing the history of a broader range of Queenslanders. Rather than a capitulation to the dense politicking in their own communities, which seek a more radical decolonisation and divestment of material culture through repatriation, Miller's and Robinson's engagements position them as both insiders and outsiders, encouraging their own communities to re-engage with institutions, thereby transforming them from within.

From two curators with reciprocal relationships to their own communities, we move to a community constituted in a very different way. In our own contribution to this collection, we, **Dalley** and **Barnwell**, travel to the tiny and remote East Kimberley town of Wyndham, home to about 800 Indigenous and non-Indigenous people. Historically, Wyndham served as a port. Now, the museum of a local historical society occupies what was once the town courthouse. Dotted across Australia, these small collecting institutions, often staffed by volunteers, play an important role in telling local stories, but they often grapple with limited resources, limited capacity and internal conflict. In a socially intimate town where everyone is known to one another, the mantle of curation takes place without the comfort of anonymity sometimes offered in larger institutions. A retreat to the defensible written evidence is one mechanism by which the museum's curator, Christine, navigates 'history by committee' and placates other museum volunteers, each with their own attitudes towards settler-colonial history and the 'History Wars'. Christine draws attention to negotiations going on behind the scenes, in which a bid by local Aboriginal people to establish their own keeping place was part of the reason for excluding material about Indigenous history at the museum. The chapter offers an insight into one local museum's efforts to revise their exhibits. Though on different scales, it and the chapter that follows by **Thomas J. Rogers**, previously of the Australian War Memorial (AWM), urges us to consider the parameters and limitations that come into play when working in institutions, regardless of their size. Museum curators battle funding mandates, institutional inertia, and long-term scheduling, meaning exhibitions are often compromised and many years in the making. This puts them at a disadvantage, limiting their ability to respond dynamically to the shorter time frames that characterise political debates, such as those that continue to take place around Australian history.

Rogers's chapter explores the question of whether the AWM addresses frontier violence – which he describes as 'violent clashes between settlers and Indigenous people between 1788 and 1928' – in its exhibitions. This relatively limited conceptualisation of frontier violence, a narrower band than many of our contributors allow, reflects, in part, the mandate of the institution that Rogers worked for, being arguably Australia's most conservative. For example, Rogers notes that the legislation that establishes the AWM's operations refers to 'active service' as the precondition for representation, a position reiterated by the museum itself in 2014 in response to criticism. Despite this, Rogers describes a set of artworks displayed by the AWM that depict frontier violence, including by Gija Aboriginal artist Rover Thomas. Though minute in the context of the AWM's overall homage to national identity, there has been an inching towards recognition of Indigenous people that includes a recent unveiling of a sculptural memorial to Indigenous servicemen, by the Aboriginal artist Daniel Boyd. Rogers captures the work that curators are doing with small projects, such as relabelling to make more visible the references to frontier violence that are in the AWM's publications and exhibitions, as well as changes in the wording of official remits. His chapter, perhaps, gestures to the slow refiguring of even the most conservative meta-narratives over time as truth-telling becomes more prominent within public discussions, and positions of complete omission become untenable.

Rounding out this second section of the book is an essay by **Chris Healy**, whose 2008 book *Forgetting Aborigines* remains a defining text in the representation of Indigenous people in Australian popular culture. In his contribution, Healy points out that public acknowledgements of colonial violence are not new and that 'commemoration – a form of remembering after the fact – as compensatory or as an antidote to "Indigenous absence" or silence is neither accurate nor useful'. He points to the body of work by First Nations intellectuals and artists who have actively remembered this history through time.

What Healy rightfully notes is that material culture and movable art by Indigenous people in Australia has long dealt with themes of history, memorialisation and violence. This extensive body of work, including by cover artist Tony Albert, already exists in Australian collecting institutions. A notable example is the work of Trawlwoolway and Scottish-Irish artist Julie Gough. A 2019 exhibition of her works entitled *Tense Past* was a powerful treatise on frontier and colonial experiences in her home of Tasmania. Held at the Tasmanian Museum and Art Gallery, the exhibition featured a range of colonial objects of the nineteenth century, repurposed to illustrate and represent violence perpetrated against Tasmania's Indigenous peoples. One particularly chilling installation was a chair, whose seat had been replaced with tens of long sharpened wooden spears inscribed with the names of Tasmanian Indigenous children stolen from their parents and titled 'Some Tasmanian Aboriginal Children Living with Non-Aboriginal People before

1840'. In a review of the exhibition, Lucy Hawthorne (2019) noted a parallel installation made by Gough to coincide with the 2019 Dark MOFO Festival held in and around Hobart. As part of *Missing or Dead*, Gough pinned almost 200 posters to installed she-oak trees, depicting Aboriginal children who were 'stolen, admitted to orphanages and/or assumed missing or dead'. Hawthorne (2019, p. 37) tells us that 'the installation site was adjacent to the extensive and well-funded Soldier's Memorial Avenue, reminding us that of the many permanent memorials around Hobart, none remember the first Tasmanians'.

Renowned Queensland Badtjala artist Fiona Foley (2018) critiqued a culture within academia that selectively recognised work in this space according to a preordained set of principles. For Foley, this had resulted in 'the erasure of many who have worked in this area for over three decades', herself included. Foley referred to her installation *Witnessing to Silence* (2004) outside the Brisbane Magistrates Court, and to the iconic work *The Aboriginal Memorial* (1987) by Indigenous curator Djon Mundine at the main entrance to the National Gallery of Australia. Along with Foley's and Mundine's installations, First Nations artists continue to take the lead in commemorating and educating audiences about Aboriginal and colonial history. This returns us to the provocation in Healy's essay, and that of this volume's afterword by **Yin Paradies**. Colonial violence is very often taken for granted as historical, as encapsulated in a set period, when the violences of colonialism that need to be publicly acknowledged, perhaps more urgently, are those continuing in the present.

References

Aird, M., Sassoon, J. & Trigger, D. (2021). 'The White-man calls me Jack': The many names and claims for Jackey Jackey of the lower Logan River, south-east Queensland, Australia. *Aboriginal History*, 45, 3–32. doi.org/10.22459/AH.45.2021

Araluen, E. (2019, 11 February). Snugglepot and Cuddlepie in the Ghost Gum. *Sydney Review of Books*. sydneyreviewofbooks.com/essay/snugglepot-and-cuddlepie-in-the-ghost-gum-evelyn-araluen/

Barker, L. (2008). 'Hangin' out' and 'yarnin': Reflecting on the experience of collecting oral histories. *History Australia*, 5(1), 09.1–09.9. doi.org/10.2104/ha080009

Barnwell, A. (2021). Keeping the nation's secrets: 'Colonial storytelling' within Australian families. *Journal of Family History*, *46*, 46–61. doi.org/10.1177/0363199020966920

Barrowcliffe, R. (2021). Closing the narrative gap: Social media as a tool to reconcile institutional archival narratives with Indigenous counter-narratives. *Archives and Manuscripts*, *49*(3), 151–166. doi.org/10.1080/01576895.2021.1883074

Batten, B. (2009). The Myall Creek Memorial: History, identity and reconciliation. In W. Logan & K. Reeves (Eds.), *Places of pain and shame: Dealing with 'difficult heritage'* (pp. 82–96). Routledge, Taylor & Francis Group. doi.org/10.4324/9780203885031

Birch, T. (2018). Recovering a narrative of place: Stories in the time of climate change. *Griffith Review*, *60*, 207–214.

Black, J. (2020). Reflexivity or orientation? Collective memories in the Australian, Canadian and New Zealand national press. *Memory Studies*, *13*(4), 519–536. doi.org/10.1177/1750698017749978

Blake, T. (2001). *A dumping ground: A history of the Cherbourg settlement*. University of Queensland Press.

Busbridge, R. (2021). Changing the date: Local councils, Australia Day and cultures of national commemoration. *Journal of Sociology*, *59*(2). Online first. doi.org/10.1177/14407833211044548

Caldwell, L. & Leroux, D. (2019). The settler-colonial imagination: Comparing commemoration in Saskatchewan and in Québec. *Memory Studies*, *12*(4), 451–464. doi.org/10.1177/1750698017720258

Casey, E. S. (2000). *Remembering: A phenomenological study*. Indiana University Press.

Chazan, M. & Cole, J. (2020). Making memory sovereign/making sovereign memory. *Memory Studies*, *15*(5), 1–16. doi.org/10.1177/1750698019900953

Chou, M. & Busbridge, R. (2019, 23 January). The culture war taking place in your own backyard: Local councils and the politics of Australia Day. *ABC News Online*. abc.net.au/religion/local-councils-and-the-politics-of-australia-day/10739410

Collins, F., Healy, C. & Radstone, S. (2020). Provincializing memory studies: The insistence of the 'here-now'. *Memory Studies*, *13*(5), 848–860. doi.org/10.1177/1750698020946415

Connerton, P. (2009). *How modernity forgets*. Cambridge University Press. doi.org/10.1017/CBO9780511627187

Curthoys, A. (2004). National narratives, war commemoration and racial exclusion in a settler society: The Australian case. In T. G. Ashplant, G. Dawson & M. Roper (Eds.), *The politics of war memory and commemoration* (pp. 128–145). Routledge, Taylor & Francis Group. doi.org/10.4324/9781315080956-4

Dalley, C. (2021). Becoming a settler descendant: Critical engagements with inherited family narratives of indigeneity agriculture and land in a (post)colonial context. *Life Writing*, *18*(3), 355–370. doi.org/10.1080/14484528.2021.1927493

Dalley, C. (2022). Pastoralism's distributive ruse: Extractivism, financialization, Indigenous labour and a rightful share in Northern Australia. *History and Anthropology*, *2*(12), 1–19. doi.org/10.1080/02757206.2022.2034622

Darian-Smith, K. & Hamilton, P. (1994). *Memory and history in twentieth-century Australia*. Oxford University Press.

Davis, B. & Heath, J. (2021). *Healing the spirit – A Birrpai perspective on the Port Macquarie penal colony and its aftermath*. Port Macquarie Historical Society.

DeLugan, R. M. (2021). *Remembering violence: How nations grapple with their difficult pasts*. Routledge, Taylor & Francis Group. doi.org/10.4324/9781003082149

Edmonds, P. (2016). *Settler colonialism and (re)conciliation: Frontier violence, affective performances, and imaginative refoundings*. Palgrave Macmillan. doi.org/10.1057/9781137304544

Foley, F. (2018, 6 July). The spectacle of Aboriginal frontier war memorial research. *ArtsHub*. artshub.com.au/news/opinions-analysis/the-spectacle-of-aboriginal-frontier-war-memorial-research-256020-2360000/

Furniss, E. (2001). Timeline history and the Anzac myth: Settler narratives of local history in a North Australian town. *Oceania*, *71*(4), 279–297. doi.org/10.1002/j.1834-4461.2001.tb02754.x

Green, C. Papertalk. 'Rain clouds' arrival'. In C. Papertalk Green & J. Kinsella, *False claims of colonial thieves* (p. 92). Magabala Books.

Grieves, G. & Spiers, A. (2021, 25 August). Counter-monuments: Challenging distorted colonial histories through public art and memorials. *Artlink*. artlink.com.au/articles/4926/counter-monuments-challenging-distorted-colonial-h/

Haebich, A. (1992). *For their own good: Aborigines and government in the south west of Western Australia, 1900–1940*. UWA for the Charles and Joy Staples South West Region Publications Fund.

Halbwachs, M. (1992). *On collective memory* (L. Coser, Ed. & Trans.). University of Chicago Press. doi.org/10.7208/chicago/9780226774497.001.0001

Harkin, N. (2018). *Archival poetics*. Vagabond Press.

Hawthorne, L. (2019). Review: Mind the gap: Julie Gough's 'Tense Past' at TMAG. *Art Monthly Australia*, *319*(36), 36–37.

Healy, C. (2008). *Forgetting Aborigines*. University of New South Wales Press.

Hobsbawm, E. & Ranger, T. O. (Eds.) (1983). *The invention of tradition*. Cambridge University Press. doi.org/10.1017/cbo9781107295636

Hodgkin, K. & Radstone, S. (Eds.) (2006). *Memory, history and nation: Contested pasts*. Transaction Publishers.

Hoelscher, S. & Alderman, D. H. (2004). Memory and place: Geographies of a critical relationship. *Social & Cultural Geography*, *5*(3), 347–355. doi.org/10.1080/1464936042000252769

Jebb, M. A. (2002). *Blood, sweat and welfare: A history of white bosses and Aboriginal pastoral workers*. UWA Press.

Johnson, M. (2005). Honest acts and dangerous supplements: Indigenous oral histories and historical practice in settler societies. *Postcolonial Studies*, *8*(3), 261–276. doi.org/10.1080/13688790500231046

Kennedy, R. & Nugent, M. (2016). Scales of memory: Reflections on an emerging concept. *Australian Humanities Review 59*(Apr/May), 61–76. australianhumanities review.org/2016/08/29/scales-of-memory-reflections-on-an-emerging-concept/

Konishi, S. (2019). First Nations scholars, settler colonial studies and Indigenous history. *Australian Historical Studies*, *50*(3), 285–304. doi.org/10.1080/1031461X.2019.1620300

Krichauff, S. (2017). *Memory, place and Aboriginal-settler history: Understanding Australians' consciousness of the colonial past*. Anthem Press. doi.org/10.2307/j.ctt1trkkdh

Latimore, J. (2019, 5 March). There are few memorials to Australia's bloody history but that's changing. *The Guardian*. theguardian.com/australia-news/2019/mar/05/there-are-few-memorials-to-our-bloody-history-but-thats-changing

Leane, J. (2014). Tracking our Country in settler literature. *Journal of the Association for the Study of Australian Literature*, *14*(3), 1–17.

Lewis, D. (2012). *A wild history: Life and death on the Victoria River frontier*. Monash University Publishing.

Logan, W. & Reeves, K. (2009). (Eds.) *Places of pain and shame: Dealing with 'difficult heritage'*. Routledge, Taylor & Francis Group. doi.org/10.4324/9780203885031

Lydon, J. (Ed.). (2014). *Calling the shots: Aboriginal photographies*. Aboriginal Studies Press.

Manning, S. (2018). Contrasting colonisations: (Re)storying Newfoundland/Ktaqmkuk as place. *Settler Colonial Studies, 8*(3), 314–331. doi.org/10.1080/2201473X.2017.1327010

McBride, L. & Smith, M. (2021). *Unsettled* (exhibition catalogue). Australian Museum.

McCabe, J. (2017). *Race, tea and colonial resettlement: Imperial families, interrupted*. Bloomsbury Publishing. doi.org/10.5040/9781474299534

McKemmish, S., Faulkhead, S. & Russell, L. (2011). Distrust in the archive: Reconciling records. *Archival Science, 11*, 211–239. doi.org/10.1007/s10502-011-9153-2

Misztal, B. (2003). *Theories of social remembering*. Open University Press.

Monument Australia (n.d.). *Conflict*. monumentaustralia.org.au/themes/conflict/indigenous

Nora, P. (1989). Between memory and history: Les lieux de mémoire. *Representations, 26*, 7–24. doi.org/10.2307/2928520

Nugent, M. (2013). Sites of segregation/sites of memory: Remembrance and 'race' in Australia. *Memory Studies, 6*(3), 299–309. doi.org/10.1177/1750698013482863

O'Malley, V. & Kidman, J. (2018). Settler colonial history, commemoration and white backlash: Remembering the New Zealand Wars. *Settler Colonial Studies, 8*(3), 298–313. doi.org/10.1080/2201473X.2017.1279831

O'Neill, C. (2016). *Roots*. Find & Connect. findandconnectwrblog.info/2016/07/roots/

Owen, C. (2016). *'Every mother's son is guilty': Policing the Kimberley frontier of Western Australia 1882–1905*. UWA Press.

Prowse, L. (2015). Parallels on the periphery: The exploration of Aboriginal history by local historical societies in New South Wales, 1960s–1970s. *History Australia, 12*(3), 55–75. doi.org/10.1080/14490854.2015.11668586

Reid, K. & Paisley, F. (Eds.). (2017). *Sources and methods in histories of colonialism: Approaching the imperial archive*. Routledge, Taylor & Francis Group. doi.org/10.4324/9781315271958

Rosenberg, S., Dean, A. & Granzow, K. (2010). Centennial hauntings: Reckoning with the 2005 celebration of Alberta's history. *Memory Studies*, *3*(4), 395–412. doi.org/10.1177/1750698010375666

Rothberg, M. (2009). *Multidirectional memory: Remembering the Holocaust in the age of decolonization*. Stanford University Press. doi.org/10.1515/9780804783330

Russell, L. (2002). *A little bird told me: Family secrets, necessary lies*. Allen & Unwin.

Ryan, L., Debenham, J., Pascoe, B., Smith, R., Owen, C., Richards, J., Gilbert, S., Anders, R. J., Usher, K., Price, D., Newley, J., Brown, M., Le, L. H. & Fairbairn, H. (2018). *Colonial frontiers massacres, Australia, 1788 to 1930* (Vol. 2.1) [Massacres map]. University of Newcastle. c21ch.newcastle.edu.au/colonialmassacres/map.php

Schlunke, K. (2010). *Bluff Rock: Autobiography of a massacre*. readhowyouwant.com/Books/search/author/Schlunke/1

Schlunke, K. (2013). Memory and materiality. *Memory Studies*, *6*(3), 253–261. doi.org/10.1177/1750698013482864

Scott, K. & Brown, H. (2005). *Kayang & Me*. Fremantle Press.

Sentance, N. (2019, 18 September). Disrupting the colonial archive. *Sydney Review of Books*. sydneyreviewofbooks.com/review/natalie-harkin-archival-poetics/

Shellam, T. (2020). *Meeting the Waylo: Aboriginal encounters in the archipelago*. UWA Publishing.

Travis Penangke, K. A. & Haskins, V. (2021, 12 April). More than a story: Family history webinar series: Collaborative family histories. University of Tasmania. youtube.com/watch?v=I_6Uk1SABKw

Wright, A. (2016). What happens when you tell somebody else's story? A history of Aboriginal disempowerment. *Meanjin* (Summer), 58–76. meanjin.com.au/essays/what-happens-when-you-tell-somebody-elses-story/

Part I: History in the landscape archive

1
Matriarch: Reclaiming the mermaid

Julia Hurst and Karen Maber

Warning: This writing contains the names of people who have passed away (with permission from Karen Maber).

Prologue

Following the personal narrative and experience of Darug and Dharawal woman Karen Maber and her late mother Aunty Margaret Slowgrove, this chapter will bring to the fore an example of Indigenous women's experience of memory, identity and survival, and of making sense of history with recollections of everyday conversations, oral history interviews and the simple act of being on the beach.

Karen's Aboriginal ancestors were etched into settler-colonial history by settler PH Phelps in 1843 in his work *Australian Aborigines, Cabramatta Tribe*. However, it was not until Karen completed her own family research that the drawing made sense to her; the memories she held as a young girl in conversation with her late mother, Margaret Slowgrove, alerted her to the many layers, experiences and swirling histories her family have endured, survived and continue to live with. Never straightforward or without controversy, this writing offers an example of how memory can exultingly push us forward to our future Aboriginal selves, beyond the confines of settler history and expectations of self, or succumb to the never-ending ache of wanting more, history.

MEMORY IN PLACE

'She': History mum and me[1]

She laps at my bones. Little by little carving a new path, it is always her, absolute and immediate, determined to keep all of us together even though she is gone. Our stories do not stop.[2]

> She is contradictory.
> She belongs to the water, but she lived on the land.

She watches us and I ache for her, myself and what I cannot know. All of it, everything that is gone, everything she represents.

> **She said, my wish for you is that you have *enough*.**
> You belong to me. I know and you *know*. You're mine.

But be careful what you say!

Am I enough?

1963	*Kogarah*
1938	**Yarra Bay**
1916	*Yarra Bay*
c. 1875	*Georges River*
1853	*Georges River, Liverpool*
1826	*Airds, Campbelltown*
c. 1800	*Chief of the Cabrogal Clan*

And my Dharug side … Namut. Malone … Dharawal. They were neighbouring nations, allowed to marry.[3]

Oh, but I haven't named the people, yes, that's important, isn't it.

> Dad never came into mum's house. Just dropped us and left. Stew on the fire. Card games for days.

---

1   This writing is based on interviews and personal communication between Margaret Slowgrove, Karen Maber and Julia Hurst. Excerpts are from interviews completed with Margaret Slowgrove and Karen Maber by Julia Hurst, 26 February 2013 and 25 July 2013, Sans Souci. Recordings are in the family's possession.
2   Karen Maber to Julia Hurst, personal communication, 14 May 2021.
3   historyofaboriginalsydney.edu.au/south-coastal/tracing-back-eight-generations-karen-maber

1. MATRIARCH

> Half the whites married the blacks and half the blacks married the whites! There was never anybody … theirs or ours or anything … just family! All in.
>
> … Dad?

Mum was born in Yarra Bay in La Perouse in 1938 … It was mum's starting point …

> I was the eldest of five.

… children should always surpass their parents.

But she was never defined by the past, she was never stuck or broken, caught between the gaps, or lonely.[4]

> How do you want more when you've got everything?[5]

PH Phelps drew us into history. So much was left unsaid.[6]

… Here's the list of people. Nine men and women. Is that enough?

1. Fanny and child
2. Piala (Black Rose)
3. Clare
4. Queen Kitty (Mali)
5. White Polly (Dahlia)
6. Kourban (Cooman)
7. Visitor or Envoy from Richmond Tribe
8. Jack (real name unknown)
9. **King George (George Charles Gilbert)**
10. Clara's boy
11. Rosa's girl[7]

Proves our existence. Don't you think?

… and so, I paint. Weaving my story through time. It's not about painting, it's about belonging, it's about being a part.

---

4   Karen Maber, personal communication, 31 October 2021.
5   Karen Maber, personal communication, 31 October 2021.
6   Karen Maber, personal communication, 31 October 2021.
7   historyofaboriginalsydney.edu.au/south-west/%E2%80%98australian-aborigines-cabramatta-tribe%E2%80%99-ph-phelps

You can't share what you haven't been passed on.

Because of who I am, because of my history.
Because we exist in spite of you, and because you make us so.

Aboriginal.

Is this history safe to share?

> I'm the eldest of five ... I'm the only one who knew my grandparents.

> In the shack, straw bed, no electricity. But the horses! Ginny and Browney – everyone jump on!

> Albert Butler and Eliza Butler.

> ... Grandmother Eliza ...

Was she black mum? *Pitch Black!* Gorgeous.

> Then my family split up.

Shell-worker

We're surrounded by the waterways.

> You don't need material for a skirt; stay home!

> She specialised in the Sydney Harbour Bridge. Twelve inches long. Dainty shells, strings of glitter down the sides. Velvet along the edge. A velvet box, shaped like a heart with satin and velvet cut on the cross. Always some glitter sprinkled on the top.

> Come help me girl!

Her eyes would sparkle.

> Sometimes we couldn't keep up

> Walking for days on the beach looking for shells
> It was a big payday for us.

My mother's mother.

Absent and connected.

1. MATRIARCH

Different shells. Different places. Different families. Different styles.

Different stories.

> Fingernail shells so opaque at Kurnell. Coloured shells at Cronulla. Jingle shells and Cockle Shells at Yarra Bay to show the light. Purple pipi shells further down the South Coast.

… a mosaic with purple pipi shells.

> You can't find the dainty shells now. They're very rare now.

This is one promise I have to keep, to show her how to do this.

I'm the only one to show her the proper way.

> The shell-work they're doing now, in my opinion, is not pretty anymore.
>
> Mum sold pairs of shoes down the main strip at LaPa.
> Mimic: *'Oh look at them!'*
> Stupid woman! Gowan wodjiwoman!
>
> Cousins dived for a zac from the pier
> Mimic: *'Oh look at them!'*
> Stupid man! Gowan wodjiman!
>
> I couldn't swim
> I didn't ask questions
> Nobody had anything
> It was who we were

It starts with mum. *It **starts** with mum. It starts with **mum**. It starts **with** mum.*

> **… we sort of got away from that for a while, didn't we?**

[Beat]

> Are they your memories or mine?
> she asked.

She squeezed her hand gently,

'they're both'.

It just felt good …

How can you begin to know me? I'm Aboriginal!

It wasn't anything we really talked about much …

The papers

> To me, the papers don't mean a thing
> It does to my children

We didn't know about papers, papers are your identification papers, a certificate, and then Aboriginality papers … to prove you're Aboriginal.

> I know where I come from, everybody that's important to me

Mum never mentioned that

> Nobody had them
> **And we never thought about that!**

Mimic: So where do you come from? What are you from? **What place?**

Nobody had them in your day
We never needed to talk about that.

> I took my nieces and their families out to LaPa. They said what about you? I said 'oh no, I **know where** I am'
>
> Politics, politics, politics.
>
> Now they won't give me 'em. But I've already taken my cousins out there. They all got.
>
> I'm the Elder.
>
> *Get up in their faces!*
>
> They say 'ello cuz, how ya goin?'
>
> *Mimic:* '… Do you remember an old couple?'

That's my grandparents you're talking about!

They know where I lived. My parents … who my grandparents were

Now they don't want to give any papers out.

I moved around the Bay

We were here before we were at LaPa.

Rearing the kids. Workin' of a nightime in the kitchen.

Trying to survive.

They're **frightened**. I'm gonna cost them … They're not interested in the originals!

What's community?

Continuing.

2

Spirit of place: The critical case for site visits in the construction of Indigenous Australian histories

Barry Judd and Katherine Ellinghaus

> They come out to the community in a big four-wheel drive – towin' flash campin' gear – looked like they'd be stayin' awhile – set up camp. The historians – they said they were – come out to help us tell our story. (Leane, 2017)

The photographs in this essay depict work done during a research project that examines the education scheme facilitated by Friedrich Wilhelm (FW) Albrecht, the superintendent at Ntaria (Hermannsburg Mission) in the Northern Territory in the 1950s and 1960s. Albrecht created a program in which young girls were taken with permission from their families, fostered and educated, but were allowed to return to family and community for holidays. Never before studied, the history of this scheme promises to provide us with a deeper understanding of the varied ways in which postwar 'assimilation' was imagined and enacted by both officials and Aboriginal people. But this project is not just about uncovering the past. It is also about finding new ways of writing history that move beyond the problems created when a discipline that is overwhelmingly staffed by non-Indigenous people disseminates knowledge about communities, individuals and places that they are not connected to, and have never visited, spoken to or stepped foot upon.

As discussed in numerous other chapters in this volume, the call for histories to be created not just from archives but also in collaboration with Aboriginal historians and using multiple sources is not new. Historians of settler colonialism are increasingly beginning to work collaboratively and in ways that are Indigenous-led (Birch, 2006, 2013; Ellinghaus & Judd, 2020; Grieves, 2005; Judd & Ellinghaus, 2020; Peters-Little, 2010). The spatial implications of this shift are explored here. One of the authors of this chapter, Ellinghaus, is one such scholar who has moved beyond solely archivally based studies to consciously engage with the Aboriginal people that she researches. She is of Irish, German and Scottish descent. The other author, Judd, works in the field of Indigenous studies, a discipline whose fundamental aim – to promote the wellbeing of living, breathing Aboriginal people through scholarly activism – sits at odds with the emphasis on archives that defines the discipline of history. While fieldwork, travel and relationality are expected in other disciplines such as anthropology and sociology, in the field of history there has been little discussion of such collaborations beyond acknowledging the need for them. What happens when historians step away from big city-based archives to search out, engage and speak with Aboriginal people who might live close by or far away in remote communities? What is gained (or maybe lost) when academic research is combined with the building of personal relationships required for authentic collaboration? How are relationships articulated through the outcomes of an academic project? What happens when the distance – cultural, experiential, sometimes geographical – between researcher and researched is traversed?

Unlike fieldwork-based disciplines, history does not yet have a language to articulate these moments, or to answer these questions. As Dalley and Barnwell argue in the introduction to this volume, multidisciplinary scholarship allows us to focus on the present as well as the past and shows the importance of a step beyond basic historical truth-telling: the building of relationships that do not reinscribe colonial power relations. In this chapter, we use the medium of photography to explore these issues. Photographs show us a glimpse of a moment in time, they show us relationality in the way bodies relate to each other and they give shape to the disembodied scholarly voice or the 'universalising Western standpoint' (Nakata et al., 2012). They situate research in particular places, give it a more colourful background of dirt and trees (or cars or buildings) rather than the black and white of the page. They commemorate our research, providing small reminders of the many small moments that are required when trusting relationships are formed between researcher and researched. The relationships depicted here began in small, everyday ways. In 2016, Ellinghaus reached out to Lorna Wilson, Judd's mother, whose life was shaped by FW Albrecht's scheme of taking Aboriginal girls out of Central Australia to be educated. At the time, Ellinghaus knew nothing of the scheme – she contacted Wilson to ask about her childhood in Mparntwe (Alice Springs) for another, short-lived research project. They stayed in touch, and have ever since, by phone and through regular visits. Our research into Albrecht's scheme is driven by Lorna Wilson's desire to tell this story; these photographs depict her as teacher rather than informant.

Historians most often use photographs in their work as evidence of the past, not the present. They imagine photographs as a way of bridging the distance between non-Indigenous Australians and Indigenous people, specifically as a medium through which settler Australians have confronted the violence of the past. Photo narrative and analysis has increasingly been applied in history as a technique to understand past relations between Aboriginal and settler Australians. Jane Lydon's *Eye Contact* (2006) and *Photography, Humanitarianism, Empire* (2016) are exemplars of current work that seeks to give insight to imperial and settler-colonial use of photography to represent Indigenous peoples for various political ends. Importantly, such work also seeks an understanding of how Aboriginal peoples have used photography since the 1930s to support their own anticolonial and imperial agendas. While historians have been interested in subjecting photographic records of Aboriginal people to various types of images and narrative analysis, the recently published monograph *Bitter Fruit: Australian Photographs to 1963* by New Zealand–based authors Michael Graham-Stewart and Francis McWhannell allows this collection of photographic images to speak for themselves. According to the authors:

> The images included here are inevitably skewed in viewpoint, most having been taken by non-Aboriginal men. But they show actual people in actual situations. This publication does not aim to fix interpretations. (Graham-Stewart & McWhannell, 2017, p. 9)

Bitter Fruit is, however, very much an outlier. The dominant utilisation of photographs in history involves analysis of the images that capture Aboriginal life in the nineteenth and twentieth centuries according to various methodological approaches drawn from structuralism, poststructuralism, anticolonialism, postcolonialism or settler colonialism. For example, historian Jane Lydon begins her 2012 book *Flash of Recognition: Photography and the Emergence of Indigenous Rights* by asking how photographs have 'aroused empathy with Indigenous suffering and discrimination, and moved viewers to action on their behalf?' She writes about how:

> photography has come to hold a privileged place as proof of distant events – such as the death of a foreign terrorist, or the plight of victims of natural disaster. The power of the image, both to create empathy and to prove what is, has made it an essential tool in the hands of humanitarians and human rights activists attempting to intervene in distant wars or tragedies. (Lydon, 2012, p. 14)

Photography has functioned as a way for settler Australians to 'know' Aboriginal people, whom they may only rarely meet in their everyday life:

> For most non-Indigenous Australians, ideas about Aboriginal people have always been formed through images and narratives, rather than relationships with real people. This is a function of distance – both geographic and social – as well as the minority status of Indigenous people, who make up a little over 2 per cent of the population. (Lydon, 2012, p. 16)

By contrast, in the photographs used in this essay, Ellinghaus is the one traversing the distance – from Melbourne to Titjikala and Mparntwe, and from archive to living, breathing person. The photographs here are not doing the work of bridging distance. Rather they *depict* distances being closed or closing – an historian coming to better understand the past through 'being here' (Judd, 2018). The photographs in this essay also flip, or maybe speak back to, the common view of the medium of colonial photography as 'trophies bagged by the colonial hunter, ciphers in a relationship characterized by distance, exploitation, and coercion' (Lydon, 2006, p. 2) or used as an 'agent of "social truth" depicting poverty and suffering for middle class consumption' (Birch, 2006; McGrath & Brooks, 2010). We are not, of course, the first to rethink the messages that photographs might convey in colonial contexts (Aird, 2015; Andrew & Neath, 2018; Hughes & Trevorrow, 2018).

Readers should note that Judd, the Aboriginal researcher, is depicted in just one of these shots. Mostly he is found behind the camera inverting the usual colonial-imperial gaze whereby the imperialist-colonialist camera determines the frame of Aboriginality. Elsewhere Judd is completely absent. Arielay Azoulay's concept of a photographic 'civil contract' is useful here to understand the significance of this shift. Azoulay points us towards the contract that exists in every photograph between the photographer, the photographed persons and the spectator, and the way in which every photograph 'bears the traces of the meeting between the photographed persons and the photographer, neither of whom can, on their own, determine how this meeting will be inscribed in the resulting image' (Azoulay, 2008, p. 11). Azoulay sees this contract as a free space that can exist separately from the usual political, economic or social structures that shape our lives. 'The relations between the three parties involved in the photographic act – the photographed persons, the photographer, and the spectator', she writes, 'are not mediated through a sovereign power and are not limited to the bounds of a nation-state or an economic contract' (Azoulay, 2008, p. 24). The photographs discussed here are of small moments between individuals; they do not depict historically significant locations, as do images in many other chapters in this collection, or well-known people. Readers should pay attention to the connections between the subjects, not between the subjects and themselves. The photographs presented here are, therefore, far removed from the types of photographic material that most historians would consider significant, important and worthy of academic engagement.

The photographs we present are different from well known and important photographic collections such as those produced at Coranderrk, Victoria, in the nineteenth century by Frederick Kruger, or those captured in Arnhem Land, Northern Territory, in the twentieth century by Donald Thomson, among other important photographic collections. Yet, these are images that contain value because they reflect the importance of relationality and its role in shaping research agendas and outputs. In the field of Indigenous studies, collaborative research with Indigenous people is seen as a vital part of research, drawing from Indigenous notions of relationality that 'make visible Indigenous peoples' connectedness with the earth and with each other' (Moreton-Robinson, 2016, p. 75). Pointing to the constant work that is required to move towards research based in relationality, these images underscore the need for researchers to be mobile in overcoming the geographic distances that often separate them from the people and communities that are the focus of their research. The images also demonstrate the need for researchers to set aside the concept of objective truth, and the research practice that seeks to (re)impose spatial distances between the researcher and those who are the subject of intellectual enquiry. A strength (and perhaps a weakness) of what these photographic images demonstrate is the 'closing of the gap' that occurs when researchers commit to relationality with the Aboriginal subjects of their research as boundaries between the personal and professional, work and life become somewhat blurred, dynamic and unstable.

The purpose of this chapter is twofold. First, by pointing to several key photographs taken during the unfolding of our research collaboration, we demonstrate the potential importance of relationality, in which the research is focused on Aboriginal peoples' histories and contemporary race relations in settler Australia. Second, the photographic fragments of our work presented here demonstrate that ethical research collaborations between Aboriginal and settler-Australian researchers and Aboriginal knowledge holders who exist outside academia, in their communities, are possible. This is important, as it provides an example of how historians might move beyond what Eve Tuck and K Wayne Yang (2012) have called the 'move to settler innocence' – by which they mean the imperative that settlers move past their own white guilt about Indigenous dispossession (and the performance of this as self-indulgence) – and engage with the issue through substantive de-colonial action. In the Australian context, this means settler action that is based in relationality of the type central to the methodological framing of works by John Bradley (2014) and Amanda Kearney (2019), and evidenced in the collaborative and exemplary research collaborations and partnerships of Aaron Corn, Joe Gumbala and Steven Wanta Patrick (Corn, 2018; Corn & Patrick, 2018).

Being There (Ellinghaus)

On my first visit in 2018 to Mparntwe to work on the Albrecht project, I met Lorna in the foyer of the hotel I was staying at. I assumed we would drive to her house and begin the interview straight away. I had a voice recorder and ethics forms in my bag and was looking forward to getting the interview done, then perhaps having a swim and some time alone (I had small children at the time). However, instead of going to her house to do the interview, Lorna took me first to the Alice Springs Old Lutheran Church Living History Collection, a museum managed by historian Olga Radke, the widow of a Lutheran pastor. It is situated in the 'old' church on the Lutheran Church Mission block – the original church was built in December 1938, the same year in which the block was established (Figure 2.1). It was the church in which FW Albrecht himself taught, preached, married and confirmed his congregation.

2. SPIRIT OF PLACE

Figure 2.1. The importance of place. Lorna and Kat at the Alice Springs Old Lutheran Church Living History Collection, 7 May 2021.
Photograph: L Jewell.

The 'new' church was built in the late 1960s. The 'Mission block' on which it sits was a place where people lived, and where Lorna herself spent much time as a child. It housed two cottages in which up to 12 children from surrounding cattle stations lived so they could attend school, supervised by 'cottage parents'. Lorna herself never lived there, as she had kin who lived nearby with whom she could stay when she moved to Mparntwe to go to primary school. But it was the place where she spent a lot of time, and the place where an important Sunday school exchange took place – a moment in which Albrecht noticed Lorna's intelligence and clocked her as a potential participant in the scheme. On that first day I was going with the flow, but later I realised that this pre-interview visit was a strategic and important step made by Lorna.

Despite our unannounced arrival, Olga was pleased to see Lorna and was happy to drop what she was doing to show us around. I learned, without being told, that Lorna's story was not just important to the two of us, but to others as well. I also saw the influence of religion in her life. Lorna talked with Olga about attending church regularly – I was surprised as she had not mentioned this before. Olga pulled out folders filled with photographs, and we looked through them. This was the first time in my career I had been deliberately shown archival material by an Aboriginal person. Since then, I have been fascinated by the differences between how historians and Aboriginal people engage with archives, how they can be traumatising (Harkin, 2020) but also put to use as 'unreliable witnesses' to educate non-Indigenous people as they were in this moment (Sentance, 2019). Now, almost every time I go to Mparntwe, we drop in at the Alice Springs Old Lutheran Church Living History Collection. (A recent visit is depicted in Figure 2.1.) Each visit is an example of Lorna deliberately emplacing me in her story – forcing me to set foot on the Mission block, to meet Olga Radke, to sit and listen, just as she did that first day before the interview could take place later that afternoon. So when she told me this life-changing story later that day, I did not need to imagine the place in which it took place:

> One day he asked a question and nobody in the class sort of knew and I didn't know either and I put my hand up and I gave him an answer and he said, 'Yeah, that's right.' Still today, I tell that story to friends … you know, my sister-in-law who is one of the church people here and she says, 'The Holy spirit was working in you … on that day'. And I think that's when he also realised that we needed more education. (Wilson, interview, 13 February 2018)

On another visit to Central Australia in May 2020, I was given an understanding of the distance between three places significant to Lorna's childhood: Titjikala, the Rodinga Siding and Mparntwe. In one day we (Wilson, Judd and Ellinghaus) traced in reverse the many journeys that Lorna undertook as a child – from her home with her mother at Titjikala to foster parents or school in South Australia or New South Wales, or into Alice Springs to attend primary school. Sometimes these journeys were in trucks or cars, and sometimes by train. Rodinga Siding was the place where Lorna could catch The Ghan when it was still a narrow-gauge railway (later the route was changed, so it is now simply a 'point of interest' on the road from Alice Springs to Maryvale). Though the historical marker at Rodinga Siding pays attention only to the history of the old Ghan railway, and the contributions of the fettlers who lived in the prefabricated concrete quarters that dominate the site today, Rodinga partially facilitated one of the most important aspects of Albrecht's scheme – the reason why participants insist they were not part of the Stolen Generations – the return of children for summer holidays (Figure 2.2).

Figure 2.2. Intimacy and distance at Rodinga Siding, May 2020.
Photograph: B Judd.

As we drove down the dirt roads (I was glad not to be driving), covering the distance much faster than would have been possible when Lorna was a student, I gained a sense of the way in which mobility and the need to travel was something ingrained in Lorna from a young child. Lorna, of course, did not just travel because of her involvement in Albrecht's scheme. Mobility was part of her everyday life, as it is for many other Indigenous people. Indeed, mobility is a core component of Central Australian Indigenous cultural practices and traditions (Musharbash, 2009; Standfield & Stevens, 2019). Lorna was part of a community that was forcibly relocated from Alice Well to Titjikala before her birth, and as a young child she travelled with her mother and brother by train and mail truck as they followed her biological father. Lorna's childhood was also shaped by extensive family travel, undertaken with her stepfather (a Luritja and Afghan man) as he followed stock and station, working the cattle in the country between Port Augusta, Alice Springs and Birdsville. Lorna is still an intrepid traveller today, and in many ways her life is an example of the concept of 'orbiting' (Burke, 2013).

As well as distance, there is intimacy in this photograph – in my arm around Lorna's shoulders, pulling her to me. We lean against the Land Rover, smiling for the camera. Looking at this photo, I am reminded of Amanda Kearney's work exploring the coexistence of intimacy and distance in Indigenous people's relationship to Country (Kearney, 2018). I wonder about the extent to which the friendship that now exists between Lorna and I is the reason I can now be taken on this journey to Titjikala and be shown these places (Figure 2.3). I think, too, of the homecomings that Lorna experienced, how after travelling such long distances and living with strangers she must have enjoyed being back with her family, particularly her mother. And yet how each homecoming the distances she had travelled and the changes she had made to herself must have come into focus:

> Every time I went back after … being at the college, Mum would buy a new dish, you know? Knife and fork, wherever she could get it, plates, pannikin. 'Don't you drink out of anybody's pannikin. Drink out of your own!' she'd say. She wanted me to be clean all the time. She understood when I went down south that I had to have clean stuff not fresh, but it had to be clean. And she kept all my things washed and cleaned all the time. So she was a good mum. (Wilson, interview, 13 February 2018)

Figure 2.3. Being here matters. Walking back from Lorna showing me where Albrecht used to camp at Titjikala, May 2020.
Photograph: B Judd.

Figure 2.3, taken at Titjikala, shows Lorna telling me how significant it was for Albrecht to make the journey to Titjikala. Titjikala is an Aboriginal community about 100 kilometres south of Mparntwe, situated inside the boundaries of Maryvale cattle station. It is where Lorna spent most of her early childhood. At that time, the people lived in humpies, fetched water from a well on foot, hunted and collected bush tucker to supplement the rations they earned as station workers and domestics. There was no school at Titjikala until the 1970s. I am depicted walking alongside Lorna but, really, I was following her as she walked and talked. Lorna is telling me how the arrival of Albrecht's car was a joyous moment for the community. How his making that journey, again and again, was a demonstration of his commitment – a gift of time and effort – that deepened Albrecht's relationships with the people at Titjikala, and made his arrival cause for celebration. Albrecht's regular visits, and the relationships they enabled him to build, meant that her mother felt comfortable enough to send Lorna into Mparntwe to go to primary school, and later watch her go even further away to high school and to train as a nurse. Behind us and to the left in this photograph, among the trees, is the place where Albrecht camped. Lorna had just led me to a better vantage point so that I can see the exact spot.

Looking at this image now, I think about how those distances that Albrecht travelled, again and again, are mirrored in my own relationship with Lorna, how going back, again and again, is at the heart of the project. In the early days of the project, I felt as though I needed to have an interview set up, or a place to visit, or some outside reason to justify going to Central Australia. Now I simply go, because I finally understand that it is the being there that matters (Judd, 2018) and that the conversations had while travelling are often the most important. As Gibson et al. and Hurst and Maber's chapters in this collection show, history is often made sense of in conversations that take place while people are driving or walking to significant places. I know, too, that as a non-Indigenous researcher from the south, I carry with me the burden of all of my kind, 'the historians' (Leane, 2017), who have come before, and who have taken knowledge and left, and not returned, or have claimed expertise on what Judd calls a 'fly-in and fly-out' basis (Judd, 2018, p. 5). I will never write about the history of Central Australia as an insider or as an expert. Yet that is not a reason to stop. Distance has defined settler Australia in so many ways. Historian Rachel Standfield (2004) has noted how, since the 1990s, mainstream Australians have simultaneously distanced themselves from Australia's dark past, the ongoing disadvantage of Aboriginal people, as well as the extreme right-wing politics of figures such as Pauline Hanson and Andrew Bolt, and positioned themselves as benign. I carry that history with me too. I did not understand it at the time, but in the very first interview that I did with Lorna, the message was there. Keep going back:

> He used to come out to Maryvale. And near the creek next to the community, he would camp there. And he would hold a service there under the Bloodwood tree. We would be so happy when we saw the dust of his truck and we could see the dust because the camp is on lower ground and he'd come along on the road was higher. We'd say, 'Ingkarta coming. Ingkarta coming'.[1] And old people to young kids, we would all rush down to the river which was pretty close to where we lived. And he would come, and greet everybody with a smile. And we were happy to see him, we would all line up, the children would hug him and the adults would shake his hand. (Wilson, interview, 13 February 2018)

---

1   Ingkarta was a term used for a respected leader in the Lutheran Church.

Sweeping the Yard (Judd)

There is a long tradition in Australian photography, starting in the nineteenth century, of Aboriginal people being the subject of staged photographs. As documented in the work of Nettelbeck and Foster (2007), Mounted Constable William Willshire, an infamous character in the history of Alice Springs and Central Australia, once famously commissioned a series of staged photographs in which he situated himself as the bringer of law, order and civilisation to the Arrernte, Luritja and other Aboriginal peoples of the region. In these photos, the long-range rifle and Willshire's command over the Aboriginal men who formed his native police force are emphasised as central components of his 'heroic' nation-building in Central Australia. The staged photos of showbiz promoter Archibald Meston (later protector of Aborigines in Southern Queensland), taken and distributed to promote his circus sideshow–like Wild Australia shows, constitute another famous example (McKay & Memmott, 2016). Historically, staged photographs were used to narrate the story of settler nation-building, civilisation and progress, while representing Aboriginal people as stone-age savages, primitive and treacherous.

The photos shown below (Figures 2.4 and 2.5) were taken when Ellinghaus visited Lorna Wilson on a short field research visit in May 2021 and stayed at her home in Alice Springs. As part of the deal, as she had done in previous visits, Wilson expected Ellinghaus to contribute in ways outside the scope of how the institution of the university defines research work. Over the course of the project, Ellinghaus has learned that entering a working relationship with an Aboriginal Elder and/or knowledge holder comes with the benefits of access to highly sought-after information, but there is also work to do. In return for agreeing to participate in research, Elders and knowledge holders often demand the researcher pay with their time and effort by working on the things that matter most to the Elder. Wilson used Ellinghaus's research visit to exchange historical information for labour directed at the task of house cleaning and yard maintenance.

MEMORY IN PLACE

Figures 2.4 and 2.5. Relationality and the servitude of forging ethical research relationships.
Photographs: L Wilson and J Judd.

The photograph on the left was staged by Ellinghaus and Wilson during Ellinghaus's visit and shows her sweeping up a patio area in Wilson's yard. It was sent to Judd in a text message intended as a humorous commentary on the relationship that had developed between Ellinghaus and Wilson. Significantly, the relationship between the two has remained good, ethical and productive over time because Ellinghaus has come to occupy a subservient role to Wilson as Aboriginal Elder and knowledge holder. It is also significant that, in assuming this position in the relationship, Ellinghaus has also submitted, perhaps unknowingly, to the ethical and cultural frameworks that inform how Wilson acts in the world and understands it to be. The photograph of yard work being undertaken demonstrates just how much the lines between the personal and the professional, between work and life, become blurred or practically meaningless in research situations where the need for relationality is given value and priority. The subservience of Ellinghaus as depicted in Figure 2.4 can also be understood as the outcome of Indigenous ethical frameworks and understandings in action. In Pitjantjatjara the term *ngapartji ngarpartji*, meaning 'in turn' or 'in return', signifies much about how ethical relationships are considered by Aboriginal peoples in Central Australia. *Ngapartji ngarpartji* aptly describes the relationality that has developed between Ellinghaus and

Wilson. A careful balancing act between rights and responsibilities, access rights to knowledge and the cultural obligations that emerge as a result. It is a relationship between two women, one older and one younger, that might be considered 'proper and right' and in accordance with Aboriginal law and culture. It works because both women understand that this is not a relationship of equals.

Several months after Ellinghaus staged her photo, Judd visited Alice Springs and found himself in a similarly subservient position in his relationship with Lorna Wilson, who is his mother. Undertaking the same yard duties that Ellinghaus had carried out months earlier, Judd staged the photo as a parody of the original. Sending it by text to Ellinghaus, both photographs have become the basis of a standing joke about what constructing research practices built on relationality with Aboriginal people means in terms of the various expectations this may give rise to. Yard duties and house cleaning is a cost Ellinghaus has deemed to be fair. For Judd, the staged photographs showing yard work replacing research work as the primary reason for visiting Wilson in Alice Springs is a reminder that skin names bequeathed, and knowledge and wisdom passed on, never come for free. Looking beyond the intended humour of these photographs, Judd believes they pose serious questions for academic researchers about whether they are personally equipped to submit themselves to a situation of subservience to an Aboriginal Elder in accordance with Aboriginal law, culture and ethics. Thinking about the photographs prompted him to send a copy of Kim Mahood's (2012) essay 'Kartiya Are Like Toyotas: White Workers on Australia's Cultural Frontier' to Ellinghaus with the message 'doesn't this sound familiar?' Mahood's essay describes the unhealthy dynamic experienced by kartiya (non-Indigenous people) in remote communities who rush in with good intentions but are unable to withstand the pressures of the job and leave, only to be replaced by other unprepared do-gooders. Mahood writes about the 'legacy of expectation and dependency, coupled with one of failure and disappointment' that is created by this process. The interactions between Ellinghaus and Wilson depicted in this essay certainly bear the weight of this phenomenon. Humour is our chosen method of dealing with this without dismissing it. For Ellinghaus, both the jokes and the housework are ways of following Sara Ahmed's (2004, p. 59) call:

> for white subjects ... to stay implicated in what they critique, but in turning towards their role and responsibility in these histories of racism, as histories of this present, to turn away from themselves, and towards others.

Conclusion

It seems both sad and hopeful to publish an essay about the importance of visits to place so soon after the lockdowns and travel bans of the global pandemic. Mobility has been necessary to deepening our understandings of the Indigenous people and communities whom we represent through our collaborative writings. In this essay, we have focused on photographs not as evidence of past colonial violence, nor as ways to commemorate or repatriate history, nor as documents that need decolonised reframings through creative practice. Rather, we have used them as evidence of the experiential learnings in place that have been critical to our ability to strengthen and maintain our research collaboration. As Elizabeth Edwards (2015, p. 248) argues, 'ultimately photographs are evidence of affect, of how people feel, and think and negotiate their world'. These images commemorate moments when the past is being remembered and communicated in ways that are deeply meaningful, even when meant as a joke. They depict communication that is only made possible by personal relationships that exist between the photographed and the photographer, relationships built over time by the simple but important method of visiting, returning and visiting again.

Acknowledgements

This chapter was written on Wurundjeri and Dja Dja Wurrung Country, and we acknowledge the Traditional Owners of Central Australia. We also thank Lorna Wilson for her editorial advice, and Beth Marsden for expert research assistance. This research is supported by ARC DP200103269.

References

Ahmed, S. (2004). Declarations of whiteness: The non-performativity of anti-racism. *Borderlands e-Journal*, *3*(2). webarchive.nla.gov.au/awa/20050616083826/http://www.borderlandsejournal.adelaide.edu.au/vol3no2_2004/ahmed_declarations.htm

Aird, M. (2015). Tactics of survival: Images of Aboriginal women and domestic service. In V. Haskins & C. Lowrie (Eds.), *Colonization and domestic service: Historical and contemporary perspectives* (pp. 182–190). Routledge, Taylor & Francis Group.

Andrew, B. & Neath, J. (2018). Encounters with legacy images: Decolonising and re-imagining photographic evidence from the colonial archive. *History of Photography*, *42*(3), 217–238. doi.org/10.1080/03087298.2018.1440933

Azoulay, A. (2008). *The civil contract of photography*. Zone Books.

Birch, T. (2006). Testimony (archive box no. 4). *Aboriginal History*, *30*, 29–32. doi.org/10.22459/ah.30.2011.03

Birch, T. (2013). The trouble with history. In A. Clark & P. Ashton, (Eds.), *Australian history now* (pp. 232–250). UNSW Press.

Bradley, J. (2014). *Singing saltwater Country: Journey to the songlines of Carpentaria*. Allen & Unwin.

Burke, P. (2013). Indigenous diaspora and the prospects for cosmopolitan 'orbiting': The Warlpiri case. *Asia Pacific Journal of Anthropology*, *14*(4), 304–322, doi.org/10.1080/14442213.2013.804870

Corn, A. (2018). Joe Gumbula, the Ancestral chorus, and the value of Indigenous knowledges. *Preservation, Digital Technology & Culture*, *47*(3–4), 77–90. doi.org/10.1515/pdtc-2018-0027

Corn, A. & Patrick, W. J. (2018). Home within: Locating a Warlpiri approach to developing and applying an Indigenous educational philosophy in Australian contexts. In J. Petrovic & R. M. Mitchell (Eds.), *Indigenous philosophies of education around the world* (pp. 168–194). Taylor & Francis. doi.org/10.4324/9781315173603-9

Edwards, E. (2015). Anthropology and photography: A long history of knowledge and affect. *Photographies*, *8*(3), 235–252. doi.org/10.1080/17540763.2015.1103088

Ellinghaus, K. & Judd, B. (2020). Writing as kin: Producing ethical histories through collaboration in unexpected places. Researching F. W. Albrecht, assimilation policy and Lutheran experiments in Aboriginal education. In S. Maddison & S. Nakata (Series Eds.), *Questioning Indigenous–settler relations: Indigenous perspectives. Indigenous–settler relations in Australia and the world series*: Vol. 1 (pp. 55–68). Springer.

Graham-Stewart, M. & McWhannell, F. (2017). *Bitter fruit: Australian photographs to 1963*. Michael Graham-Stewart.

Grieves, G. (2005). The politics and ethics of writing Indigenous histories. *Melbourne Historical Journal*, *33*, 1–5.

Harkin, N. (2020). Weaving the colonial archive: A basket to lighten the load, *Journal of Australian Studies, 44*(2), 154–166. doi.org/10.1080/14443058.2020.1754276

Hughes, K. & Trevorrow, E. (2018). 'The nation is coming to life': Law, sovereignty, and belonging in Ngarrindjeri photography of the mid-twentieth century. *History of Photography, 42*(3), 249–268. doi.org/10.1080/03087298.2018.1521571

Judd, B. (2018). Introduction to special issue: Being here matters. *Learning Communities: International Journal of Learning in Social Contexts [Special Issue: Ethical relationships, ethical research in Aboriginal contexts: Perspectives from central Australia], 23*, 2–11. doi.org/10.18793/LCJ2018.23.01

Judd, B. & Ellinghaus, K. (2020). F. W. Albrecht, assimilation policy and the education of Aboriginal girls in Central Australia: Overcoming disciplinary decadence in Australian history. *Journal of Australian Studies 44*(2), 167–181. doi.org/10.1080/14443058.2020.1754275

Kearney, A. (2018). Intimacy and distance: Indigenous relationships to Country in Northern Australia. *Ethnos, 83*(1), 172–191. doi.org/10.1080/00141844.2016.1236827

Kearney, A. (2019). Interculturalism and responsive reflexivity in a settler colonial context. *Religions, 10*(3), 199–217. doi.org/10.3390/rel10030199

Leane, J. (2017) Historians. *Overland, Oodgeroo Noonuccal Poetry Prize Issue.* overland.org.au/previous-issues/2017-oodgeroo-noonuccal/poetry-prize-jeanine-leane/

Lydon, J. (2006). *Eye contact: Photographing Indigenous Australians*. Duke University Press. doi.org/10.2307/j.ctv125jfqq

Lydon, J. (2012). *Flash of recognition: Photography and the emergency of Indigenous rights*. New South Publishing.

Lydon, J. (2016). *Photography, humanitarianism, empire*. Bloomsbury. doi.org/10.5040/9781474235532

Mahood, K. (2012). Kartiya are like Toyotas. *Griffith Review, 36*, 26–46.

McGrath, P. F. & Brooks, D. (2010). *Their Darkest Hour*: The films and photographs of William Grayden and the history of the 'Warburton Range controversy' of 1957. *Aboriginal History, 34*, 115–141. doi.org/10.22459/ah.34.2011.05

McKay, J. & Memmott, P. (2016). Staged savagery: Archibald Meston and his Indigenous exhibits. *Aboriginal History, 40*, 181–203. doi.org/10.22459/AH.40.2016.07

Moreton-Robinson, A. (2016). Relationality: A key presupposition of an Indigenous social research paradigm. In J. M. O'Brien & C. Andersen, (Eds.), *Sources and methods in Indigenous studies* (pp. 69–77). Routledge, Taylor & Francis Group.

Musharbash, Y. (2009). *Yuendumu everyday: Contemporary life in remote Aboriginal Australia*. Aboriginal Studies Press.

Nakata, N. M., Nakata, V., Keech, S. & Bolt, R. (2012). Decolonial goals and pedagogies for Indigenous studies. *Decolonization: Indigeneity, Education & Society 1*(1), 120–140.

Nettelbeck, A. & Foster, R. (2007). *In the name of the law: William Willshire and the policing of the Australian frontier*. Wakefield Press.

Peters-Little, F. (2010). Introduction. In F. Peters-Little, A. Curthoys & J. Docker (Eds.), *Passionate histories: Myth, memory and Indigenous Australia* (pp. 1–6). ANU Press. doi.org/10.22459/PH.09.2010

Sentance, N. (2019, September). Colonial archives: Archival poetics. *Sydney Review of Books*. sydneyreviewofbooks.com/review/natalie-harkin-archival-poetics/

Standfield, R. (2004). 'A remarkably tolerant nation'?: Constructions of benign whiteness in Australian political discourse. *Borderlands e-journal, 3*(2). webarchive.nla.gov.au/awa/20050616083909/http://www.borderlandsejournal.adelaide.edu.au/vol3no2_2004/standfield_tolerantnation.htm

Standfield, R. & Stevens, M. (2019). New histories but old patterns: Kāi Tahu in Australia. In V. Stead & J. Altman (Eds.), *Labour lines and colonial power: Indigenous and Pacific Islander labour mobility in Australia* (pp. 103–132). ANU Press. doi.org/10.22459/LLCP.2019.05

Tuck, E. & Yang, K. W. (2012). Decolonization is not a metaphor. *Decolonization: Indigeneity, Education & Society, 1*(1), 1–40.

3

Memory-lines: Ethnographies of colonial violence in Central Australia

Jason Gibson, Jennifer Green and Joel Perrurle Liddle

It is often while driving with people in Central Australia that stories are shared. The engine hums, the chassis shakes and people begin to talk. Traversing long distances means passing by and crossing over ancestral, historical and personal stories of kin and Country, sometimes in rapid succession. On one occasion, two Anmatyerr Elders, Huckitta Lynch and Ronnie McNamara, called out over the din of the Toyota engine to recount the story of an attack in the 'olden' times. Ronnie bent over into the cabin where Jason Gibson was driving and, speaking loudly into his ear, remarked that during the time of 'the war' Anmatyerr men had used fire as their primary weapon. He continued: 'They made *rwa* (fires) everywhere around the station at Angkwerl (Annas Reservoir). Killed whitefellas too. We made trouble everywhere.'[1] The archive, too, records these events, noting that the thatched roof of the Annas Reservoir homestead was set alight by a large group of Aboriginal men who waited outside with their spears at the ready. The exact reasons for the attack on Annas Reservoir are not known, but there is evidence to suggest that access to resources, or perhaps the rape of a young Anmatyerr girl, had sparked the hostility (Kimber, 1991, p. 11).

---

1   The spellings of words in Indigenous languages in this chapter follow conventions used in published dictionaries of these languages. Where appropriate, alternative spellings in different languages, for example in Warlpiri and in Kaytetye, are given.

Whatever the cause, the 1884 Annas Reservoir attack was followed by a brutal response from the authorities, whereby the notoriously violent Mounted Constable William Willshire (see Griffiths, this volume), other police and Aboriginal native police pursued and shot dead a number of Anmatyerr people ('The late outrage', 1884, p. 5).

Indigenous people retain memories of these events and other examples of frontier violence through modes of historical and cultural practice involving the recounting of oral narratives, visits to Country (Gibson, 2020, pp. 183–209) and, more recently, through the construction of monuments and the hosting of large-scale memorial events. The spectre of colonial violence looms large over parts of Central Australia, and some placenames imposed by settler-colonists are a continual reminder of the role of violence in the annexation of Indigenous lands. Skull Creek, for example, is said to take its name from the bleached bones left there after a punitive party shot numerous Indigenous people in response to an attack on the Barrow Creek Telegraph Station in 1874. Blackfellows Bones Bore (Itarlentye), a place roughly 100 kilometres north-east of Alice Springs and discussed at length below, similarly marks the site of police shootings in the late nineteenth century. In Anmatyerr Country, Wirmbrandt Rock (traditionally known as Mwetyek), on the edge of Lake Lewis, is named on colonial maps after Constable Erwein Wurmbrand, a man remembered by local people as *tyerrenherrenhe nthurre*, an excessive or 'quick shooter' (Strehlow, 1960, p. 73).[2] A street in Alice Springs retains the name of the notorious Mounted Constable Willshire, despite decades of community protests and recent lobbying to the Alice Springs Town Council for its name to be changed.

This chapter examines contrasting forms of commemoration of colonial violence in Central Australia and addresses the different ways that the violence of the late nineteenth and early twentieth centuries has been remembered. Conceptualised as 'memory-lines', we visualise these stories as moving through time and space, shaped by social context and relationships. Their passage is enabled and marked in diverse and dynamic ways, such as memorials in place, social and oral memory, published texts derived from oral recordings and, increasingly, new media such as film and other creative artworks or online resources. The passage of remembrance through time raises questions about the nature of 'living memory' and of the impacts of a past known through 'memory, through family stories, through lived

---

2 Strehlow's spelling, as it appeared in his field diary entry, has been transposed to a modern Arandic orthography (see David Moore in Kenny, 2018, pp. 101–140).

experience and being in place' and a past learned through 'history', including written texts and commemorative plaques (Krichauff, this volume). To tease out these differences, we adopt a spatial/geographic approach to observe how acts of memorialisation might differ across associated cultural/linguistic regions and show how distinctive historical relationships with settler-colonial society have produced different ways and means of remembering violent encounters. Our general focus is on an area of Central Australia to the north of Alice Springs, bifurcated by the Stuart Highway, where the land is associated with Arrernte, Anmatyerr, Kaytetye and Warlpiri peoples (Figure 3.1).

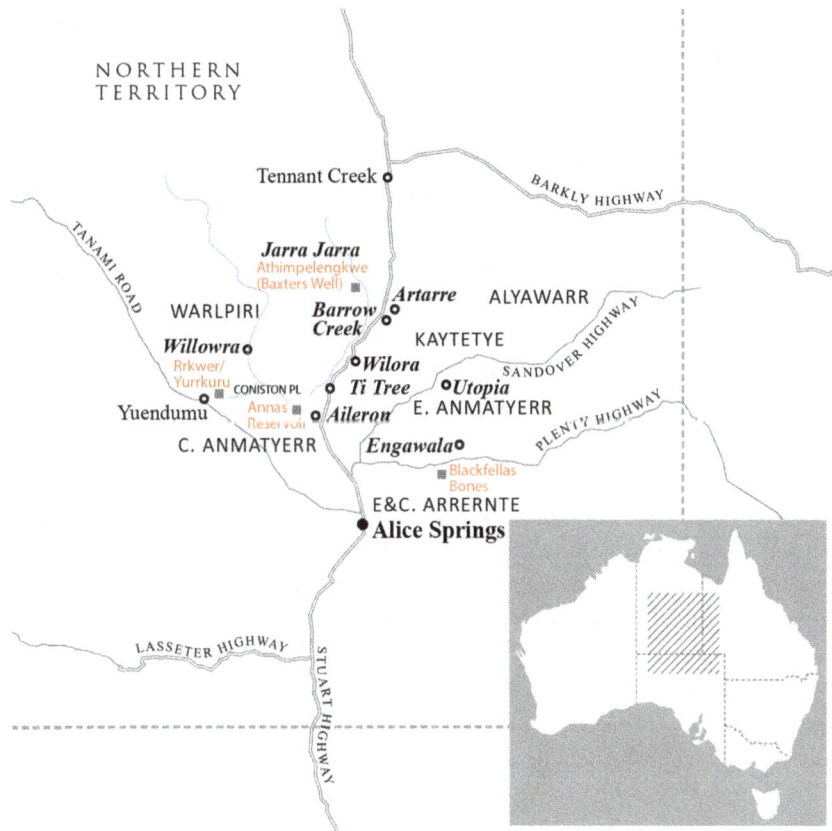

Figure 3.1. Map of the Central Australian region, showing key places mentioned in text.
Map: Jennifer Green.

Notwithstanding complex cultural and ceremonial links between these Indigenous peoples and the interpenetration of social relationships across the broader region, we first consider the country and peoples residing to the west of the Stuart Highway, then those to the east. As is the case with other arbitrary lines that delineate borders and boundaries, to differing degrees their geographic significance may be retrofitted to match underlying Indigenous ontologies. For example, across the Anmatyerr region, the notion of *altwerl-thayt* 'west side' and *ingerr-thayt* 'east side' is a common point of regional differentiation in the Anmatyerr vernacular, and the highway itself provides a convenient, if imprecise, point of reference (Green, 2010, pp. vii, viii).

Growing global debates about the removal of monuments of known perpetrators of colonial violence (Levinson, 2018; Mitchell, 2003) and processes of 'truth-telling' have reverberated across Australia (McKenna, 2018). In the Australian context, 'truth-telling' has been proposed as a means of 'clarifying historical truths' and paying respect to previously unrecognised victims and/or their descendants (Appleby & Davis, 2018, p. 504). Inspired by the release of the *Uluru Statement from the Heart* in 2017, which outlines processes for treaty-making and truth-telling, community debate about how to remember complex, shared colonial histories and acknowledge violent conflict has intensified. This chapter thus advances an ethnographic and historical consideration of this process from a Central Australian context. We ask how memories and stories of frontier violence, which may contain narratives that do not necessarily fall into conventional invader/resistor distinctions, are recognised according to the varying social-political positions of different Aboriginal communities. Moreover, we argue for a deeper understanding of past events and the ways they have been remembered, which permits a full consideration of Aboriginal agencies and interpretations. Drawing upon oral histories, we examine how memories of such events mark junctures of historical periodisation (between precolonial, colonial and postcolonial lifeways), emphasise feelings of immense loss and tragedy, and invite readers to consider themes of coexistence involving both settler-colonist and Aboriginal experience.

Early interactions

The spatial/geographic analysis also has historical context. The colonial frontier swept across Central Australia at an uneven pace and utilised different tools to subordinate the original occupants. No doubt ecological factors also played a role, as riverine country and water sources were prized by all, and mountain ranges presented a challenge for some forms of transportation. The first recorded European incursion into Arrernte and Anmatyerr Country was in 1860, when John McDouall Stuart reached Central Australia after several thwarted attempts. The expedition was instrumental to the establishment of the Overland Telegraph Line linking the north and south of the continent; by 1872, the line was operational and had almost bisected Anmatyerr lands (Devitt & Urapuntja Health Service Council, 1994, p. 25). Along this central corridor and to the east of it, pastoral entrepreneurs petitioned for greater police presence to protect their livelihoods and check against Aboriginal spearing of cattle and horses (Gillen, 1968).

In contrast, the lands to the west of the telegraph line, which progressively became less watered, were left largely unexplored. Some people in this area, often bilingual speakers of Warlpiri and Anmatyerr, lived on pastoral leases, while others grew up on gazetted Aboriginal reserves that had not been widely utilised for pastoralism; these people later moved to missions and other government settlements and have since received far greater attention from a range of scholars and Aboriginal advocacy groups than other Aboriginal people (Rowse, 1990).[3] As is explained below, this attention and support has assisted with the establishment of counter-monuments (offering alternative histories to those monuments erected to the dominant group) and with the communication of histories of violence.

To the east, however, people came to know settler-colonists via the distinctive experience of living on a remote and largely unruly pastoral frontier. Some Arrernte and Alyawarr people were dispersed and moved east into western Queensland and north towards Lake Nash and elsewhere (Lyon & Parsons, 1989). Frontier brutality and killings undoubtedly contributed significantly to their dislocation and exile from traditional Country. Arthur Groom's account of Indigenous people fleeing north in the 1920s is powerfully illustrative of how these dispersals played out: 'It appeared they were not wanted somewhere, and had been warned off. They had come through an area new and strange to them, tired, dispirited, and lethargic' (Groom, 1963, p. 10). Accounts of the past on the eastern side are rarely published and thus little-known, and memories of frontier violence are maintained principally

---

3   Although a very rough and ready metric, a search by language name of the Australian Institute of Aboriginal and Torres Strait Islander Studies (AIATSIS) print collection shows that the number of Warlpiri catalogue items far exceeds the totals for their easterly and south-easterly neighbours (Anmatyerr, Alyawarr and Kaytetye). While a search for Arrernte yields results on a par with Warlpiri, these records are predominately associated with Alice Springs and with Hermannsburg (aiatsis.gov.au/collection/search-collection).

in oral form (but see Bowman & Central Land Council, 2015). The archival record is also quite patchy, and although more recent oral historical material has been generated through land claim and then native title research, these records are seldom known beyond the local context and may be subject to access conditions. Here colonial violence has been largely forgotten by the wider public. There are no public observances or monuments to act as mnemonics for darker histories. As such, the way the region either remembers or forgets these difficult pasts has been somewhat shaped by institutional, political and legal determinants. Improved communication technologies and changing public attitudes have also combined to lift the veil on cultures of collective secrecy around such atrocities in some regions, but less so in others. The sympathetic public gaze is unevenly distributed.

Coniston monuments

We begin to the west of the Stuart Highway, with the Coniston killings of 1928. As the last large-scale atrocity committed against Aboriginal people by settler-colonists, and one of the better-known Australian 'massacres', the story of Coniston looms large in the national consciousness. Numerous books have been published, and documentary films made, about the shootings, and the details of these terrible events have been scrutinised by historians, lawyers and anthropologists. Aboriginal oral histories and eyewitness accounts were gathered during the late twentieth century when survivors were still alive to share their stories (Batty & Kelly, 2012; Bowman & Central Land Council, 2015, pp. 88–94; Bradley, 2019; Cataldi, 1996; Cribbin, 1984; Kimber, 2003; Koch, 1993; Read & Read, 1993; Rubuntja & Green, 2002, pp. 29–34; Vaarzon-Morel, 1995). Even Keith Windshuttle, the chief conservative protagonist in the divisive 'History Wars' debates of the 1990s, has acknowledged the extent of the atrocities (Windshuttle, 2000, p. 9). Former conservative senator for the Northern Territory and minister for Indigenous affairs Nigel Scullion also supported annual moves for a 'solemn commemoration' of the event so that it is 'never forgotten' (Parliament of Australia, 2018). Given the attention that these events have received in recent decades, we provide only a very brief synopsis of their history and instead focus on the forms of remembrance and memorialisation that have emerged.

Towards the end of the 1920s, after years of prolonged drought, opportunistic and hungry Anmatyerr, Warlpiri and Kaytetye people came into closer contact with the small number of settler-colonists. These predominantly male frontiersmen had spread out across the vast arid terrain, eking out

3. MEMORY-LINES

a marginal life under the watchful eye of the country's traditional custodians. Angered by the sight of cattle spoiling scarce food and water resources and encroaching upon rich cultural sites, and outraged by witnessing the abuse of Aboriginal women, Indigenous people along the Lander and Hanson rivers began confronting the new arrivals. In 2006, Anmatyerr/Warlpiri Elder Paddy Willis Kemarr recounted a story told to him as a boy about the disreputably cruel pastoralist Nugget Morton, who had been attacked following his harsh treatment of Aboriginal women. The 'old people', he explained, 'gathered together into a fighting group and attacked Morton just before daybreak, while he was sleeping … They smashed him about with boomerangs' (Kemarr, 2006). Morton apparently recognised some of his attackers and shot one of them dead with his revolver (Bowman & Central Land Council, 2015, p. 92; Wilson & O'Brien, 2003, p. 137). Almost a month earlier, a dingo trapper named Fred Brooks – who had similarly 'taken' an Aboriginal woman – was killed by an aggrieved Warlpiri man called Kamalyarrpa Japanangka or 'Bullfrog'. This incident took place at Brooks Soak (called Rrkwer in Anmatyerr and Yurrkuru in Warlpiri) on Mount Denison Station (see Figure 3.1). The response from the police, joined by a small group of pastoralists, was brutal, and between August and October 1928, a group led by Mounted Constable William George Murray terrorised the region.

The number of dead officially tallied as 31, however, other accounts suggest the number could possibly have been as high as 150 (Central Land Council, 2018; Cribbin, 1984; Kimber, 1991). News of the killings captured international attention, with British humanitarian groups joining with their Australian counterparts to successfully call for a full federal government inquiry. As with all the previous enquiries into earlier acts of frontier violence in Central Australia, the inquiry exonerated the perpetrators, finding that the shootings were 'justified'.

Some Aboriginal people had long been asking for memorials to those who were killed, and there are now two monuments to the Coniston massacres, both erected in the past 20 years. The first was unveiled in September 2003 at Rrkwer/Yurrkuru (Brooks Soak) on the 75th anniversary of the murders (see Figure 3.2). A plaque attached to the memorial rock states that the murder of Brooks led to the killing of many innocent Aboriginal people across the region and includes the text, 'We will remember them always', translated into Warlpiri, Anmatyerr and Kaytetye (Central Land Council, 2018; Monuments Australia, n.d.). With support from the Central Land Council, large numbers of people gathered for the unveiling of the monument,

61

women performed traditional dances, and the descendants of victims and perpetrators met for the first time. The great-niece of Constable Murray, Liza Dale-Hallett, read a personal statement of sorrow and reconciliation. Speaking of a 'shared history' of colonial encounter characterised by 'difficult and painful pasts', she appealed for a future of 'diversity and equal rights' (McCarthy, 2009, p. 8). Outside the Aileron Roadhouse, on the journey back to Alice Springs after the event, Dale-Hallet and Napaljarri, a Warlpiri descendant of the man who killed Brooks, stood for a photo opportunity holding the gifts they had exchanged. Napaljarri repeated a line that had featured in the formal proceedings of the event several days before: 'Ah, two murderers' daughters together!' (see also Vaarzon-Morel, 2016b).[4] A difficult moment met with dark humour and fellowship. The exchange was not meant to lessen the gravity of the Coniston tragedy, but rather could be read as an attempt to afford a level of generosity between people and begin to erode presumed barriers between them.

Figure 3.2. At the Coniston memorial site: Lesley Stafford, Jason Gibson and Huckitta Lynch, 2008.
Photograph: Mick Ngal Turner.

---

4   Jennifer Green was present when this exchange occurred at Aileron. Although the term 'daughter' was used, a Napaljirri would be a great-grandchild of a Japanangka.

The location of the Rrkwer/Yurrkuru memorial (Figure 3.2) is close to where Brooks was killed, not at one of the many places where Murray's party rampaged and Aboriginal people were murdered (Read, 2008, p. 33; Vaarzon-Morel, 1995). The stone monument stands out as a Western/European form of memorialisation on a European pastoral lease (although a portion of this land was returned to Traditional Owners in 2014). Travelling within the vicinity of the memorial site in 2008, Anmatyerr men were keen to take Jason Gibson to this monument and recount the story of the Coniston shootings. These elderly men had never received any formal schooling, could not read the plaque and showed no interest in having it read to them. Instead, they encouraged their visitor to learn more about what happened via the inscriptions as a means of augmenting the far more expansive, complex and detailed stories that they shared as the group continued to drive. While the purpose of the trip was to record ancestral 'Dreaming' stories in situ (at the places where these ancestors visited and resided), a detour to the cave where Bullfrog had hidden was added. These men believed that the events that unfolded there upset or jeopardised a provisional, yet deeply unequal, balancing of Indigenous and non-Indigenous interests in the region. Stopping at the old monument to Fred Brooks, erected by his long-time friend Randal Stafford, the men again commented that it was the unjust killing of Brooks that had led to the further deaths of so many of their family members. Indeed, as was stated in evidence in the Brooks Soak land claim, some descendants of those brutally murdered in retaliation for Brook's killing did not bear 'any animosity' towards him (Olney, 1992a, pp. 23–25). The process of site visitation, incorporating Western-style monuments within a distinctively Aboriginal landscape, raised complicated matters of intercultural difference, misunderstandings and asymmetries of power.

A second stone memorial was built in 2008 at Athimpelengkwe (Baxters Well, Figure 3.3), a site less known in the published accounts of the Coniston shootings, but well known to Kaytetye, Anmatyerr and Warlpiri people. Like the monument at Brooks Soak, the Athimpelengkwe structure stands at a site a long way from main roads, townships and communities and is unlikely to receive significant visitation from tourists or non-resident travellers, yet its intention is to generate public recognition of the extent of Murray's murderous rampage. Built by Indigenous Volunteers Australia and the people of Alekarenge (a community to the east of the Stuart Highway) with assistance from the Central Land Council and Newmont Gold Mines, the memorial stands at one of the many places where people were killed as the reprisal party moved north along the Hanson River. As Kaytetye Elder Tommy Thompson Kngwarraye recalled:

> The police went on horseback along the side of the creek, following the people's tracks. They travelled and shot people as they went along. There were two Aboriginal trackers who knew the country. They showed the police where the people were. (Kngwarraye, 2003)

Oral history accounts from senior people connected to this country have explained that people from surrounding areas were attacked at Athimpelengkwe where they had gathered for ceremonies (Koch, 1993, pp. 66–71). According to Thompson, they had gathered for a type of ceremony known as *ltharte* and were unaware of the impending trouble (Kngwarraye, 2003). Others believe that the 'ceremony was staged at Athimpelengkwe at the request of the police as a trick to get people together, and that in the massacre that followed there was an underlying message that ceremonies should no longer be performed' (Turpin, 2005, p. 42).

Figure 3.3. The memorial at Athimpelengkwe (Baxters Well) in 2008.
Photograph: Jane Hodson, courtesy Central Land Council.

Figure 3.4. The late Tommy Thompson Kngwarraye speaking at the Coniston Memorial event, 2003.

Photograph: Roger Barnes.

Constructed with affordable red brick blocks and concrete, the base of the Athimpelengkwe monument is unassuming (Figure 3.3). The attached plaque recognises two of the landholding groups that hosted these ceremonies – those from Tyarre-tyarre (in Warlpiri Jarrajarra or Jarra Jarra) and those from Errweltye. On top of the monument stand two large stones sourced from these lands (McCarthy, 2009, p. 10). Placing these stones in this way was presumably no small matter. What might, at face value, be understood as a monument to the fallen simultaneously stands as a statement on traditional land tenure and the ongoing importance of local Kaytetye and Warlpiri cultural practices. More than the monument at the site of the Brooks murder, this monument directly addresses those killed by the punitive party and draws in highly local and specific Aboriginal conceptions of place and personal relationships. A banner displayed on the day of the monument's unveiling quoted Thompson (Figure 3.4) as saying:

> We old people are thinking and talking about the history at Athimpelengkwe and we want to make it a public place. We want to make it a place where everyone can know what happened. We want to tell people about the place where the blood and bodies of our relatives lie.[5]

The eastern region

As detailed above, the sequence of reprisals known as the Coniston massacres had an immediate and fatal impact on the lives of Warlpiri, Anmatyerr and Kaytetye peoples. In the eastern region, however, where colonial violence has largely been 'forgotten' by the public, and where the archival record is patchy, there are no monuments or public observances to crimes of the past. In some cases Indigenous Elders and their families have retained memories associated with the events, and possess knowledge of the key places where violence occurred. The retelling of these stories nonetheless has been inhibited (Elliot, 2008). Stories associated with the killing of people by settler-colonists in this part of the region mark the juncture of historical periodisation, between precolonial and colonial lifeways. The stories are infused with feelings of loss and tragedy, but also framed within ideas of mutual ignorance or misunderstanding, as both black and white confronted each other, mystified by each other's presence.

As much as the Annas Reservoir conflict subdued some of the resistance, Alyawarr, Anmatyerr and Arrernte people continued to kill cattle. Reprisals involving groups of stockmen and police often 'working beyond the law' were carried out (Kimber, 1991, p. 13). Anmatyerr Elder Eric Penangk has described this period of history as a time when his ancestors would regularly flee to the hills for safety. Stories of hiding in the range country, retreating to caves and using the rough, rocky terrain to avoid punitive parties travelling on horseback were common among his senior family members. In the hills, people's tracks would be invisible to the unskilled outsider eye. Constable Willshire's own record of these events, written from the perspective of the pursuer, concur with Anmatyerr memory: 'We tried very hard to arrest them, but we were almost helpless in the big ranges compared with those savages, as they leap from rock to rock, and then

---

5   The text on the banner was sourced from Green's 2003 recording of Thompson.

suddenly disappear' ('The outrages by natives', 1884, p. 31). Nonetheless, police, settlers and trackers went on bloody forays reaching well beyond the 'settled' region.

At Itarlentye, now also known as Blackfellows Bones Bore and named for the human remains left there after the killings, one of these punitive parties shot a large number of Anmatyerr people.[6] Itarlentye is located on the Mount Riddock Pastoral Lease, on the eastern side of Ongeva Creek. Nearby, there are ruins of stone huts and other debris from a mid-twentieth-century mica-mining camp (Figure 3.5). Although within a region that is generally associated with Eastern and Central Arrernte (Henderson & Dobson, 1994, p. 10), Itarlentye is close to communities who may more readily identify with other Arandic languages, such as Akarre, Akityarre, Ikngerrepenhe, Eastern Anmatyerr and Alyawarr (see Figure 3.1).

Figure 3.5. Ruins at Itarlentye (Blackfellows Bones Bore).
Photograph: Craig Elliot.

---

6   Recorded as 'Etalinja' by TGH Strehlow on the *Songs of Central Australia* map. Carl Strehlow glosses *etalinja* as meaning 'continuous' or 'unceasing' (Kenny, 2018, p. 193).

The 1884 reprisals, organised by police and a band of volunteers, spread out across the region in two groups, led by mounted constables Willshire and Daer ('The outrages by natives', 1884, p. 31). Historian Mervyn Hartwig (1965, pp. 397–398) estimated that between 50 and 100 Anmatyerr people were killed during these reprisals (see also Purvis, 1940, p. 176; Young, 1987, p. 160), and while the incident has been referred to in a number of sources (O'Reilly, 1944, p. 117; Olney, 1992b, pp. 8–9; Perkins, 1975, p. 19; Strehlow, 1932, p. 108; Strehlow, 1971, p. 588), precise details of what happened at different localities are difficult to determine from the archival record.

Memories of Itarlentye

Historical archives contain only the slimmest details of what occurred at Itarlentye, but for the descendants of those shot, the memory is remarkably present. The few known recorded oral histories associated with the killings at Itarlentye are worth recounting in detail. The most significant accounts were recorded in Anmatyerr by linguist Jennifer Green with senior Anmatyerr men Tommy Bird Mpetyan and Ken Tilmouth Penangk (Figure 3.6). The first recording was made in 1983, almost 100 years after the event, and the second in 1995. These are clearly not eyewitness accounts but recollections of events that have been retold over several generations. As Tilmouth states, they are stories that 'the olden time people used to tell us' (Bowman & Central Land Council, 2015, p. 91). The cycle – from the initial recording through to community consultations with the authors of these interviews or their descendants – took place over a timespan of almost four decades. The community consultations at Alcoota and Mulga Bore in 2020 were led by Joel Perrurle Liddle, an Arrernte-speaking Indigenous researcher related to the families affected by the Itarlentye atrocities. Joel's close relation, Charles Perkins, recalls how people from his mother's family, 'including her mother, her mother's sister, and a number of aunts and uncles', were involved in the massacre that took place there (Perkins, 1975, p. 19).[7]

---

7   Charles Perkins was the first cousin of Joel's paternal grandmother, Emily Perkins Kngwarraye/Angale.

Such processes of engagement with troubled and confronting histories, and the return of archival materials, are theoretically and culturally complicated, resource intensive and time-consuming (Barwick et al., 2020). They are, however, of immense value to processes of truth-telling that aim to do justice to local stories, where the potency of history and memory coalesce in particular landscapes, people and places (Dalley & Barnwell, this volume; Griffiths, this volume). As we demonstrate below, in such instances, 'the mode of storytelling' (Dalley & Barnwell, this volume) – the nuances of verbal artistry, the words chosen, and their interpretations – adds an important dimension to ongoing understandings of how these traumatic histories are remembered and retold. These are 'living documents' (Griffiths, this volume); they add emotional and contextual contours to the sparse facts that can be gleaned from a reading of archival sources alone. It is also significant that in the various stages of the process we describe in this chapter, from the recording of oral histories in the 1980s and 1990s, to the consultations with community members regarding these recordings in 2020, the primary mode of communication has been in Eastern Arrernte and Eastern Anmatyerr (the first languages of the people concerned). While at times discussions switched to Aboriginal English, the medium of communication remained in these languages, enabling researchers to better ascertain the intentions of the individuals involved.

Figure 3.6. Ken Tilmouth and child at Amwely, Alcoota Station, July 1995.
Photograph: Jennifer Green.

Speaking with Green in 1995, Tilmouth explained how his ancestors, members of the Atwel and Ilkewartn Country groups in Anmatyerr Country, had been travelling together searching for food. Hungry, dehydrated and tired, they ascended a hill hoping to locate soakages that might assuage their thirst. A decision was made to go to a place known as Itarlentye where they could meet up with others who presumably might be able to share food and water. Tilmouth's recounting of the story from this point is exceptionally detailed and equally emotive:

> From there they went on towards the hill, and the man in front looked from the top of the hill and then said, 'Eh, there's lots of whitefellas down there …' And the whitefellas saw them, the poor things. They saw the man standing on top of the hill … They loaded their guns and mounted their horses … It was too late. By the time they met it was too late. The whitefellas started killing, started shooting. Right there.
>
> The poor old people tried in vain to defend themselves with spears. Others started to run away in terror. They shot at them and chased them and kept shooting at the poor things. Several of my grandfathers, from my father's and my mother's side, were killed … There used to be many men in Ilkewartn and Atwel countries. There used to be lots, but they shot them … The horses rode over them, really shouldered them. You know what shoulder'em means? Put them in the shoulder with the horse. Go alongside them and push them over with the horse's shoulder. The poor things. Others were shot. Some were shot so that their backs broke, and others were shot in the side … The whitefellas kept on shooting, oh, jinkles.[8] Another went into a cave, and he was shot inside the cave … The bones of the dead lay all over the place … They weren't buried, nothing. The poor things just lay in the open, just as if they had been shot like bullocks. The shields and all were lying in the open. (Penangk, 1995)[9]

Ken Tilmouth's father's father, a skilled *ngangkar* or 'traditional healer' named Charlie Penangk, survived the ordeal:

---

8   'Jinkles' is a local colloquialism probably derived from 'by Jingo' and used as an exclamation of surprise or strong emotion.
9   Other extracts from this recording can be found in Bowman and Central Land Council (2015, pp. 91–92).

He started to breathe, and he opened his eyes. He picked up his spears and then set off, escaped. He cried all the way. The hills dragged him along – and he kept going, mourning all the way. And others who had escaped the terror waited for him at a soakage called Arrkweny.

The survivors, in tears and shaken by the terror, regrouped at Mount Bleechmore (Kwepal or Awerrepwenty) and began covering themselves with white ash as part of their mourning ritual. As Ken stated, his grandfather was 'a good doctor'. As is sometimes claimed in oral accounts of these atrocities, some who escaped were credited with special powers – to render themselves invisible, protect themselves and divert bullets with song (Campbell et al., 2015). Others, as we describe below, escaped by 'playing dead' (see also Martin & Pascoe, this volume).

Knowledge of what had occurred at Itarlentye spread far and wide and was shared across the generations. When Theodor George Henry (TGH) Strehlow arrived at the site in 1932 his Arrernte assistant, Tom Lywenge, knew of the atrocities and referred to the place as *lalbala bon* (the bones of 'nomads'), meaning the place where the bones of those who had traditionally walked the country lay (Strehlow, 1932, pp. 21a, 126). Rather than using common, generic Arrernte designations for 'people' such as *arelhe* or *tyerrtye*, the use of *lalbala* makes specific reference to those earlier generations of people who were not yet familiar with white people. Here lay the bones of the 'old people' who first confronted white men.[10]

In 1983, 12 years before Tilmouth told this story, Tommy Bird Mpetyan recalled the story of Itarlentye in an oral history interview recorded on reel-to-reel tape. It was part of a project instigated by the Central Australian Aboriginal Media Association to record oral histories with senior people in several Central Australian communities. Green covered areas on the Stuart Highway and to the east, where she had skills in local languages and long-term connections. Bird's account vividly recreates the moments when the two groups became aware of each other's presence, before the shooting started:

---

10   TGH Strehlow glosses *atua lalbala* as 'nomad men'. The term *lalbala* does not appear in Kenny (2018), and its source is uncertain. It is possible it could be based on a form of the word *urlaylp* 'kurdaitcha', which is found in several Arandic languages (see Green, 2010).

> Right, then they were close up, and from a hill on the west side a big mob emerged. Well one bastard sang out, 'Hey, look out for the *arrenty* [monsters]!' The monsters were about to drink water … And when the whitefellas saw the Aboriginal people they said, 'Look out, there's a big mob of animals!' The whitefellas said that there were five hundred animals coming. 'Five hundred animals coming.' Because they didn't know anything about Aboriginal people. They were the same, level in ignorance of each other. And then the horses started galloping. (Mpetyan, 1983)

Bird also noted the lucky survival of Ken Tilmouth's grandfather:

> [He] … had been shot in the thigh … went into a cave to lay down and when that whitefella saw him, he pretended to be dead. He tricked him. And that whitefella said, 'Oh, he's dead.' But he just had a flesh wound. He pretended. (Mpetyan, 1983)

Part of the power of the spoken narrative derives from the intonation Bird imparts to the phrase 'Oh, he's dead' (spoken in English). Once rendered in written text, some of the vital performative aspects of an oral history, which can be heard in the recording, are lost. Bird's impersonation of the whitefella's summary appraisal of the consequences of his violent actions has a quality that is hard to forget – the way the words were uttered by the perpetrator encapsulates an attitude of shocking indifference. Bird's performance of the oral history, in particular his impersonation of the voice of the shooter, conveyed meaning in a way that a stone monument or plaque could never do.

The drama of the event is also imparted in the terminologies that were used for the unknown other. In Bird's account, Aboriginal people thought the pale strangers were *arrenty* (non-human, monsters), a description noted in other 'first encounter' stories in inland Australia (Charola & Meakins, 2016, p. 31; Gibson, 2015a, p. 45; Strehlow, 1967, p. 8). Conversely, the whitefellas are reported as calling the Indigenous people 'animals'– in Tilmouth's version, his countrymen were 'shot like bullocks' and not even accorded burial rites (Pascoe & Martin, this volume; Vaarzon-Morel, 1995, p. 45). Whatever might be said about the historical asymmetries of these words and their use, each 'side' did not view the other as akin to themselves.

Yet it is also Bird's reflections on the reasons for this event that make these recordings so significant. Rather than dichotomies of domination and resistance, his framing of the story evokes the more complicated matters of cross-cultural misunderstandings and asymmetries of power. Perhaps people could only be so cruel, and behave in ways beyond moral codes or notions of law – and kill 'just for nothing' – if they did not know each other?[11] Even though the punitive party had shot and killed innocent Anmatyerr people, Bird suspected that each side was equally unaware and perhaps perplexed by the other:

> They didn't know Aboriginal people – they were completely ignorant about Aboriginal people. And Aboriginal people were absolutely *myall* when it came to whitefellas. Well, both were equally ignorant … They were the same, level in ignorance of each other. (Mpetyan, 1983)

Here the language employed to describe of 'acts of othering' (Griffiths, this volume) is used reciprocally. Bird's use of the term 'myall' evokes the perception of a people not yet used to the presence of settler-colonial society. But, he asserts, both sides were as *myall* as each other. The term 'myall' is used in Central Australia to mean 'unaware', 'inexperienced', 'ignorant' or even 'wild' (Dixon et al., 1990, p. 171), but its origins may be traced back to Indigenous languages of Sydney, where *mayal* is glossed as 'stranger' (Troy, 1994). The terminology sets up a distinct historical periodisation, between a time when Aboriginal people and settler-colonists were indeed strangers to each other, and a time when they later became entangled. Speaking from a time when Aboriginal people had endured settler-colonial incursions since the late 1870s, which persisted in distinctive new social and cultural milieus alongside pastoralists for over a century, these Anmatyerr Elders remembered these events as key markers in regional histories that included complex relationships with settlers. The 'myall' or 'nomads' were regarded by subsequent generations as inexperienced and unable to navigate the new social domain.

However, what is perhaps most remarkable about these comments is the generosity displayed towards the perpetrators of violence. How could men whose family members had been killed and injured by people meting out extreme violence describe the two groups as 'equally myall', exhibiting 'the same level of ignorance of each other'? The generosity of these comments could be explained simply as a type of accommodation offered to the non-Indigenous person conducting the interview. Was this, for example, an instance of James C Scott's (1990) notion of the 'public' and 'hidden' transcript, whereby a member of a subjugated class offers

---

11 Vaarzon-Morel (2016b) refers to this as 'incomprehensible moral logic'. See also Vaarzon-Morel (2022, p. 4).

a version of history acceptable to the dominating group, while at the same time maintaining a covert version (the hidden transcript) out of earshot and away from the surveillance of the powerful? Having known both men, and having conducted fieldwork in Anmatyerr communities for decades, we suggest that this is unlikely. Both Bird and Tilmouth possessed a bigheartedness and a willingness to share knowledge within their communities, but also with others, and, like many of their generation, demonstrated a deep commitment to accurate oral historical recollection. Both men wished for people to know the correct version of events and recognise these complexities. Their histories of Itarlentye are intended to bring greater recognition of a largely unknown historical event, but also to emphasise coexistence as a theme.

Bird's notion of 'mutual ignorance', however, is indeed a challenge to conventional thinking about relations on the colonial frontier, and it includes the implication that both black and white are responsible for overcoming their ignorance and learning to understand each other. But rather than exonerating the perpetrators of these atrocities, it highlights the need for more nuanced forms of thinking about the complexities of culture contact. As anthropologist Michael D Jackson (1998, p. 109) argues:

> Rather than cementing estrangement, culture contact always entails, in some measure, for each party, stratagems of reconfiguring the horizons of their own humanity … Though every … encounter begins in strangeness and separation, that gap is gradually, though seldom utterly, closed.

The need for these 'reconfigurations' was certainly present on the unruly pastoral frontier, and it continues to offer space for both sides of this history to join in finding ways to recollect and comprehend this tragic past.

The resilience of memory

The 'spatial' aspect of colonisation has resulted in different ways of remembering the past, and these forms of memorialising reflect dynamic practices and shifts in attitude. Roadside memorials to mark the sites where Indigenous lives have been lost in motor vehicle accidents may now be seen, even on remote roads (Vaarzon-Morel, 2016a), and we are witnessing shifts away from taboos that prohibit speaking the names of the dead, even as respectful cautions are now routine. These serve to keep memories salient rather than to efface them. In Central Australia's west, monuments to the

Coniston killings have been permitted entry to the conventional renderings of Australia's 'negative self-history' (Rowse & Waterton, 2018, p. 12). With support and encouragement from representative organisations and others, including successive state and territory governments, these communities (often led by Warlpiri people) have been actively engaged in the work of counter-monuments and annual memorialisation events. As a relatively recent event, the Coniston killings are immediate history, but they are also supported by forms of evidence that are generally acceptable to conventional history-making: they were recorded in official archives, captured global attention, were subject to judicial inquiries and have been the topic of multiple oral history projects. They have also, now, been embraced as part of the Australian nation's difficult heritage.

The silent casualties of Itarlentye, although not locally forgotten, have not been memorialised in the same way as the Coniston killings. One reason for this may be that the killings at Itarlentye and surrounds occurred about 50 years before the Coniston reprisals. Audio recorders had only just been invented and were not used in Central Australia until much later, at the beginning of the twentieth century (Gibson, 2015b). Moreover, eyewitness survivors of the Itarlentye killings did not live to see the arrival of the Aboriginal rights movements of the 1970s and 1980s, when representative bodies such as lands councils, Aboriginal media and other organisations were established and scholarly interest in these oral histories increased. As we have argued above, documentation of these histories from those living east of the highway had also received far less attention. Since writing this chapter, we have noted developing interest in the violence that occurred at Itarlentye. When we started, Itarlentye did not appear on the now influential map of *Colonial Frontier Massacres in Australia* produced by researchers at the University of Newcastle (Ryan et al., 2018), yet, in the interim, mounting evidence must have passed 'the minimum threshold' for its inclusion (Dalley & Barnwell, this volume). There is also a mood for changing the official name of Blackfellows Bones Bore, although the reasons have nothing to do with the murders that took place there. Rather, the word 'blackfellow' has been identified as being 'discriminatory or derogatory' (NT Place Names Register, n.d.).[12] This judgement is indicative of a cautious and pre-emptive move on the part of local bureaucracy, as it attempts to respond to changing public attitudes towards racially prejudiced language. However,

---

12 The term 'blackfella/blackfellow', while a 'stigmatising label' in some contexts, has been repurposed (and sometimes respelled) by some Aboriginal groups and used as a positive marker of identity.

acknowledging the site's dark history – a fact currently embedded in the placename – would require more nuanced approaches. The complex ways in which both Tilmouth and Bird discuss the site demand a less generic response, one open to perhaps unexpected solutions that derive from Aboriginal community perspectives and aspirations.

Listening to these accounts of colonial violence is confronting – the impact does not lessen over time. And while processes of truth-telling have been likened to the 'talking cure' of some psychological therapies, there is no automatic efficacy in speaking one's mind unless the framework of a community contextualises and recognises the act. Adorno's (2006, p. xv) assertion that 'the need to lend a voice to suffering is a condition of truth' requires a sympathetic listener and will not necessarily heal the harm that has been done. It may be the case that the Australian nation is ready to come to terms with these complex and nuanced histories, and, as Krichauff (this volume) writes, this may facilitate 'non-Aboriginal Australians' recognition of their implication in the colonial process'.

The way in which Anmatyerr people tell these stories, however, is not intended primarily to address national concerns, but to accommodate local concerns and histories. Younger generations are told these stories not only to illustrate acts of resistance and domination, but also to bring past injustices into the present and inspire personal and collective reflexivity. To use the language of Connerton (2008, p. 63; see also Connerton, 1989), these memories serve 'a practicable purpose in the management of one's current and ongoing purposes'. Arrernte man Shaun Angeles, for example, has suggested that Elders continue to speak of these tragedies, not simply to reiterate the deleterious effects of colonial dispossession, violence and inequity, but to remind the coming generations of their relative freedom:

> I remember one time at Napperby and an old *atyemeye* [classificatory mother's father] of mine sat all the young men down and talked about these stories. In particular, he spoke about a specific group of Anmatyerr men (I can't remember where) who were in an *urrempele* ceremony camp but had to flee due to the killings. He explained to us that a group of young men had been forced to run from their bush camp and hide from the reprisal group, and how this happened over a number of days as they kept running and hiding, then running again … I think old man wanted to make a point to all of us about how easy we have it these days compared to our old men, specifically during the massacres. (Shaun Angeles, personal communication to Jason Gibson, 2 August 2020)

3. MEMORY-LINES

These sentiments are echoed in other accounts of violence that highlight resilience and survival in the face of great odds. Such histories instil in younger generations a sense of optimism grounded in the knowledge of where they have come from (Martin & Pascoe, this volume). As Bradley and Kearney (2009, p. 470) have observed in relation to Yanyuwa people's relationship to a specific place, 'through the act of remembering, people trigger emotional and political engagements'. We add, however, that these people–place–history engagements work as memory-lines to move across generations, draw in specific kin relationships and genealogical lineages, and intersect with larger shared histories.

Conclusion

The monuments to those killed in the Coniston massacres, and oral histories such as those of Itarlentye, speak to an entangled story of colonial coexistence; they are reminders of recently lived cruelties and privations, as well as the long-term, systematic negation of Aboriginal agency. The accounts that we have outlined in this chapter are rich in detail – of kin relations, the specifics of place, and of the cultural practices that so often form a backdrop for these accounts of colonial crimes and outrage. But they also attend to other aspects of these complex histories – acts of heroism or kindness, humour or rare moments of levity, and also reflections on what must be the most significant question: 'How could this happen?' Although neither Bird nor Tilmouth were born at the time of the tragic events they recall, those that were relayed their experience via an evidently detailed and affective oral retelling. Time will tell what is remembered in future retellings of such histories and which details of such memory-lines are maintained.

As the 'memory-line' of the Itarlentye incident has moved through space and time, it has been remembered through social and oral memory, and now also via archival recordings. In 2020, when family groups at Alcoota and Mulga Bore listened to the recordings of Bird and Tilmouth, many were shocked to learn of the dramatic events that occurred at Itarlentye all that time ago. The vivid and detailed accounts captivated audiences; while many just listened intently, others began to energetically embody and act out the actions of the key protagonists. Gripping imaginary reins, one man enacted the movements of the punitive party riders as they used their horses to knock people down. During another part of the story, he used hand and wrist movements to suggest that people used woomeras and spears in self-defence. This performative re-imagining, made in response to hearing archival recordings that had been returned to relevant communities and locales, may now play a part in the future trajectory of this memory-line. Such detailed and evocative stories needed to be shared with related families and other Aboriginal people from the region. It was seen as critically important that these historical events be known locally among younger generations of Arrernte and Anmatyerr people, but also that they be shared more widely with a diffuse Indigenous and non-Indigenous public.[13]

As the nation incrementally opens up avenues for the truth to be told about crimes like those that occurred at places such as Itarlentye, there are few remaining senior people who have spoken directly with those personally affected. It is generally acknowledged, however, that the 'affect' of this violence does not stop with those who were eyewitnesses. Consideration of Indigenous perspectives on colonial-era violence provides a crucial counterpoint to one-sided perspectives on the impacts of colonialisation. Its absence significantly limits the very possibility of address and the chances of fostering meaningful dialogue with the past in the present (although further archaeological and archival research may offer some scope for this). Aboriginal people are leading the way in terms of readying the nation for more nuanced histories of these interactions. They speak directly to complexities of the past, point out the diversity of regional experiences, and call upon both white and black Australians to move from narratives of estrangement to those that produce greater entanglement.

Acknowledgments

The authors would like to thank the descendants of Tommy Bird (particularly Colin Bird) and Ken Tilmouth for granting permission to publish excerpts from these important oral histories. We would also like to thank the following for their vital feedback: Petronella Vaarzon-Morel, Tim Rowse, Skye Krichauff, Myfany Turpin, Michael Cawthorn, Craig Elliott, Sarah Hayes and Yin Paradies.

---

13 For example, see Perkins (2022, especially Episode 3).

References

Adorno, T. W. (2006). *History and freedom: Lectures 1964–1965*. Polity Books.

Appleby, G. & Davis, M. (2018). The Uluru statement and the promises of truth. *Australian Historical Studies*, *49*(4), 501–509. doi.org/10.1080/1031461X.2018.1523838

Barwick, L., Green, J. & Vaarzon-Morel, P. (Eds.). (2020). *Archival returns: Central Australia and beyond*. Sydney University Press.

Batty, D. & Kelly, F. (Producers). (2012). *Coniston* [DVD]. PAW Media.

Bowman, M. & Central Land Council. (2015). *Every hill got a story: We grew up in Country*. Hardie Grant Books.

Bradley, J. J. & Kearney, A. (2009). Manankurra: What's in a name? Placenames and emotional geographies. In L. Hercus & H. Koch (Eds.), *Aboriginal placenames: Naming and re-naming the Australian landscape*. Aboriginal History Monograph, 19 (pp. 463–479). ANU E Press. doi.org/10.22459/AP.10.2009.19

Bradley, M. (2019). *Coniston*. UWA Publishing.

Campbell, A., Long, C., Green, J. & Carew, M. (2015). *Mer Angenty-warn alhem: Traveling to Angenty Country*. Batchelor Institute Press.

Cataldi, L. (1996). The end of the Dreaming?: Understandings of history in a Warlpiri narrative of the Coniston massacres. *Overland*, *144*, 44–47.

Central Land Council. (2018). Time to tell the truth. Remembering the Coniston massacre 1928–2018. clc.org.au/time-to-tell-the-truth/

Charola, E. & Meakins, F. (Eds.). (2016). *Yijarni: True stories from Gurindji Country*. Aboriginal Studies Press.

Connerton, P. (1989). *How societies remember*. Cambridge University Press. doi.org/10.1017/CBO9780511628061

Connerton, P. (2008). Seven types of forgetting. *Memory Studies*, *1*(1), 59–71. doi.org/10.1177/1750698007083889

Cribbin, J. (1984). *The killing times: The Coniston massacre 1928*. Fontana/Collins.

Devitt, J. & Urapuntja Health Service Council (1994). *Apmer anwekantherrenh, our Country: An introduction to the Anmatyerr and Alyawarr people of the Sandover River Region, Central Australia*. Urapuntja Health Service.

Dixon, R. M. W., Ransom, W. S. & Thomas, M. (1990). *Australian Aboriginal words in English: Their origin and meaning*. Oxford University Press.

Elliot, C. (2008). Social death and disenfranchised grief: An Alyawarr case study. In K. Glaskin, M. Tonkinson, Y. Musharbash & V. Burbank (Eds.), *Mortality, mourning and mortuary practices in Indigenous Australia* (pp. 103–120). Ashgate Publishing. doi.org/10.4324/9781315248646

Gibson, J. (2015a). John McDouall Stuart remembered in Central Australia. In F. Cahir, A. Inglis & S. Beggs (Eds.), *Scots under the Southern Cross* (pp. 41–52). Ballarat Heritage Press.

Gibson, J. (2015b). Central Australian songs: A history and reinterpretation of their distribution through the earliest recordings. *Oceania*, *85*(2), 165–182. doi.org/10.1002/ocea.5084

Gibson, J. (2020). *Ceremony men: Making ethnography and the return of the Strehlow Collection*. State University of New York Press.

Gillen, F. J. (1968). *Gillen's diary: The camp jottings of F. J. Gillen on the Spencer and Gillen expedition across Australia, 1901–1902*. Libraries Board of South Australia.

Green, J. (2010). *Central and Eastern Anmatyerr to English dictionary*. IAD Press.

Groom, A. (1963). *Flying doctor annual*. Dean & Son.

Hartwig, M. (1965). *The progress of white settlement in the Alice Springs district and its effects upon the Aboriginal inhabitants, 1860–1894*. Unpublished doctoral dissertation. University of Adelaide.

Henderson, J. & Dobson, V. (1994). *Eastern and Central Arrernte to English dictionary*. IAD Press.

Jackson, M. (1998). *Minima ethnographica: Intersubjectivity and the anthropological project*. University of Chicago Press.

Kemarr, P. W. (2006). Interview recorded by Jason Gibson, Ti Tree. Audio recording kept at the Anmatyerr Knowledge Centre, Ti Tree.

Kenny, A. (Ed.). (2018). *Carl Strehlow's 1909 comparative heritage dictionary: An Aranda, German, Loritja and Dieri to English dictionary with introductory essays*. Monographs in Anthropology Series. ANU Press. doi.org/10.22459/CSCHD.08.2018

Kimber, R. G. (1991). 'The end of the bad old days: European settlement in Central Australia, 1871–1894'. Eric Johnston Lecture 5. *State Library of the Northern Territory Occasional Papers*, (25), viii–24. territorystories.nt.gov.au/10070/718182

Kimber, R. G. (2003, 11 December). Real true history: The Coniston massacre (Part ten). *Alice Springs News*. alicespringsnews.com.au/1041.html

Kngwarraye, T.T. (2003, 31 July). Interview recorded by Jennifer Green, Tennant Creek. Transcribed and translated from Kaytetye by Alison Ross and Myfany Turpin. Central Land Council collection.

Koch, G. (Ed.). (1993). *Kaytetye Country. An Aboriginal history of the Barrow Creek area*. Institute for Aboriginal Development Publications.

The late outrage by natives at Alice Springs. (1884, September 17). *The South Australian Advertiser*, 5.

Levinson, S. (2018). *Written in stone: Public monuments in changing societies*. Duke University Press. doi.org/10.2307/j.ctv1198wqp

Lyon, P. & Parsons, M. (1989). *We are staying: The Alyawarre struggle for land at Lake Nash*. IAD Press.

McCarthy, Teresa. (2009). *Remembering the Coniston massacre. Territory stories*. Northern Territory Library. hdl.handle.net/10070/715097

McKenna, M. (2018). *Moment of truth: History and Australia's future. Quarterly Essay 69*. Black Inc.

Mitchell, K. (2003). Monuments, memorials, and the politics of memory. *Urban Geography*, *24*(5), 442–459. doi.org/10.2747/0272-3638.24.5.442

Monuments Australia. (n.d.). *Coniston Massacre*. monumentaustralia.org.au/display/80059-coniston-massacre

Mpetyan, T.B. (1983). Interview recorded by Jennifer Green, Angkwel outstation. Transcribed and translated from Anmatyerr by Jennifer Green. Original recordings archived at AIATSIS, CAAMA_03, CAAMA_07, CAAMA_11.

NT Place Names Register. (n.d.). *Blackfellows Bones Bore*. ntlis.nt.gov.au/place names/view.jsp?id=10930

Olney, H. (1992a). *Yurrkurru (Brookes Soak) land claim*. Report No. 43. Findings, recommendation and report of the Aboriginal Land Commissioner, Mr Justice Olney, to the Minister for Aboriginal and Torres Strait Islander Affairs and to the Administrator of the Northern Territory. Australian Government Publishing Service.

Olney, H. (1992b). *Harts Range land claim*. Report No. 44. Findings, recommendation and report of the Aboriginal Land Commissioner, Mr Justice Olney, to the Minister for Aboriginal and Torres Strait Islander Affairs and to the Administrator of the Northern Territory. Australian Government Publishing Service.

O'Reilly, M. (1944). *Bowyangs and boomerangs: Reminiscences of 40 years' prospecting in Australia and Tasmania*. Oldham, Beddome and Meredity.

The outrages by natives. (1884, 20 September). *Adelaide Observer*, 31.

Parliament of Australia. (2018, 24 August). *Remembering the Coniston Massacre* [Media release]. parlinfo.aph.gov.au/parlInfo/search/display/display.w3p;query=Id%3A%22media%2Fpressrel%2F6166575%22

Penangk, K. T. (1995). Interview recorded by Jennifer Green. Transcribed and translated from Anmatyerr by Jennifer Green. Digital recording deposited with the Central Land Council (identifier CLC-JGA_HIST_19950704).

Perkins, C. (1975). *A bastard like me*. Ure Smith.

Perkins, R. (Director). (2022). *The Australian wars* [TV series]. SBS Television. www.sbs.com.au/ondemand/tv-series/the-australian-wars

Purvis, A. (1940). *Heroes unsung*. Unpublished manuscript.

Read, P. (2008). The truth that will set us all free: An uncertain history of memorials to Indigenous Australians. *Public History Review, 15*(June), 31–46. doi.org/10.5130/phrj.v15i0.810

Read, P. & Read, J. (Eds.). (1993). *Long time, olden time: Aboriginal accounts of Northern Territory history*. Firmware Auto-Publishing.

Rowse, T. (1990). Enlisting the Warlpiri. *Continuum, 3*(2), 174–200. doi.org/10.1080/10304319009388171

Rowse, T. & Waterton, E. (2018). The 'difficult heritage' of the Native Mounted Police. *Memory Studies, 13*(4), 737–751. doi.org/10.1177/1750698018766385

Rubuntja, W. & Green, J. (2002). *The town grew up dancing: The life and art of Wenten Rubuntja*. Jukurrpa Books.

Ryan, L., Debenham, J., Pascoe, B., Smith, R., Owen, C., Richards, J., Gilbert, S., Anders, R. J., Usher, K., Price, D., Newley, J., Brown, M., Le, L. H. & Fairbairn, H. (2018). *Colonial frontiers massacres, Australia, 1788 to 1930* (Vol. 2.1) [Massacres map]. University of Newcastle. c21ch.newcastle.edu.au/colonialmassacres/map.php

Scott, J. C. (1990). *Domination and the arts of resistance: Hidden transcripts*. Yale University Press.

Strehlow, T. G. H. (1932). *Book I: Field diary (1) 1932*. Unpublished manuscript. Strehlow Research Centre.

Strehlow, T. G. H. (1960). *Book XXVI: Field diary (26) 1960*. Unpublished manuscript. Strehlow Research Centre.

Strehlow, T. G. H. (1967). *Comments on the journals of John McDouall Stuart*. Libraries Board of South Australia.

Strehlow, T. G. H. (1971). *Songs of Central Australia*. Angus and Robertson.

Troy, J. (1994). *The Sydney language*. Australian Dictionaries Project and the Australian Institute of Aboriginal and Torres Strait Islander Studies (AIATSIS). williamdawes.org/docs/troy_sydney_language_publication.pdf

Turpin, M. (2005). *'Form and meaning of Akwely': A Kaytetye women's song series from Central Australia*. Unpublished doctoral dissertation. University of Sydney.

Vaarzon-Morel, P. (2016a). Continuity and change in Warlpiri practices of marking the landscape. In W. Lovis & R. Whallon (Eds.), *Marking the land: Hunter-gatherer creation of meaning in their environment* (pp. 201–230). Routledge, Taylor & Francis Group. doi.org/10.4324/9781315668451

Vaarzon-Morel, P. (2016b, 2–4 December). *For a cultural future: Re-figuring the Coniston massacre*. Paper presented at the Annual Meeting of the Australian Anthropological Society, University of Sydney.

Vaarzon-Morel, P. (2022). Hope in a time of world-shattering events and unbearable situations: Policing and an emergent 'ethics of dwelling' in Lander Warlpiri Country. *Australian Journal of Anthropology*, 33(S1), 77–91. doi.org/10.1111/taja.12433

Vaarzon-Morel, P. (Ed.). (1995). *Warlpiri women's voices: Our lives our history*. IAD Press.

Wilson, B. & O'Brien, J. (2003). 'To infuse an universal terror': A reappraisal of the Coniston killings. *Aboriginal History*, *27*, 59–78. doi.org/10.22459/ah.27.2011.06

Windschuttle, K. (2000). The myths of frontier massacres in Australian history, Part I: The invention of massacre stories. *Quadrant*, *370*, 8–21.

Young, E. (1987). Resettlement and caring for the country: The Anmatyerre experience. *Aboriginal History*, *11*(2), 156–170. doi.org/10.22459/AH.11.2011.16

4

Tommy Burns and the challenge of truth-telling on the pastoral frontier in the Gulf Country of northern Australia

Richard Martin and Fred Pascoe

Kurtjar Country in the south-east Gulf Country of northern Australia was the scene of intensive colonial violence beginning in the 1860s with the arrival of white explorers and settlers. Multiple published sources indicate the scale of violence to which Aboriginal people were subjected, including correspondence published in the newspapers *The Brisbane Courier* (Carpentaria, 1868) and *The Queenslander* (e.g. Yeneen, 1874). Estimates published by Edward Curr, drawing on information from the sub-inspector of native police, William E Armit, indicate that hundreds of people 'fell by the rifle' across the district (Curr, 1886–87, p. 306), with other Aboriginal people also suffering severely from European diseases like measles, erysipelas (a bacterial skin infection) and venereal disease (see also Evans, 1988, pp. 96, 98, 99, 139n; Memmott, 1993, p. 1; Adams et al., 2018). Kidnapping of Aboriginal women and children was also reported, with Police Magistrate Henry writing in 1874 that 'the stealing of Aboriginal women and children' was 'a matter of frequent occurrence' and 'a recognised custom' at Normanton (Police Magistrate, 1874). However, apart from these sources, the impacts of colonisation on Aboriginal peoples of the south-east Gulf Country are generally poorly understood, with many details of historical incidents either not recorded, lost or destroyed (many relevant sources were destroyed in a fire at the Normanton police station and courthouse in 1969; Normanton Police, 1984).[1] Moreover, Aboriginal perspectives on colonial-era violence were generally not recorded in newspaper sources, archival documents and histories produced by non-Indigenous people, leading to partial and one-sided accounts of the impacts of colonisation in written records that privilege the perspectives of the colonisers.

Aboriginal oral histories from this region provide insight into colonisation and its impacts on Kurtjar people that are not captured in non-Indigenous records. For example, Kurtjar Elder Rolly Gilbert recalled the perfidy of the explorer Captain Cook in a speech to the International Savanna Symposium in Brisbane in 1985. Gilbert stated:

> That Captain Cook, that Jew, he was travelling in the boat on the ocean. Then he came out to see Australia. A couple of blokes were in the boat and himself. He said: 'We go ashore in Australia,' and they did come to shore, and saw these couple of Aboriginal people standing by the beach. They were going to do them over, like … shoot them down, and another fellow said, 'You had better not do that. They might give a good idea where the other people might be'. And so they did. They pointed out where the Aborigines had their main camping area. So they set off and found the tracks of Aborigines where they were hunting around the area. Then they went back to the boat and set up the people to explore and go down the countryside and shoot the people down, just like animal. They left them there lying for the hawks and the brows. I couldn't see that was very right. Everything what they done, some people shot off into the woods trying to save themselves. So they save themselves by going across creeks with a lot of crocodiles and things. They had to cross to go into the woods to save themselves. (Gilbert, cited in Chase, 1985, pp. 168–169)

---

1 While the cause of this fire is unknown, some local Aboriginal people have suggested it was deliberately lit to destroy local records about colonisation and hide the crimes of living (non-Aboriginal) people's forebears. The suggestion that the fire was deliberately lit was frequently made to Dr Martin during fieldwork at Normanton, beginning in 2010 and continuing into the time of writing.

Like related stories recorded elsewhere around Australia in the 1970s and 1980s, this 'Captain Cook story' contradicts official historical sources, conveying an Aboriginal perspective on Cook that repudiates his depiction as a European culture-hero and the founding father of Australia (see Kolig, 1979; Mackinolty & Wainburranga, 1988; Maddock, 1988; Rose, 1984; see Rose, 1991, for related Captain Cook stories from other parts of Australia). Instead, Captain Cook is presented in this story as a murderer who 'shoot[s] the people down' without compunction.

Kurtjar oral history stories told by Rolly Gilbert to the linguist Paul Black in the late 1970s and early 1980s provide additional detail about the actions of the native police and white pastoralists. For example, in a document entitled *About Kurtjar Land* (co-credited to Rolly Gilbert), Black and Gilbert record that:

> White people began moving in on our land long before any of us now alive were born. History books tell us that white people began settling in the area in the late 1860s, at which time the town of Normanton was also started. Our old people who passed away years ago would sometimes tell us about these early days, the *nokotingk*, or 'no good' times [from English 'no good' plus the suffix *ingk*, i.e. 'in']. The white men would drive us away from the places they wanted. They drove us away from our soak at Rdeekirranch, or Skull Hole, so that their cattle could have water. They shot many of our people there, and you could still see the bones in recent years, before the last flood ... Butcher Pallew's father was shot at Lntheerr, but by playing dead he was able to get away later and live to tell what happened.[2]
> (Gilbert & Black, 1980, p. 1)

In this account, Aboriginal oral histories are explicitly distinguished from what 'history books tell us', with these local histories providing details that history books lack, including accounts of Aboriginal resistance. Later in the same document, Black and Gilbert describe a place of such resistance, called Chinaman Creek – so named because a Chinese person was reportedly killed by Aboriginal people there – as well as other responses to violence, including the movement of Aboriginal peoples around the region to avoid violence, and their gradual assimilation into the pastoral industry on properties that were known to provide refuge during the *nokotingk*.

---

2   The spelling of Kurtjar words has been amended from the original to assist non-specialist readers.

However, with the politicisation of research about colonial violence during the 'History Wars' in Australia in the 1990s and 2000s (Macintyre & Clarke, 2003), attention has increasingly turned away from the explication of Aboriginal oral history accounts of colonial violence such as Captain Cook stories and towards the meticulous analysis of colonial documents. Eschewing the looser but in some respects wider veracity of Aboriginal oral accounts of colonisation, historians have instead focused on identifying incidents that appear in historical records. For example, the work of historian Lyndall Ryan et al. (2018) utilises historical records to show the incidence of violence occurring around the continent (see also further discussion in the introduction to this collection). Due to the paucity of records about places like Normanton, these meticulously researched maps suggest that no violence took place along the east coast of Cape York between Normanton and the Ducie River (north of Aurukun). In these maps, the evidence contained in Aboriginal histories, such as those collected by Black in collaboration with senior Kurtjar people like Rolly Gilbert and other deceased Aboriginal knowledge holders, is disregarded. These absences suggest that alternative methodologies are required to understand the incidence of violence across the continent, particularly in areas like Kurtjar Country. Yet, efforts to understand the truth claims of Aboriginal oral histories have dwindled since the 1980s, while the wealth of information contained in linguists' and anthropologists' records – and in Indigenous testimony in land claims and native title proceedings – has remained largely unaddressed by historians.

In the *Uluru Statement from the Heart* (ulurustatement.org/the-statement/view-the-statement/), Indigenous people who gathered at Uluru for the 2017 National Constitutional Convention called for 'truth-telling about our history' to build a 'fair and truthful relationship with the people of Australia and a better future for our children'. Since that time, the Victorian Government has announced a formal inquiry into colonial violence, entitled the Yoorrook Justice Commission (established in May 2021, see yoorrookjusticecommission.org.au/). Other Australian state governments have indicated plans to follow this initiative in lieu of any Commonwealth response. At the same time, other institutions, like museums, art galleries and libraries, have responded to Indigenous leaders' calls for 'truth-telling' in relation to violence, with the Australian Museum, for example, producing an exhibition entitled *Unsettled* (curated by Laura McBride and Dr Mariko Smith), which purports to 'uncover … the untold histories behind this nation's foundation story', including 'the hidden stories of devastation, survival and the fight for recognition' (Australian Museum, n.d.). This exhibition draws on historical documents, large-scale artworks, objects and firsthand accounts by Indigenous people to 'illuminate … the power of truth-telling to realise change'. However, questions remain about the appropriate research methodologies to document colonial violence, particularly as many incidents went undocumented in colonial records, and multiple and sometimes contradictory accounts of other incidents proliferate in parts of Australia, such as the south-east Gulf Country, where living memories of the *nokotingk* endure. In settings like this, Captain Cook stories and other Aboriginal histories of the colonial frontier continue to circulate, challenging straightforward historicist interpretations with powerful alternative truths about what happened. At the same time, oral histories of colonisation remain susceptible to criticism as contemporary people's stories about the colonial past are typically multiple, variable and inconsistent.

This chapter responds to the call for 'truth-telling about our history' in the Uluru Statement by providing an account of Kurtjar leader Fred Pascoe's personal connections to a colonial atrocity (see Figure 4.1).[3] In sharing this story, Fred describes his aspiration to produce 'history as told by us, as told by a black man for a change rather than a whitefella, [and to] have that history put down'. In our discussion that follows Fred's story, we draw out tensions between Aboriginal and non-Aboriginal histories of the past, as suggested by this quotation, and discuss some of the issues it raises. As Fred further states, this story asks us to consider the role of Aboriginal history in the construction of cultural identity, particularly among young Aboriginal people, but also among non-Indigenous Australians ('white people'):

---

3   In this chapter, we draw on an account of a murder, elicited in a conversation between non-Indigenous anthropologist Richard Martin, Kurtjar Aboriginal man Fred Pascoe, and Aboriginal curator and director of the University of Queensland Anthropology Museum, Michael Aird. This conversation took place at Karumba near Normanton on 2 July 2021, with Michael Aird participating via telephone. We additionally draw on the results of Richard Martin's research with Kurtjar people and neighbouring Aboriginal peoples conducted since 2010, including genealogical research, interviews, cultural mapping and archival research with Kurtjar people.

> [Our goal] is to have young Kurtjarra[4] fellas feeling optimistic: out of all the trials and tribulations that their ancestors went through, *the fact is we are still here* … We have a very successful cattle station [Delta Downs]. We are about to get access to the rest of our traditional Country that we never had [through the Kurtjar People's native title claim, QC2015/006, which was successfully resolved in 2022]. This is our perspective of our history in our backyard and the impacts of [the] whiteman coming into this country. Initially we struggled, but we adapted. To give them our perspective that they won't get from a textbook that they read. To tell the whole story, not just the bad stuff. I would like young people to have a sense of hope and optimism for the future, [and] for them to know where they have come from and that is their identity as a Kurtjarra person … [At the same time], I'd like to go some way to one day we might get to an Australia where the white people do acknowledge that there was a society and a race of people living in this country well before [non-Indigenous people arrived]. (Pascoe, interview, 2 July 2021)

We begin with Fred's story, followed by a discussion of the challenges of 'truth-telling' about colonisation in settings like the south-east Gulf Country, where the paucity of official records requires researchers to engage with Aboriginal histories of the region. In so doing, we build on recent historical accounts of incidents like the shooting of Aboriginal man Yokununna at Uluru in 1934 by Northern Territory policeman Bill McKinnon (see McKenna, 2021), which solicits perspectives from Yokununna's relations, including his brother's grandchildren. Our account of Tommy Burns's life and death differs from this and related histories by rejecting the assertion that 'the whole truth' (McKenna, 2021, p. 212) can be 'uncovered' in the archive and repatriated to Aboriginal people. Instead, like other contributions in this collection by Jason Gibson, Jennifer Green and Joel Perrurle Liddle, and Barry Judd and Katherine Ellinghaus, our discussion of Fred's story about his great-grandfather Tommy Burns indicates that histories of colonisation cannot begin and end in the archive but must engage in dialogue and negotiation with Aboriginal people. In so doing, we take inspiration from Minoru Hokari's insistence on collaboration between academics and Aboriginal storytellers and historians, 'not to dichotomise "our history" and "their history"' but 'in order to share ways of constructing the past' (Hokari, 2005, p. 214).

---

4   The label Kurtjar refers to a language and identity group of the south-east Gulf of Carpentaria. Kurtjar people pronounce the name of this word variously. In the discussion that follows, we have rendered Fred Pascoe's pronunciation of Kurtjar as 'Kurtjarra'. Other Kurtjar people pronounce this word as 'Kurtjar', 'Kurtijara', or 'Kurrtjar'. The Kurtjar people's native title claim uses the spelling 'Kurtjar'.

Figure 4.1. Fred Pascoe (far right) with Carpentaria Land Council Chairperson Murrandoo Yanner and Kurtjar Elders Joseph Rainbow (the named applicant on the Kurtjar native title claim) and Warren Beasley (a Kurtjar speaker and senior knowledge holder) during a break in the hearing of the Kurtjar people's native title claim at Delta Downs, 29 August 2019.
Photograph: Richard Martin.

Murder at Dorunda

Fred Pascoe is a Kurtjar man from the south-east Gulf Country (see Figure 4.2). Fred grew up in Normanton but maintains tradition-derived connections through his mother's parents to the Smithburne River on Delta Downs Station as well as the Staaten River on modern-day Vanrook Station. Fred's story is about the life and death of Tommy Burns, his great-grandfather (Fred's mother's father's father), who was traditionally associated with Dorunda to the north of Delta Downs. Fred's father was a Kuuku Y'au/Kaanju/Wuthathi man from the Lockhart River area of Cape York.

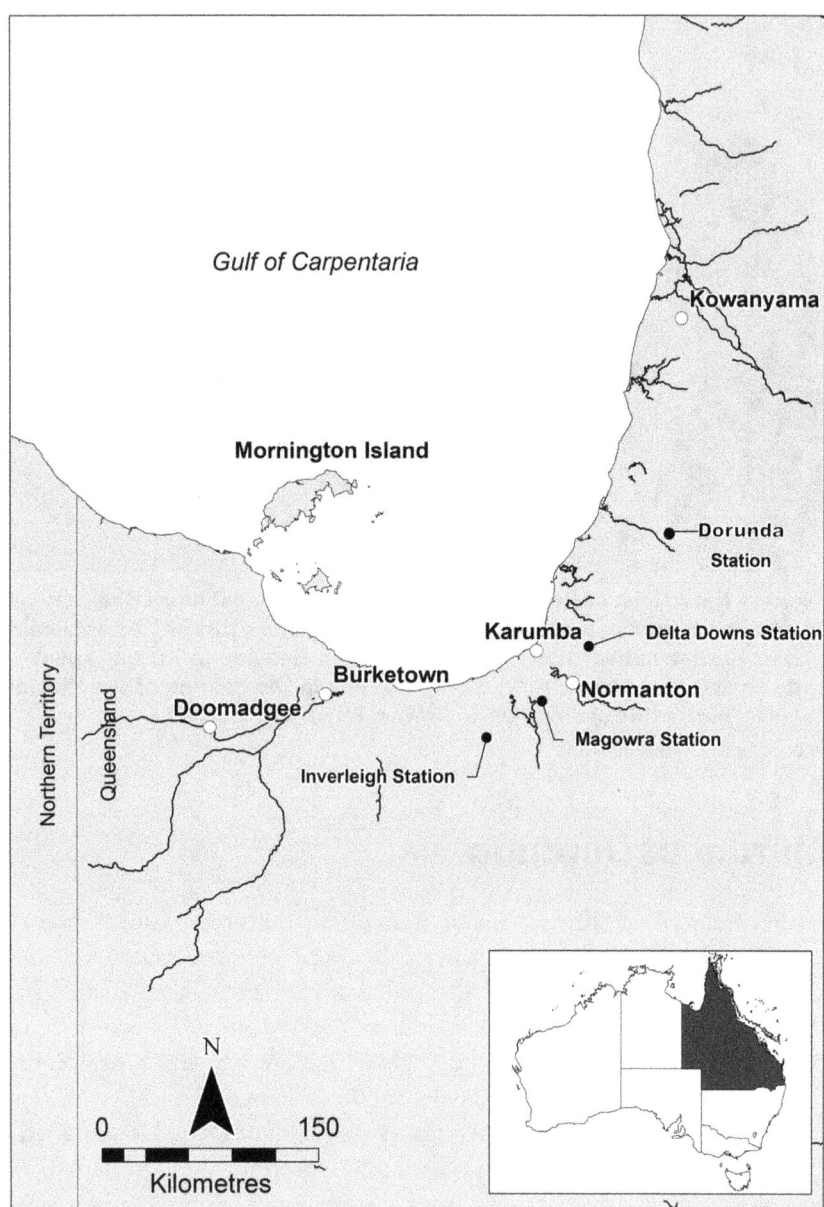

Figure 4.2. The south-east Gulf Country, showing Normanton and Delta Downs Station.
Map: Courtesy of Richard Martin.

4. TOMMY BURNS AND THE CHALLENGE OF TRUTH-TELLING

In our interview, Fred recalls how he came to know about his great-grandfather's story via his mother's father and mother's father's brother, whom Fred calls his 'grandfathers'. Fred explains how his great-grandfather Tommy (whom Fred calls his 'old boy') was an accomplished cattleman who worked with a white lessee named Jack Bell on stations around the south-east Gulf Country in the first half of the twentieth century. Fred states:

> As a kid … Tommy … worked with Jack Bell, who drew the blocks of Myravale and in his life owned Myravale, Macanoni Island, Double Lagoon Station and Dorunda Station [cattle station leases]. Jack Bell educated him in the ways of horses and cattle and Tommy became basically his right-hand man and … went on to manage and run Dorunda for him. (Pascoe, interview, 2 July 2021)

As Fred explains, Tommy Burns came to manage Dorunda on behalf of Jack Bell.

At that time, Dorunda was an 'outstation' (or subsidiary dwelling), which was connected to Myravale Station, where Jack Bell lived.[5] Fred further explains:

> Every dry season, after the wet, Tommy would take all his boys … Bob, Don, Noble, Nardoo, [and] Neville … to Dorunda along with other Kurtjarra men, [while] … the girls … stayed at Myravale … Tommy and his sons … basically ran Dorunda for Jack [and] Tommy became a very successful cattleman.

Fred indicates that Aboriginal men like Tommy Burns became indispensable to the cattle industry in this and other parts of northern Australia in the late nineteenth and early twentieth centuries. Aboriginal men worked as stockmen, while Aboriginal women's labour was focused on the main station homestead at Myravale (see McGrath, 1987; May, 1994).

Fred explains that Tommy Burns's traditional connections to Dorunda aided his work with cattle at that location. In our interview, Fred describes Dorunda as Tommy's 'traditional run', using a word ('run') associated with

---

5   At the time of writing, Dorunda was owned by Gulf Coast Agricultural Company, which describes it as a 110,010-hectare property running about 3,000 head of breeding cattle. The company further states: Dorunda was established in 1885 and named after the steamer SS *Dorunda*, which was the first vessel to carry beef from Queensland to Great Britain in 1881 … Dorunda is a hidden oasis, abundant with pristine natural waters, the largest of which is the remarkable 20 kilometre-long permanent freshwater lake, fed by numerous waterfalls in the wet season. (gulfcoast.com.au/discover/our stations/)

the cattle industry (referring to a limited grazing area or exercise lot for animals) to identify what anthropologists would describe as Tommy Burns's clan 'estate', 'range' or 'domain'.[6] Fred explains:

> Obviously, Dorunda being part of his traditional run he knew the country inside out. That was the reason why Blackfellas were so valued by Whiteman at that time; because they knew Country. Particularly in the wet season, [Aboriginal people] … knew where the high country was [and] where permanent waterholes were in the dry, and the Whiteman used that to his advantage. If he could teach them horse and cattle skills, which for whatever reason Aboriginal people picked up very very quickly and became very good at it, they were then an invaluable resource to the Whiteman. These large cattle stations basically had to rely on those Blackfellas running the show for them and providing the labour for them to continue. (Pascoe, interview, 2 July 2021)

Tommy Burns's role involved managing a team of Aboriginal workers engaged in managing cattle. In the first half of the twentieth century, such work was labour-intensive, requiring the regular mustering and branding of calves (and cattle), which were typically roped from horses and hauled to a bronco ramp or tree, where they would be secured to the ground for earmarking, branding and castrating (if male) (see Martin, 2019, p. 62). With few yards and no fences until the mid-twentieth century, mustering was difficult and dangerous, and involved many arguments over where 'cleanskins' (unbranded animals) belonged. 'Poddy-dodging', or the theft of unbranded calves, was rife.

Fred goes on to explain how his ancestor, Tommy Burns, was murdered by a neighbouring pastoralist who was jealous of his success at stealing cattle:

> Tommy became very successful, so successful that my grandfather told me he was actually killed by one of the neighbouring whitefellas. In them days, 'poddy-dodging' or stealing one another's cattle was a way of life. That was how most whitefellas got ahead in this country, how they got established, by rounding up 'cleanskins' or stealing some else's calves … Tommy was very good at it, and in the end it was to his detriment, because he actually got killed. The story I was

---

6   Anthropologists typically distinguish between an 'estate' and a 'range' using the definitions provided by Stanner, with an 'estate' described as 'the traditionally recognised locus … of some kind of patrilineal descent-group', a 'range' as 'the tract or orbit over which a group … ordinarily hunted and foraged to maintain life' (which normally included the estate) and a 'domain' as an estate and range together (see Stanner, 1965, p. 2).

told was that he was shot in the head with a .22 calibre rifle, and he was then struck with a single-pronged spear to make out that wild Murris – wild Blackfellas [i.e. Aboriginal people living in the bush] – had speared him … This old whitefella when he shot Tommy, he had two Aurukun blackfellas with him. He actually got the spear from one of those Blackfellas and stuck it in old Tommy's head and made out that he was speared by a Blackfella.

Fred then describes what happened next:

His sons found him. They were on their way back to Dorunda from Myravale. In those days it was all wagon and dray, and they were on their way back with supplies. It was getting into the wet season months, so they stocked up. And they found him pretty much two or three days gone in his camp dead. They dug a hole and pretty much rolled the old fella in to the hole right beside him, which is now in pretty close proximity to where Dorunda Homestead is … [T]hey in fact built a horse yard over the old fella's grave, and that's where he lies today. (Pascoe, interview, 2 July 2021)

Figure 4.3. Members of the Kurtjar people examine the area near Tommy Burns's grave at Dorunda, 21 June 2016. From left: Cedric Burns, Irene Burns, Joseph Rainbow, Lance Rapson.
Photograph: Richard Martin.

Tommy Burns's date of death was recorded as 27 September 1948. On his death certificate, which was certified by Jack Bell, his cause of death was pencilled in as 'Found dead', with no further information provided.[7] No inquest was conducted, and no one was ever charged.[8] Indeed, according to the official records, Tommy Burns was not murdered. Tommy Burns is scarcely mentioned in official records at all. He was buried at Dorunda (Figure 4.3).

Given the lack of documentation about Tommy Burns, how is his story to be told? Who was Tommy Burns?

Who was Tommy Burns?

Decades before the events at Dorunda, on the other side of the world, a white boxer named Tommy Burns (real name Noah Brusso, no relation to Tommy Burns at Dorunda) was the heavyweight champion of the world. Burns won the heavyweight championship in Los Angeles on 23 February 1906. He held the title until December 1908, when he fought Jack Johnson, an African American boxer, at the Sydney Stadium in Australia. Jack Johnson's victory in that match, at the height of the Jim Crow era in the United States, made him the world's first Black American world heavyweight boxing champion and an international celebrity, including in Australia. Jack Johnson's subsequent bout with James J Jeffries, in what was dubbed the 'fight of the century', overshadowed the life and career of the white boxer Tommy Burns, who faded into obscurity after his loss to Jack Johnson.[9] So how did an Aboriginal man on the Australian frontier come to be named after the white heavyweight boxing champion who lost to Jack Johnson? The answer takes us back to the south-east Gulf Country in the 1900s, where the American race politics embedded in the name 'Tommy Burns' collided with Australian race relations on the colonial frontier.

---

7   Queensland Death Certificate, Tommy Burns, C4436/1948.
8   Inquests were generally performed in this period if there were evident external injuries such as gunshot or spear wounds.
9   Two years later, in a fight convened to 'prov[e] that a white man is better than a Negro', Jack Johnson fought and won the 'fight of the century' against former undefeated heavyweight champion James J Jeffries, triggering race riots around the United States. Indeed, the University of Queensland Anthropology Museum collection includes a carved boomerang that commemorates Jack Johnson's 1910 fight with James J Jeffries, created at Deebing Creek mission near Brisbane, c. 1910–14.

4. TOMMY BURNS AND THE CHALLENGE OF TRUTH-TELLING

On his death certificate, Tommy Burns is described as 'about 50' at the time of his death in 1948, giving him an estimated birth year of around 1898, 30 years after the town of Normanton was established; his birth does not seem to have been officially registered. On his death certificate, his place of birth is listed as 'Staaten River, Normanton, Queensland'. No further official records about Tommy Burns's life have been located, apart from occasional references to his working life on the stations.[10]

Fred Pascoe's account of Tommy Burns's life provides further detail about his origins, suggesting that Tommy Burns was the child-survivor of a colonial-era massacre. Fred states:

> As told to me by those old fellas, by my grandfathers, Nardoo and Bob Burns ... Tommy Burns, was in a traditional camp that got raided by the [Queensland Native] Mounted Police ... We estimate from stories told by my grandfather that he was about 8 to 10 years old. So it would have happened in about 1910. I believe Jack Bell was part of the [Queensland Native] Mounted Police party, and the story goes when they raided the camp Tommy took off and Jack hit him over the head with a stirrup iron [used for mounting a horse]. Normally kids like that were bashed to death with a sapling, rather than waste a bullet on them. [But] Jack liked the look of Tommy, he was a sturdy, solid young fella. So, he said, 'I will take this young fella and see what I can do with him'. (Pascoe, interview, 2 July 2021)

Fred Pascoe describes his great-grandfather as the only survivor of this massacre, whose life was spared by one of the members of the Native Mounted Police party. In this account, perversely and disturbingly, Tommy is raised by a person involved in the massacre, who is named as the pastoralist Jack Bell.[11] Thus, based on Fred's account, Tommy Burns survived a colonial-era massacre as a child only to be murdered in middle age. Tommy Burns's life was, therefore, bookended by violence.

---

10 The association of Tommy Burns with the Staaten River is consistent with Kurtjar people's oral history about him, which generally associates him with Dorunda and Red River (which runs into the Staaten River). In his evidence in the Kurtjar people's native title claim, Richard Martin expressed the view that Tommy Burns held traditional country around Dorunda. On his death certificate, Tommy Burns's place of birth is identified as Staaten River.
11 Another member of the family likewise indicates that he was told by his grandfather (Tommy Burns's son) that Tommy Burns 'was a wild kid here, from the wild tribe ... Jack Bell stole him and named him and grew him up' (Lindsay Edwards, interview, 8 July 2016).

However, like the circumstances surrounding Tommy Burns's violent death, there are no official records to substantiate the assertion that Tommy Burns survived a massacre or was kidnapped by Jack Bell.[12] While Tommy Burns's murder is consistently detailed in Kurtjar oral history, Fred Pascoe's account of Tommy Burns's origins is not, with other Kurtjar people tending to suggest Tommy Burns 'walked up ... follow the Red River down right to Dorunda Station', and from there to Myravale, where he 'mated up' (i.e. married) a Kurtjar woman named Judy and started working for Jack Bell (Warren Beasley, interview, 21 July 2015). In these accounts, the context whereby Tommy Burns started working with Jack Bell is typically not emphasised, with Tommy Burns simply said to have 'walked up' to Myravale.[13]

Similar accounts of Aboriginal children who survived massacres by running away, or hiding, are also common across Queensland, with related accounts documented by other researchers in Aboriginal oral histories of the Gold Coast (south-east Queensland), Central Queensland, and elsewhere (Michael Aird, personal communication, 2 July 2021; Anna Kenny and Kim de Rijke, personal communication, 10 July 2021). In our research experience, such accounts share common features and typically suggest that the child was the last survivor of a group or 'tribe', and often that the child escaped by hiding in a log or by breathing through reeds while submerged underwater. Of course, the widespread incidence of such stories reflects similarities in Aboriginal people's experience of colonial violence, including kidnapping and the disruption of traditional kinship ties associated with colonisation: Tommy Burns was dislocated from his close relations, and while his death certificate names his parents, these names are generally not known to Kurtjar people and not associated with the broader set of Kurtjar ancestors.[14] However, such stories are also clearly cultural myths, combining elements of both history and legend, much like Rolly Gilbert's account of Captain Cook that we described in the introduction, or indeed the story of Moses in the Bible's Book of Exodus, who likewise escaped a genocide to be raised by his oppressors.

---

12   Jack Bell, the pastoralist, enters the records in the first post-Federation Queensland electoral roll in 1903, when he was working as a stockman at Magoura, south-west of Normanton, before leaving the district. He reappears in the 1930s and 1940s, when he is regularly referred to at Myravale in newspaper stories and other records. There is no indication in the records that he worked with the Queensland Native Mounted Police or participated in colonial-era massacres. See e.g. Little (1939).

13   When Richard Martin put it to the senior Kurtjar man Warren Beasley that Tommy Burns may have been a survivor of a massacre, Warren Beasley replied, 'I didn't hear that myself' (interview, 3 July 2021).

14   Tommy Burns was described by another anthropologist as a 'floater', this term being borrowed from studies of birds, where it is used to indicate an individual member of a species whose movements exceed the territory of its consociates.

The mythic elements of this story, and the inconsistencies in the record, return us to the questions we raised in the introduction about the appropriate research methodologies to document colonial violence and understand what really happened when white people arrived, and the impact they had on Aboriginal peoples like the Kurtjar.

Truth-telling about colonial violence

Our discussion of Tommy Burns's life produces a variety of conclusions.

Firstly, and most significantly, Australia's colonial frontier was shockingly violent, and this violence continued after the turn of the twentieth century. As Fred Pascoe puts it:

> The violence is an integral part of our history. From about 1900 to the 1930s, anybody that didn't come in from the bush to the cattle stations was shot or poisoned. (Pascoe, interview, 2 July 2021)

Indeed, as Tommy Burns's murder at Dorunda indicates, murderous violence continued after World War II, and in some respects continues into the present. The impacts of such violence, apart from loss of life, included the loss of languages and peoples, with multiple groups not surviving into the present. In the context of the south-east Gulf Country, this includes the decline of the group Walangama, who occupied Country to the east and south-east of Kurtjar people's lands, as well as the loss of other languages and identity groups. Reflecting this, Fred states:

> I just want the true story to be told about colonisation. Don't say that James Cook landed here and discovered this country and thinking everything was peaceful. It wasn't. My people died for their country … My people have been at wars for hundreds of years. And we didn't race overseas to fight some other man's country or for his country or fight his battles. We actually died in our own country, for our country. And none of that is recorded or talked or even acknowledged to the full extent. (Pascoe, interview, 2 July 2021)

While such violence is widely acknowledged by Australian historians, Fred's interview indicates his view that the 'true story' of colonisation remains to be acknowledged in its 'full extent' across Australian society, particularly in communities like Normanton, which are remote from metropolitan centres.

Second, while the temptation remains to periodise colonial violence prior to Federation and peremptorily close the frontier, Fred focuses on the continuing and lasting effects of colonisation:

> The lasting effect of colonisation has been the loss of identity, the loss of cultural practices, initiations, ceremonies such as dance and the stories that have been lost. Everything was handed down orally or in dance form or art form, so if the artist is no longer there to pass that down, if he or she was shot, well that's gone. It has had a lasting impact ... There is very much a direct link with colonisation and the loss of identity in young people today.

As Fred Pascoe indicates, cultural loss is an enduring legacy of colonisation, and such loss continues to be felt by Kurtjar people today, and Kurtjar people yet to be born. The violence of colonisation therefore continues, in some respects, in perpetuity, demanding restitution and compensation, as well as open acknowledgement of the impacts of past crimes.

Our discussion of Tommy Burns's life further suggests that truth-telling about Australia's past must go beyond the meticulous analysis of official records to engage with Aboriginal oral histories. Along with Fred Pascoe's account of Tommy Burns, Rolly Gilbert's Captain Cook story and discussion of the *nokotingk*, or 'no good' times, Kurtjar people maintain knowledge of other incidents, including Aboriginal resistance:

> Them whitefella used to chase them other mob and them old fella they used to get behind a tree with a spear or boomerang and *bang*, they used to do the shooting, but the old fella used to get their payment back. (Warren Beasley, interview, 16 July 2015)

Accounts like this, and others presented in this collection by Jason Gibson, Jennifer Green, and Joel Perrurle Liddle, and Barry Judd and Katherine Ellinghaus, add incalculably to our understanding of colonisation by restoring Aboriginal perspectives on colonisation and responses to it. Confining research solely to colonial sources means stories like that of Tommy Burns are too often missed by historians.

However, our discussion also illustrates tensions between Aboriginal oral histories and other accounts of colonisation. Fred Pascoe's story about Tommy Burns indicates that oral histories are not necessarily straightforward accounts of what happened and should not be solely interpreted as such. Instead, they have a looser but wider veracity that reflects Aboriginal people's experiences of colonisation. By utilising research and interpretive methodologies that listen and respond carefully to oral histories, inconsistencies that may arise between Aboriginal and non-Aboriginal histories of colonisation may come to be reconsidered as revealing other insights into Australian colonisation rather than simply being wrong. For example, Fred Pascoe's belief that Tommy Burns survived a massacre cannot be verified and exists in some tension with other Kurtjar people's accounts of his origins, but also reflects a fundamental truth about the impacts of colonisation on Aboriginal people's connections to kin and Country.

Our interview indicates that oral histories also reflect Aboriginal people's current lives and aspirations, as stories of the past contribute to the construction of contemporary cultural identities. In regions like the southeast Gulf Country, where Aboriginal people maintain stories about specific incidents of violence and those responsible for them, this results in sensitivities that may not be present in other settings. For example, Fred Pascoe notes that Kurtjar people believe they know who killed Tommy Burns. As Fred explains:

> I know who killed him, but I got to be careful, as it has never been proven. The descendants of that man are still alive today. I have to be careful, as it will be my word against theirs. They bandied another story around that a Blackfella took off from Maggieville [Station] and rode in two days up to Dorunda … and killed the old fella. He was supposed to have killed him because he was upset with him, then rode back and was back at Maggieville the next Monday morning having breakfast, which defies belief. They have spread that story around, that he was actually killed by another Blackfella. The killer's descendants are still in the region. (Pascoe, interview, 2 July 2021)

These sensitivities exist in some tension with national calls for truth-telling that may understate the living connections between contemporary communities and colonial violence. As Fred Pascoe's account of Tommy Burns's life suggests, these sensitivities include consideration of the living descendants of alleged perpetrators, as well as attention to the politics of small-town Australian life with its manifold connections between families.

Fred Pascoe's account also indicates tension between different interpretations of the past. Asked to reflect on how he feels about the colonial experience in his family's story, Fred says:

> Obviously, it angers me. It angers me … that mainstream Australia put their head in the sand when it comes to this type of stuff. You know, they say that Australia was 'discovered', well no, Australia

> wasn't discovered, there was a race of people that were here well before any Dutchman or any Englishman come sailing down the coast. And those people actually put in their logbooks and their diaries that they encountered *people*, human beings in the continent that we call Australia. And yet their perceived superiority of their culture and their race and their religion, that was so racist that they didn't acknowledge the religion and the systems and the society that was already here, and had been here for thousands and thousands of years. So that angers me that that true history is not really taught or really acknowledged in this country. (Pascoe, interview, 2 July 2021)

However, Fred's account of his great-grandfather's life also demonstrates pride in Tommy Burns's achievements in the cattle industry, as well as pleasure in Tommy Burns's poddy-dodging skills and ability to outsmart neighbouring pastoralists. Fred also insists, as we quoted in the introduction, that he wishes for young Kurtjar people to feel 'optimistic' about their future, notwithstanding the injustices of the past. As he puts it: 'out of all the trials and tribulations that their ancestors went through, *the fact is we are still here* … Initially we struggled, but we adapted.' These comments indicate the need to emphasise and acknowledge cultural continuity and strength as well as violence and cultural loss in representing colonisation and its impacts on Aboriginal people in Australia.

Acknowledgements

The authors wish to thank Michael Aird, who participated in the interview with Fred Pascoe on 2 July 2021. Richard Martin wishes to thank Warren Beasley and other senior members of the Kurtjar people for their support and assistance with his research at Normanton since 2010.

References

Adams, S., Martin, R., Phillips, S., Macgregor, C. & Westaway, M. (2018). Truth-telling in the wake of European contact: Historical investigation of Aboriginal skeletal remains from Normanton. *Archaeologies*, *14*(3), 412–442. doi.org/10.1007/s11759-018-9354-x

Australian Museum. (n.d.). *The Australian Museum's Unsettled Exhibition*. australian.museum/exhibition/unsettled/

Carpentaria. (1868, 9 June). *The Brisbane Courier*, 3.

Chase, A. (1985). Aboriginal perspectives: A comment. In J. C. Tothill & J. J. Mott (Eds.), *Ecology and management of the world's savannas* (pp. 166–167). Australian Academy of Science.

Curr, E. M. (1886). *The Australian race: Its origin, languages, customs, places of landing in Australia, and the routes by which it spread itself over that continent.* (Vol. 2). Government Printer.

Evans, R. (1988). Introduction: 'Keeping white the strain' & Part one: 'The nigger shall disappear'. In R. Evans, K. Saunders & K. Cronin (Eds.), *Race relations in colonial Queensland: A history of exclusion, exploitation and extermination* (pp. 1–146). University of Queensland Press.

Gilbert, R. & Black, P. (1980). *About Kurtjar land: A statement by the Kurtjar people of Normanton, Queensland.* Manuscript and recording held by the Australian Institute of Aboriginal and Torres Strait Islander Studies, Canberra.

Hokari, M. (2005). Gurindji mode of historical practice. In L. Taylor, G. K. Ward, G. Henderson, R. Davis & L. Wallis (Eds.), *The power of knowledge, the resonance of tradition* (pp. 214–222). Aboriginal Studies Press.

Kolig, E. (1979). Captain Cook in the Western Kimberleys. In R. M. & C. H. Berndt (Eds.), *Aborigines of the West: Their past and their present.* UWA Press.

Little, W. C. (1939, 23 November). The Lower Norman and Flinders watersheds. *Townsville Daily Bulletin*, 12.

Macintyre, S. & Clark, A. (2003). *The history wars.* Melbourne University Press.

Mackinolty, C. & Wainburranga, P. F. (1988). Too many Captain Cooks. In T. Swain & D. B. Rose (Eds.), *Aboriginal Australians and Christian missions.* Australian Association for the Study of Religions.

Maddock, K. (1988). Myth, history and a sense of oneself. In J. Beckett (Ed.), *Past and present: The construction of Aboriginality.* Aboriginal Studies Press.

Martin, R. (2019). *The Gulf Country: The story of people and place in outback Queensland.* Allen & Unwin.

May, D. (1994). *Aboriginal labour and the cattle industry: Queensland from white settlement to the present.* Cambridge University Press.

McGrath, A. (1987). *'Born in the cattle': Aborigines in cattle country.* Allen & Unwin.

McKenna, M. (2021). *Return to Uluru.* Black Inc.

Memmott, P. (1993). *Report to the minister for family services and Aboriginal and Islander affairs on the proposed appointment of Aboriginal trustees for the transferable reserve lands at Normanton.* Unpublished report. Aboriginal Environments Research Centre, University of Queensland, St Lucia, Queensland.

Normanton Police. (1984). Letter to staff at the Queensland State Archives (QSA). QSA, item 1610147.

Police Magistrate. (1874, 25 October). Letter to Colonial Secretary. Queensland State Archives, item 846930, COL/A200, 1874/2424.

Rose, D. B. (1984). The saga of Captain Cook: Morality in Aboriginal and European law. *Australian Aboriginal Studies, 2,* 24–39.

Rose, D. B. (1991). *Hidden histories: Black stories from Victoria River Downs, Humbert River and Wave Hill stations.* Aboriginal Studies Press.

Ryan, L., Debenham, J., Pascoe, B., Smith, R., Owen, C., Richards, J., Gilbert, S., Anders, R. J., Usher, K., Price, D., Newley, J., Brown, M., Le, L. H. & Fairbairn, H. (2018). *Colonial frontiers massacres, Australia, 1788 to 1930* (Vol. 2.1) [Massacres map]. University of Newcastle. c21ch.newcastle.edu.au/colonialmassacres/map.php

Stanner, W. E. H. (1965). Aboriginal territorial organization: Estate, range, domain and regime. *Oceania, 36*(1), 1–26. doi.org/10.1002/j.1834-4461.1965.tb00275.x

Yeneen, J. P. (1874, 14 February). In the Gulf Country no. 1. *The Queenslander,* 9.

5

Searching for Retribution Camp

Billy Griffiths

At first I can't make out the inscription, even though I am searching for it. Smooth new bark has grown into the cuts, bulging around the incision, preserving the words on the trunk. I run my hand across the surface, tracing the grooves, feeling the letters: R-E-T-R-I-B-U-T-I-O-N. And below, in slightly larger hand, 'CAMP' (see Figure 5.1).

Figure 5.1. Retribution Camp boab.
Photograph: Darrell Lewis.

Figure 5.2. The author at Retribution Camp boab.
Photograph: Darrell Lewis.

We are in the boab belt, the 'western wilds' of the Victoria River District in the Northern Territory, between Katherine and Kununurra. This is Ngarinyman Country: near the northern end of Judbarra (Gregory National Park). It has taken us much of the morning to track down this particular boab, which rises grandly out of long, thick grass. I step back to take it in as a whole. It is immense (see Figure 5.2).

It is hard not to be captivated by boabs (*Adansonia gregorii*). They are the charismatic megafauna of the botanical world; their bulbous trunks and knobbled limbs lend themselves to anthropomorphism. Ernestine Hill affectionately described the boab as the 'friendly ogre of the great Northwest': 'a grizzled, distorted old goblin with a girth of a giant, the hide of a rhinoceros, twiggy fingers clutching at empty air, and the disposition of a guardian angel' (Hill, 1934, p. 23). But boabs are more than guardian angels; in remote arid areas, they are life itself. Their soft, fibrous wood can trap so much moisture that the trunk visibly swells and shrinks with the seasons. Even in drought, 'sweet water' can be sucked from the wood or scooped from its hollows. In the nineteenth century, certain boabs along the police track between Derby and Halls Creek had jam tins dangling from their trunks for the convenience of thirsty travellers.

Although the wood is of no value as timber (except to drive away mosquitoes when burned), the fruit is tasty and full of potassium tartrate, tartaric acid and vitamin C; the leaves, roots and gum are also edible, as is the sprout of a young tree, which can be eaten like asparagus. Indigenous peoples have lived with boabs for millennia, taking the seed pods from camp to camp, playing a crucial role in their evolution and distribution across the north-west of Australia. People learned to make rope and nets from the fibrous bark, and glue from the pollen. They converted trunks into watercrafts and painted and engraved others for spiritual and ceremonial purposes. They imbued these remarkable trees with story, transforming them into vessels of memory and lore (Baum, 1995; Rangan et al., 2015; Wickens & Lowe, 2008).

My companion, historian and archaeologist Darrell Lewis, presses himself against the trunk of the boab, arms outstretched. He moves in this way around the tree, placing hand to hand, using his arm span to estimate its girth: some 50 feet in circumference, we calculate, or 16 metres. Perhaps 20 metres tall.

Lewis has been here many times before and has systematically photographed, measured and mapped every marking on this boab, most of which were carved during the 1890s. He has wrapped the trunk in plastic film, working with a felt-tip pen to softly capture the contours and cuts, creating an enormous scroll of frontier history. 'It's the most heavily marked historic boab I have ever encountered,' he tells me. He points out the familiar carved names of cattle men, duffers, drovers and other frontier opportunists. There are also more enigmatic markings: crosses, hearts and emu tracks; a boxer swinging a punch; a rider on his horse; a hand and forearm decorated in the style of west Arnhem Land rock art; the name 'Café Francais'. The markings are evocative of life on the early cattle stations, the banter and mobility of the workers, both Indigenous and non-Indigenous, and the increasing familiarity and connections across cultures.

But among all the markings, it is the ominous name before me that stands out. Retribution Camp. Retribution for what? What sinister event is intimated by this name? The tree attends to my questions silently. Nearby Retribution Creek runs past Retribution Bore.

***

Since arriving in this Country a few days earlier, frontier violence has been at the fore of our minds. Darrell Lewis and I have been surveying a part of the range south of Jasper Gorge, on Ngaliwurru land. We have been searching for the site of a massacre where as many as 60 people may have been killed. The place is known as Kanjamala.

Our unusual mission has elicited many impromptu conversations about the frontier. Over a cup of tea one morning, a couple of cattlemen related a dozen historical accounts of violence against Aboriginal people in the district and elsewhere: beatings, shootings, poisonings and large-scale massacres. As the late Deborah Bird Rose wrote in her landmark book *Hidden Histories*, 'violence and bloodshed, invariably ruthless and sometimes orgiastic in their excesses, were key features' of the Victoria River frontier, as was resistance (Rose, 1991, p. 20). The stories are as shocking in their brutality as they are in their insouciance. They involve characters such as the second manager at Victoria River Downs, Jack Watson, who once asked the local constable, William Willshire, to procure a particular Indigenous man's skull for him, so that he could use it for a spittoon. Like many settlers in the Victoria River District, Watson cultivated a reputation for being 'hard on blacks'. When he was at Lawn Hill, he was known for having on his station '40 prs of black's ears nailed round the walls, collected during raiding parties after the loss of many cattle speared by the blacks' (Lewis, 2021, p. 13).

But, officially, there was no war in the Victoria River District. Nor were there treaties. While the government deemed dispossession to be legitimate, it could not endorse the violent force that was used to seize the land, so a sinister, half-conscious language of denial emerged on the frontier. Historian Bain Attwood has interrogated this denial in its historic and contemporary forms, noting how settlers often projected 'their own savagery onto the Aboriginal people' to 'blame them for most of the violence that occurred or excuse their own violence in the name of the civilization they claimed for themselves' (Attwood, 2017, p. 27). At the heart of the denial were acts of othering. Women became 'gins', men 'myalls' and children 'piccaninnies'. Violence, when recorded, was coded as 'dispersing the blacks', 'quieting down the blacks' – or, simply, 'retribution'. Rose described how, in the nineteenth and early twentieth centuries, different parts of the Victoria River District became known as 'quiet nigger' country or 'bad nigger' country: 'What Europeans called "bad nigger" country was country in which Aboriginal people were able to resist invasion' (Rose, 1992, p. 12).

The war was waged over a generation; the frontier lasted a century. Keeping quiet, destroying evidence, hiding in euphemisms – these were part of the culture of the cattle stations. The routines and habits of forgetting created an immediate and lasting absence in the historical record (Healy, 2008; see also Healy, this volume). Gordon W Broughton observed 'a freemasonry of silence' during his trip from the Kimberley to Darwin in 1908. When outsiders came to the region, locals 'kept their mouths shut' (Broughton, 1965, p. 53). Crimes turned into whispers that eventually became too soft to hear.

***

Lewis first learned of the massacre at Kanjamala in 1977 when he was working for the Northern Land Council. He arrived in Yarralin and drove around over the hot months of September and October with a small group of Ngarinyman, Ngaliwurru, Jaminjung and Wardaman men, helping to record their knowledge and mapping Country as part of a land claim (Lewis, 1977). At one stage, as they drove along the only track that goes through Bulls Head Pocket on Victoria River Downs, the men pointed across the pocket to where the ranges formed a rough right angle and said: 'That's Kanjamala' and 'Big mob bin got shot there'.

A few years later, when Lewis returned with his partner Deborah Bird Rose, they followed up the story of Kanjamala with Jaminjung Elder Big Mick Kangkınang, 'the man who knew everything' who was born about 1905. Big Mick told them the story he had heard as a child: how, long ago, a group of Aboriginal people were having a corroboree at Kanjamala, and how a party of white men surrounded them in the night and attacked at first light, killing 'big mob' – so many that the survivors never went back to bury the bodies (Lewis, 2012, p. 154; Rose, 1991, pp. 93–99).

Later, when Lewis was undertaking a PhD on the early history of the Victoria River District, he was able to suggest a link between this oral history and events recorded in contemporary newspapers and the journals of the notorious police constable William Willshire. He argued that the Kanjamala massacre was connected to the well-known attack on the white teamsters John Mulligan and George Ligar in May 1895. In his book, *A Wild History: Life and Death on the Victoria River Frontier* (2012), Lewis identified the probable perpetrators and drew together the documentation of the attack, which includes these Indigenous oral histories, a few secondary accounts and an annotated 1890s newspaper clipping. What is striking, though perhaps not surprising, is that so much of the story remains shrouded in silence.

What we know from the documentary record is that Mulligan and Ligar were bringing two wagonloads of stores to Victoria River Downs homestead when they were attacked at the western end of Jasper Gorge after dark on 14 May 1895. After being besieged for three days, the teamsters, bloody and wounded, abandoned the wagons and rode towards the nearby station, Auvergne. The Indigenous men who had conducted the raid then began to carry away a large amount of the supplies. Mounted Constable Willshire came across their wagons a few days later and sent word of the raid to the manager of Victoria River Downs, Jack Watson. By late May, 20 armed and mounted men had gathered at the attack site in Jasper Gorge. After spending a few days collecting the scattered goods, Watson led a large party into the ranges, following a trail of battered cans and spilled flour. He was intent on retribution.

They were gone for one night and two days – a remarkably short time for a punitive expedition – and returned with three Aboriginal women as prisoners. These women, who had clearly been badly treated, were handed into the care of Willshire. They escaped the next day. There is no contemporary record of this punitive expedition; there are some later murmurs, but no conventional primary sources. But would we expect there to be? Willshire had a record of ruthless violence against Aboriginal peoples, as Jason Gibson, Jennifer Green and Joel Perrurle Liddle explore in this volume with their dissection of the crimes at 'Blackfellows Bones'. Willshire had faced murder charges in 1891 for his role in killing two Aboriginal men at Tempe Downs Station in Central Australia and he was careful about what he recorded in the wake of the trial (Nettelbeck & Foster, 2007). In his police journal accounts, which were addressed to his superior, there is no mention of discharging a weapon, not even to shoot a cow for meat. But in his book, published in 1896, he bragged in general terms about open battles, with phrases such as 'Not one man escaped' (Rose, 1991, pp. 29–31; Willshire, 1896, pp. 75–76).

There is another curious piece of evidence that strengthens the link between the attack on the teamsters and the Kanjamala massacre that Big Mick Kangkinang referred to. It is a clipping from the *Northern Territory Times* of 14 June 1895 that found its way into the office of State Records of South Australia. The article describes the teamster attack. Someone – we don't know who – cut it out of the newspaper, kept a copy and wrote in black ink at the bottom of the clipping: 'And sixty were shot' (Lewis, 2012, p. 154).

5. SEARCHING FOR RETRIBUTION CAMP

Was this the Kanjamala massacre that Big Mick Kangkinang referred to?

We set out in 2019 in the hope of answering this question. We followed the directions that Lewis had been given by Big Mick Kangkinang and other Aboriginal men, moving across the flat and onto the range south of Jasper Gorge. If the group was as large as 60 people, they would have camped near a permanent water source, which are few and far between on top of the range. This part of the country is accessible only by foot or helicopter. Even cattle do not make it up here, allowing lilies to grow in the waterholes and leaving stone tool scatters and hunting blinds undisturbed. We camped by the waterhole and moved methodically outwards on both sides of the creek.

With the documentary record marked by telling silences and archival noise, we were searching for a 'smoking gun': old brass rifle and pistol cartridge cases.

***

Over the past few years, a team of researchers at the University of Newcastle, led by historian Lyndall Ryan, has been collecting testimony of colonial massacres, corroborating the evidence and plotting the locations on a map of Australia. Hundreds of entries now dot the continent, like bullet holes on the landscape (Dalley & Barnwell, this volume; Ryan et al., 2019).

The project is a direct response to the so-called History Wars that were waged at the turn of the new millennium and that came to centre on the work of Keith Windschuttle. In his 2002 book *The Fabrication of Aboriginal History*, Windschuttle sought to radically recast the history of settler Australia. He argued that frontier violence was an invention of 1960s counterculture, that historians had grossly exaggerated the extent of these violent encounters and that there had been no historic wars on Australian soil. Ryan's early work on Aboriginal Tasmanians was one of Windschuttle's main targets. He chased her footnotes, questioned her methods, disputed dates, events, sources – with the sole goal of diminishing the core argument of her work: that Australia was invaded, that dispossession was brutal, bloody and often warlike, and that Indigenous Australians had resisted, suffered enormously, but survived.

While Windschuttle's allegations of fabrication were quickly and comprehensively exposed as ill-founded and his own historical methods revealed to be deeply flawed, the provocation of the History Wars generated a rich vein of historical research on the Australian frontier.

Historians, archaeologists and curators exhumed bodies from the colonial archives, counted the dead, probed the nature of cross-cultural encounters, documented the military strategies and resources of the invaders, and, region by region, revealed the ubiquity, variety and trauma of frontier violence in Australian history (Griffiths, 2016, pp. 139–142; Ryan, 2001).

The colonial frontier 'Massacres Map' is Ryan's great rebuff to Windschuttle's accusations, and, by focusing as it does on dates, documents and numbers, it is a response played out on the very battleground where Windschuttle began his war. The map seeks to present black-and-white evidence of a confronting and bloody truth. Yet so much of this history remains grey.

After three days, we called off our search for Kanjamala. We found no bullet casings, nor any other signs of European occupation such as broken glass, rusted tins or worn-out horseshoes. On our return, we continued to scan the landscape from the helicopter, tracking water sources on top of the range. This is the third time that Lewis has surveyed this remote country for the site of the massacre.

If we had found bullet casings, would that have made the Indigenous oral history any more true? Why do we elevate the written account, when, in this case, the only people who might have documented these events would have been the perpetrators of the crime? It was a narrow obsession with documents – and 'official' ones at that – that formed Windschuttle's blinkers. Yet the case of Kanjamala reveals the inadequacies of the documentary record, which is always partial, always incomplete, always containing telling silences as well as insight.

The process of truth-telling called for in the *Uluru Statement from the Heart* (Referendum Council, 2017) demands that historians make space for other forms of evidence. It calls for a reckoning with the culture of the frontier, not just individual events. It asks Australians to listen to the testimony of survivors.

Lewis has been collecting stories from both sides of the frontier since he first came to the region in 1971. He weighs them up carefully, testing them for accuracy, parsing the tall tales from the 'hidden histories'. He often turns to what he describes as 'the outback archive' to verify or enrich an account: the histories that are imprinted in the land, such as inscribed water tanks, engraved cattle skulls and 'living documents' like marked boabs (Lewis, 2014).

Sometimes, as at Kanjamala, bullet shells are all that would be needed to confirm a story. 'If there's just one shell in remote country', Lewis tells me:

> then perhaps it's some lone fella having a shot at a wallaby for dinner. But if there are dozens, even hundreds, far from a stockyard, a hut site or an old track, in an area where other sources suggest a massacre occurred, then I would take that as pretty firm evidence that it was the site of a massacre.

Lewis has compiled many of these stories into an epic book, officially launched in Darwin on 5 June 2019. He calls it *The Victoria River District Doomsday Book* and has made it available online via the Northern Territory Library (Lewis, 2021). It contains all the scraps of historical insight he has accumulated over the decades, ordered according to the cattle stations in the district, with details of the station managers, the numbers of livestock and notable events: fires, floods, thefts, spearings and massacres. It is a vast, sprawling web of memory about the region and its characters.

In some instances, Lewis has been able to tie the 'outback archive' to local oral histories, such as with a boab on Carlton Hill Station engraved with the words 'Attack Spring'. But he has had no such luck with the 'Retribution Camp' boab. The events it alludes to will not find their way onto the massacre map. The carved name rests in the realm of suggestion. It is a fragment, a clue. There is no known historical account or oral history of a 'punitive expedition' in the immediate area. This boab appears to stand testimony to an otherwise undocumented event during the long period of warfare between Ngarinyman peoples and early settlers. 'It's where the punitive expedition must have camped.' Lewis reflects. 'Not where they shot people, but where they camped.' Perhaps this was the last place where the men spoke of their acts of 'retribution'. Perhaps carving the name was a bonding experience, a compact of complicity. 'The strategy of silence,' Rose observes, 'was maintained through, and reinforced, white mateship in the bush' (Rose, 1991, p. 23).

***

I gaze up at the boab, this beautiful, old tree, signed with a statement of murder. How many generations has this tree been witness to? How many thousands of people have camped beneath it? It's hard to say. Boabs can live for a millennium, but they are unlike most other trees. There are no regular annual rings to count, and size is not always a good indicator of age. They are the world's largest stem succulent. Some trees grow tall, others stay squat. All fluctuate during their lives according to their water content. And they are amazingly resilient. Once mature, their moisture-rich wood makes them virtually fireproof. Boabs toppled in storms, with their shallow roots exposed, can resprout and grow, spreadeagled, for centuries. But, at some point in time, without warning, a boab ceases to be a boab. Its once strong trunk collapses inwards, and the soft, fibrous wood bleaches and erodes into the wind. As Penny Miller records of the South African baobab: 'When the tree dies the process is Othello-like – a pillar of Herculean strength and nobility, disintegrates into a mound of pulp' (Miller, 1979, p. 285). While a red gum remains a part of its ecosystem long after its death – perhaps for as long as it did in life – a boab's demise is frighteningly instant. It dies, withers and collapses within a year. A tree that may have lived for some 1,000 years, maybe more, a constant in a time of dramatic change, disintegrates in a few short months, like paper turning to dust. The living document dies, taking with it the history it once preserved. All that remains is a shallow scar in the earth where the giant once stood.

Acknowledgements

I owe a great debt to Darrell Lewis for guiding me around the Victoria River District and sharing his love of boabs. This piece is stronger for his incisive edits. Milton Jones, owner of Coolibah Station, generously provided free helicopter transport to and from Kanjamala. I am also grateful for comments from Ash Barnwell, Cameo Dalley, Rani Kerin, Cameron McKean and Alexandra Roginski. Peter Rose and Amy Baillieu helped enrich an earlier version of this essay that appeared in the *Australian Book Review*.

References

Attwood, B. (2017). Denial in a settler society: The Australian case. *History Workshop Journal, 84*, 24–43. doi.org/10.1093/hwj/dbx029

Baum, D. A. (1995). A systematic revision of Adansonia (Bombacaceae). *Annals of the Missouri Botanical Garden, 82*(3), 440–471. doi.org/10.2307/2399893

Broughton, G. W. (1965). *Turn again home.* Jacaranda Press.

Griffiths, T. (2016). *The art of time travel: Historians and their craft.* Black Inc.

Healy, C. (2008). *Forgetting Aborigines*. University of New South Wales Press.

Hill, E. (1934, 8 May). The friendly baobab. *The West Australian*, 23.

Lewis, D. (1977). *Report on field work for the Jasper Gorge – Kidman Springs land claim*. Northern Land Council.

Lewis, D. (1993). *In western wilds: A survey of historic sites in the western Victoria River District*. National Trust of Australia (Northern Territory).

Lewis, D. (2012). *A wild history: Life and death on the Victoria River frontier*. Monash University Publishing.

Lewis, D. (2014). The 'outback archive': Unorthodox historical records in the Victoria River District, Northern Territory, Australia. *Australian Archaeology*, *78*(1), 69–74. doi.org/10.1080/03122417.2014.11682001

Lewis, D. (2021). *The Victoria River District doomsday book* (2nd ed.). Self-published. doi.org/10.31235/osf.io/kfmnz

Miller, P. (1979). *Myths and legends of Southern Africa*. T. V. Bulpin.

Nettelbeck, A. & Foster, R. (2007). *In the name of the law: William Willshire and the policing of the Australian frontier*. Wakefield Press.

Rangan, H., Bell, K. L., Baum, D. A., Fowler, R., McConvell, P., Saunders, T., Spronck, S., Kull, C. A. & Murphy, D. J. (2015). New genetic and linguistic analyses show ancient human influence on baobab evolution and distribution in Australia. *PLOS ONE*, *10*(4), e0119758. doi.org/10.1371/journal.pone.0119758

Referendum Council. (2017). *Uluru Statement from the Heart*. Final report of the Referendum Council. referendumcouncil.org.au/final-report.html#toc-anchor-ulurustatement-from-the-heart

Rose, D. B. (1991). *Hidden histories: Black stories from Victoria River Downs, Humbert River and Wave Hill stations*. Aboriginal Studies Press.

Rose, D. B. (1992). *Dingo makes us human: Life and land in an Australian Aboriginal culture*. Cambridge University Press.

Ryan, L. (2001). Postcolonialism and the historian: The Aboriginal history wars. *Bulletin of the Australian Historical Association*, *92*, 31–37.

Ryan, L., Debenham, J., Pascoe, B., Smith, R., Owen, C., Richards, J., Gilbert, S., Anders, R. J., Usher, K., Price, D., Newley, J., Brown, M., Le, L. H. & Fairbairn, H. (2019). *Colonial frontier massacres in Australia, 1788–1930* (Version 3.0). University of Newcastle. c21ch.newcastle.edu.au/colonialmassacres/

Wickens, G. E. & Lowe, P. (2008). *The baobabs: Pachycauls of Africa, Madagascar and Australia*. Springer. doi.org/10.1007/978-1-4020-6431-9

Willshire, W. H. (1896). *The land of the dawning: Being facts gleaned from cannibals in the Australian Stone Age*. W. K. Thomas.

Windschuttle, K. (2002). *The fabrication of Aboriginal history: Vol. 1. Van Diemen's Land 1803–1847*. Macleay Press.

6

The South Australian frontier and its legacies: Remembering and representing the Mount Bryan murders

Skye Krichauff

In July 1844, according to written records, a group of Ngadjuri people separated around 200 sheep from a flock belonging to John Hallett, whose shepherds had recently occupied land in the Mount Bryan district, approximately 100 miles (160 km) north of Adelaide. Two days later, at daybreak, five armed Europeans led by Hallett's overseer, William Moore Carter, made a surprise attack upon the group, wounding four Aboriginal people, two of whom subsequently died.

I grew up in Booborowie Valley, which neighbours the Mount Bryan district. Our nearest town was Hallett, named after John Hallett. I was the fifth generation of my family to live on land my maternal family purchased in the 1870s. During my childhood and adolescence in the 1970s and 1980s, I never heard any mention of the Mount Bryan murders, or of other violent encounters with Aboriginal people. Nor did my friends and I ever hear stories of cross-cultural friendship or accommodation. Throughout my youth, I did not hear or know the word Ngadjuri. To my knowledge, no Aboriginal people lived in the district, and the current imperative to acknowledge Country and pay respects to Traditional Owners was unimaginable. Since learning the history of European occupation and Aboriginal dispossession as a young adult, understanding this 'not knowing' in the region in which I grew up has been a major impetus for my research.

This chapter draws on archival records, published histories, interviews with Aboriginal and settler descendants, and personal experience to trace community memory and oral histories of the Mount Bryan murders at the local level – the Mount Bryan district of South Australia's mid-north. I am currently employed as a research fellow for the Australian Research Council linkage project 'Reconciling with the Frontier'. Ongoing research for this project and research conducted between 2010 and 2013 for my doctoral thesis indicates that a myriad of colonial injustices are overlooked when the focus is primarily on physical conflict between Aboriginal people and colonists. While research that focuses on physical confrontations and deaths may serve the purpose of both drawing attention to the brutal realities of Aboriginal dispossession and shaking colonial foundation narratives of peaceful and unproblematic settlement, such a focus should not come at the expense of understanding other, enduring aspects of colonial violence. A narrow understanding of frontier violence can not only inhibit deeper understanding of enduring – and more pressing – legacies of colonialism, but also unintentionally work to distance non-Aboriginal people from their implication in the colonial process.

**

The Mount Bryan murders and their remembrance – or, more pertinently, lack of remembrance – in community memory is a worthy case study for several reasons. First, the case was significant in its day. From a rich archival record held by State Records of South Australia and court reports published in Adelaide newspapers, it is possible to hear Aboriginal witnesses' accounts, to provide a nuanced and relatively detailed account of events and, consequently, to expand knowledge of frontier life. Second, the case is mentioned in several published histories produced from 1985 onwards. Thus it is possible to both analyse historians' representations and local residents' remembrances of the Mount Bryan murders, raising broader questions regarding the influence of publicly available accounts of frontier violence on Australians' historical consciousness. In addition, one of my interviewees was the author of a local history and had a family connection to the Mount Bryan killings. Her observations regarding her own and her family members' acknowledgement of this connection demonstrate a range of positions taken by settler descendants when learning of frontier violence.

The Mount Bryan murders in the historical record

An empirically based, forensic analysis of the historical evidence is not the purpose of this chapter. Nonetheless, a brief summary of information contained in the historical record lays a foundation from which to analyse if – and how – the Mount Bryan murders have been remembered and represented over the generations.

On 21 August 1844, the South Australian police commissioner Boyle Travers Finniss informed Governor Grey that he had been notified by stockholder John Hallett of an 'affray' at Hallett's Mount Bryan Station. Finniss was concerned that some Aboriginal people may have been injured and asked the governor if the relevant local magistrates had forwarded a report (Finniss, 1844). Grey had received no such report and ordered Finniss to make enquiries (Grey, 1844a, 1844e). Protector Moorhouse subsequently proceeded to Mount Bryan with an Aboriginal interpreter and a police party (Grey, 1844b).

On his return, Moorhouse provided a detailed report dated 7 October. It is worth noting that European occupation of the mid-north had only recently commenced and was confined to a few scattered pastoralists and their employees and stock, whose huts and head stations were isolated and distant from each other. Moorhouse had been serving as the protector of Aborigines since mid-1839 and was conscientious about his role in ensuring Aboriginal people's accounts of events were conveyed to the relevant authorities. Through an interpreter, Moorhouse spoke with Aboriginal people at various stations on his way to Mount Bryan.

Fourteen miles distant from Mount Bryan (at Dr Browne's Booborowie Station, the closest station to Hallett's Mount Bryan Station), Aboriginal people – who had heard firsthand from those present at the attack – told Moorhouse that one man and one woman had been killed (Moorhouse, 1844a). At Mount Bryan, Hallett's employees showed Moorhouse sheep skins and bones and Aboriginal ovens at the site where Aboriginal people had camped with sheep, all of which indicated sheep had been taken. Moorhouse was unable to meet with any Aboriginal witnesses at Mount Bryan: the Aboriginal people he met with at Browne's station informed him that those present at the affray had left the district and gone to the Murray

River (112 km distant). On his return to Adelaide, Moorhouse travelled via George Hawker's station, where Hawker and fellow magistrate Henry Price had commenced hearing the case.

Moorhouse enclosed the sworn depositions of Hallett's overseer, William Carter, and shepherd Charles Spratt in his report to the governor. In Carter's sworn statement he claimed that, on learning sheep had been taken, he organised a surprise dawn attack on the Aboriginal group, and that during the recovery of the sheep, he 'slightly' wounded an Aboriginal man named Williamy with a sword (Grey, 1844d). Moorhouse reported that this statement differed greatly from a verbal account Henry Price had overheard six weeks earlier, in which Carter claimed to have:

> fought the blacks, killed a man and a woman, the woman was with child, and he had set a bulldog upon her, which tore open the belly and womb – he took the child out of the womb and gave it to the dog to eat. (Moorhouse, 1844a)

This brutal remark, attributed to Carter, shocked government officials and was an impetus for the governor's, advocate general's, police commissioner's and protector's determination to learn the truth of events at Mount Bryan (see Grey, 1844c, 1884d, 1884f; Price, 1844; Smillie, 1844a; 'Supreme Court criminal side: Tuesday, 26 November', 1844, p. 3). Moorhouse also reported the unlawful manner in which 'Kangaroo Jack' (Pinpa Ngaltya) had been arrested on suspicion of stealing Hallett's sheep (Moorhouse, 1844a). Having reviewed Moorhouse's report, Advocate General George Smillie was scathing of Hawker and Price's enquiry. Smillie was not impressed that the magistrates' primary concern was the loss of Hallett's sheep and not injuries done to Aboriginal people, or that only Carter and Spratt had been examined. He recommended that all five Europeans present at the conflict be examined before the Grand Jury (Smillie, 1844a). On Smillie's recommendation, the colonial secretary wrote to Edward Eyre, resident magistrate and sub-protector at Moorunde, asking him to enquire among the 'natives of the Murray' who was to blame and how many people were killed (Grey, 1844c, 1884f). Price and Hawker were reprimanded by the governor and compelled to explain their poorly conducted enquiry (Grey, 1844c, 1844f; Hawker & Price, 1844). Price was asked to provide a sworn affidavit verifying Carter's brutal statement. He responded that it was Mr Stein whom Carter told, and that he (Price) took no action because he believed Carter's shocking claim was an 'unblushing falsehood' – 'a detail of imaginary slaughter or at least … a gross exaggeration' typical of Carter's social status and dubious character (Price, 1844). If Price's deduction was correct, and Carter thought such a claim would impress those with whom he was speaking, this nevertheless tells us much about Carter's character, the sentiments of the people with whom Carter socialised, and the morals and attitudes of the earliest Europeans with whom the Ngadjuri were in sustained contact.

In November 1844, Pinpa Ngaltya (Kangaroo Jack) was tried in the Supreme Court for stealing Hallett's sheep and acquitted, with the court reporter noting that the main purpose of the trial was not to try Kangaroo Jack, but to ascertain whether 'a great cruelty had been exercised towards the blacks' ('Supreme Court criminal side: Friday, 29 November', 1844, 3CD). In early December, Moorhouse met a man named Pari Kudnatya who had witnessed the Mount Bryan affray; he informed Moorhouse that 'Mr Hallett's men wounded four natives, three men and one woman. One man and one woman died ... The Natives buried the dead bodies' (Moorhouse, 1844b).

Moorhouse, Pari Kudnutya and three policemen (one of whom was a native constable) travelled to Mount Bryan, where Pari Kudnutya led the group to the place where the man and woman were buried. However, on searching the graves, they found them empty. Further searching revealed the remains of a fire containing human teeth and hand and feet bones (Moorhouse, 1844c). By this time, Carter had left the district. The men present on Hallett's station – namely Charles Spratt, William Smith and Charles Pritt – were brought to Adelaide, tried at the Police Commissioner's Court and committed on the charge of feloniously killing Ngunnirri Burka and Mary-Ann ('Police commissioner's court', 1845, p. 3C).

In early February 1845, three other Aboriginal witnesses – Parnkari Waritya, Wimma Warrintpinna and Pulpurra Munarta – confirmed Pari Kudnutya's evidence (Smillie, 1845a). Unfortunately, in court, Pari Kudnutya made no mention of Carter who, by his own account and the evidence of other shepherds, was known to have taken a leading part in the attack (Smillie, 1845a). Pari Kudnutya's lack of reference to Carter in court may reflect Aboriginal law, whereby friends and relatives of the perpetrator can be punished in lieu of the perpetrator if the perpetrator is not present. Or it may be that Pari Kudnutya was overwhelmed by the unfamiliar experience of being in a courtroom filled with Europeans, compelled to answer questions he may or may not have understood. Regardless, the outcome shows that the British legal system did not recognise or accommodate cultural incompatibilities between Aboriginal and British law, and that the applicability of British law and procedures in such cases was not challenged – even by government officials sympathetic to Aboriginal people.

There is no reference to a dog or an unborn baby in any evidence provided by Aboriginal or European witnesses in court or in the multitude of private correspondence between relevant (and sympathetic) government officials. Because Carter's shocking comments were an impetus for sustained government investigations, and because determining their veracity was at the forefront of government officials' and the presiding judge's minds, this suggests that Price's opinion (i.e. that Carter's claim was a 'blushing falsehood') was likely correct.[1]

When Hallett was questioned, he refused to answer one of the questions put to him, causing the advocate general and governor to question Hallett's position as a 'gentleman' and commissioner of the peace (Finniss, 1845a; Smillie, 1845a). Spratt, Smith and Pritt were tried at the Supreme Court on 12 March. The case stalled when the Aboriginal witness mistook Spratt for Carter. Spratt, Smith and Pritt were bound over until the upcoming sessions in June with the hope that, by then, Carter would have been captured and charged (Smillie, 1845b). A police party was dispatched to the Mt Gambier district in South Australia's south-east to secure Carter and the governor requested 'every assistance' from relevant authorities in Port Phillip (Grey, 1845a, 1845b, 1845c, 1845d). Carter, aided by a stockowner named Leake, absconded to Van Diemen's Land. Despite reducing government expenditure across a range of areas, Governor Grey authorised the exorbitant sum of £20 to continue the police search for Carter and requested assistance from the governor of Van Diemen's Land (Grey, 1845e, 1845f, 1845g). Despite all efforts, Carter could not be located, and the case was eventually dropped (Finniss, 1845b).

John Hallett sold his Mount Bryan run to Joseph Gilbert in 1850 ('1851 Pastoral lease diagram', 1850). Large portions of it were resumed by the colonial government in the 1870s and subdivided into 640-acre farming blocks.

---

1   The only hint I can find that Mary-Ann may have been pregnant is that Pari Kudnutya stated that Mary-Ann was shot in the stomach (Moorhouse, 1844b; 'Police commissioner's court', 1844, p. 3A). Carter, being the person he was, may have targeted Mary-Ann's stomach because she was pregnant.

Community memory of Mary-Ann and Ngunnirri Burka's murders

As mentioned above, the Mount Bryan murders were not part of the community memory I absorbed while growing up in the district in the 1970s and 1980s; it was not until conducting archival research in the early 2000s that I became aware of them. This lack of knowledge of frontier conflict – and, more generally, of historical Aboriginal presence – was evident during fieldwork and interviews conducted between 2010 and 2013 when I asked mid-northern settler descendants what they knew about the Aboriginal people of the area, and if any stories dating back to the colonial era had been passed down through their families. There were no stories; Aboriginal people were absent in settler descendants' historical consciousness, and a sense that Aboriginal people's histories were disconnected with the history of their own family – and the history of the district – was evident.

I have sought to understand this disconnect (Krichauff, 2017). For the purpose of this chapter, suffice to say that I found the most powerful way the past is known among settler descendants is through being in place, through family stories and through lived experience – both the lived experience of the interviewees *and* his/her/their forebears. Unsurprisingly, my interviewees were most knowledgeable about their own family, and their sense of the history of the district began with the arrival of their first forebear in the district. As such, when analysing settler descendants' historical consciousness, it is necessary to consider the nature and extent of interviewees' *and* interviewees' forebears' experiences with Aboriginal people. Regarding the latter, it is necessary to distinguish between pastoralists (and their employees) who resided in the mid-north from the early 1840s, and freeholders who arrived from 1870 (after the pastoral runs were subdivided), and to learn when an interviewees' forebear arrived in the district (Krichauff, 2019). It is also important to recognise that very few Ngadjuri have lived in the wider mid-north since the 1870s. Shockingly, within 30 years of European occupation, Aboriginal populations had declined to 10 per cent, largely through introduced diseases. Regarding the extended Mount Bryan district, two Aboriginal people were recorded by census collectors as living near Mount Bryan in the 1871 census ('Aboriginal population of South Australia', 1871). By 1891, the census collectors did not record any Aboriginal people in the entire Burra County – a large area that included the Mount Bryan, Hallett, Booborowie and Burra districts. It was not until the late 1980s that those who now identify as Ngadjuri learned of their Ngadjuri heritage and began the process of reconnecting with their ancestral Country. The decades-long physical absence of Aboriginal people in the district is not evidence of wishful thinking or denialism on behalf of the colonisers, but a grim reality of the outcome of British colonisation that is openly spoken of by Ngadjuri descendants (Copley & McInerney, 2022; Krichauff, 2020, p. 428; Warrior et al., 2005, p. 6).

The vast majority of mid-northern settler descendants are descended from freeholders who had limited or no contact with nineteenth-century Ngadjuri. Tellingly, freeholder descendants had no stories of Aboriginal people dating back to the colonial era; nor did they have stories of early pastoralists (such as John Hallett or Joseph Gilbert). Very few descendants of pastoralists continue to live in the mid-north; those I spoke with have a sense of history that begins with the arrival of *their* forebears (i.e. in the pastoral era), which, when pressed, includes stories of Aboriginal people.

This widespread lack of acknowledgement of the pastoral era is reflected in the content of information boards and commemorative plaques of mid-northern towns, which present the district's history as beginning with the arrival of 'pioneering' freeholders, and the formation of towns and district councils in the late 1860s and 1870s.[2]

Published accounts of the Mount Bryan murders (written histories and websites)

Interestingly, the absence of information about early pastoralists is not reflected in local written histories – most of which were published from the late 1960s to the 1980s to celebrate the centenaries of local towns and districts. Although these histories usually include a section on the pastoral years, few refer to Aboriginal people. Of the Hallett/Mount Bryan written histories, one 1968 publication simply notes that several of the early pastoralists 'roamed with the Blacks' to discover their waterholes (Mattey, 1968, p. 24). In *Hallett: A History of Town and District*, published in 1977, author Marlene Richards states that 'the pastoralists' problems included

---

2   The exception is towns named after pastoralists, such as Hallett and Laura, in which case the origin of the name is explained.

attacks from Aborigines', but that 'the only references to be found to the Aboriginals in this district deal mainly with the ways in which they helped the early pastoralists' (Richards, 1977, p. 16).

Ruth Stolte's *Razorback Range Country* (1985) is the first published history to refer to the 1844 conflict at Hallett's station; Stolte covers it in a lengthy paragraph (pp. 17–18). In *Resistance and Retaliation* (1989), Alan Pope devotes a chapter to the Mount Bryan killings (pp. 113–119). Both Stolte and Pope base their description of the affray on their interpretation of Moorhouse's 7 October report.[3] *Ngadjuri: Aboriginal People of the Mid-North Region of South Australia*, co-authored by Fred Warrior (a Ngadjuri man), Fran Knight, Adele Pring and Sue Anderson, was published in 2005.[4] Warrior et al.'s half page account of the Mount Bryan conflict (p. 83) is a condensed summary of Pope's account and includes a full transcript of Moorhouse's 7 October report (pp. 84–85). Stolte, Pope and the authors of *Ngadjuri* overlooked, or were unaware of, numerous relevant records filed in the colonial secretary's outgoing correspondence, the advocate general's correspondence and the police commissioner's correspondence. Problematically, Stolte, Pope and Warrior et al. promulgate Carter's brutal boast, which (as these primary sources indicate) was unsubstantiated and seemingly false.

Stolte's, Pope's and the *Ngaduri* authors' representations of the Mount Bryan murders illustrate the influence of revisionist histories that began emerging in the 1970s, best exemplified by Henry Reynolds's popular *The Other Side of the Frontier* (1981). Pope emulates Reynolds in providing ample evidence of South Australia's violent frontier and Aboriginal resistance but, regarding the Mount Bryan murders, overlooks important details, inserts unfounded assumptions, confuses the chronological order of events and does not include relevant contextual information. In 2012, Rob Foster and Amanda Nettelbeck's *Out of the Silence: The History and Memory of South Australia's Frontier Wars* was published. Foster and Nettelbeck provide a more comprehensive and accurate account of the Mount Bryan murders.

---

3   Stolte does not use footnotes or endnotes, and her references to sources are placed at the end of the chapter and are not specific (see Stolte, 1985, p. 26). The State Records of South Australia Government Record Group (GRG) sources Stolte examined for the Mount Bryan murders are not differentiated, for example, 'Reports, SA Archives, 1842–1844'. Pope's examination of the archival sources is limited to several letters held in the Colonial Secretary's Incoming Correspondence file and a Supreme Court hearing published in the *Southern Australian*, 3 December 1844, p. 3.
4   Significantly, this is the first mid-northern history that focuses on the Ngadjuri.

They recognise variations in settlers' responses to frontier violence and conclude that two Aboriginal people died as a result of the conflict at Mount Bryan (Foster & Nettelbeck, 2012, pp. 82–84).

From 2018, the Mount Bryan murders were included on the University of Newcastle's online map of *Colonial Frontier Massacres in Australia, 1788–1930* (hereafter 'Massacres Map'; Ryan et al., 2018) and its more widely known duplicate, *The Guardian* newspaper's interactive digital map, 'The Killing Times' (2022). The entry was removed from both online maps in March 2022 after a review of the historical documents found that the case did not fit the Newcastle research team's definition of a 'massacre' – namely, 'the deliberate and unlawful killing of six or more defenceless people in one operation'.[5]

The influence and perceived authority of published histories

Regarding the impact of written histories on mid-northern settler descendants' historical consciousness, I found that although my settler-descendant interviewees generally had a copy of the local history book on their bookshelves, and while they accepted the information contained within it as authoritative and factual, most gave no indication that they had read it and could not remember specific stories or details (Krichauff, 2017, pp. 147–164). This is exemplified by my interviewees' lack of reference to Stolte's account of the Mount Bryan murders; *Razorback Country* had a local readership, but when I conducted interviews between 2010 and 2013, the Mount Bryan murders had not become part of community memory or local residents' historical consciousness. Only one interviewee, Marlene Richards (the author of *Hallett* – to whom I will return), mentioned the murders, and she had not become aware of them through Stolte's book.

In making sense of this, the findings of memory scholars such as Pierre Nora (1996), Dominique LaCapra (1998) and Geoffrey Cubitt (2007) are useful. These scholars point out differences between the past known through memory (which is subjective and emotional and juxtaposes temporalities)

---

5   The 'Massacres Map' and the 'Killing Times' Mount Bryan entry rested solely on Pope's (mis)interpretation of the records, as outlined above. On communicating my concerns and sending the research team a detailed list of relevant primary sources and a summary of my findings, the team reviewed the entry and removed it from both online maps in March 2022.

and the past known through history (which is objective, detached and distances previous times from the present). Not surprisingly, I found that the past known through memory, through family stories, through lived experience and being in place, impacts more powerfully on settler descendants' historical consciousness than the past learned through 'history' (such as through written texts, history lessons, commemorative plaques and information boards). While the information contained in local histories may be generally considered by mid-northern settler descendants to be 'accurate' and 'true', and, thus, while local histories (and, by implication, wider histories) may have a certain *authority* over oral stories, local histories do not necessarily have greater *influence* on settler descendants' consciousness (Krichauff, 2017, pp. 147–164).

When evaluating the influence of written histories, the interviewees' age, life experiences and connection with the district require consideration. Older interviewees (those in their 80s and 90s) made no reference whatsoever to local written histories when asked about the history of the district, while younger people who were unsure about events or details would suggest that such information may be found in the written history. Outside the private family group or local community, and over the years, published local histories take on an authority and legitimacy, and become an increasingly important (and, for some people, sole) reference about the past. For people with no ties to the district – people with no family stories or community memory to draw on – written histories may be their only source of information, and the information contained in them is uncritically accepted as factual. In such cases, information learned through written sources may become part of that person's memory. These findings are applicable to Ngadjuri descendants. Fred Warrior became aware of the Mount Bryan murders through working with his co-authors, and the wider Ngadjuri community was informed of the murders by Fred and through the publication of *Ngadjuri* (Sue Anderson, personal communication, 5 September 2021; Vince Copley, personal communication, 2018 and 2021; Adele Pring, personal communication, 5 September 2021). This finding – that published information is widely and uncritically perceived as authoritative and is particularly influential among those who have no alternative memory to refer to – is applicable at the wider level.

Problems with a narrow understanding of frontier violence as principally physical violence

The Newcastle researchers focused their attention on 'massacres' of six or more defenceless people. While other frontier violence scholars do not structure their research around a particular number, most likewise focus on incidents of physical violence between Aboriginal people and colonists that resulted in deaths. And, as evidenced by the 'Massacres Map' entries and Pope's and Stolte's accounts of the Mount Bryan murders, it is often settler brutality and Aboriginal defencelessness that are highlighted. As demonstrated by the Australian History Wars of two decades ago, a preoccupation with numbers and types of killings can inadvertently induce a perception of, and/or obsession with, a 'hierarchy' of violence whereby Aboriginal deaths and colonists' brutal acts are the focus, rather than expanding understandings of the ubiquitous and multifaceted violence of European occupation and colonialism.

'The South Australian Frontier and its Legacies' project team aims to capture as many incidents of settler–Aboriginal violence in colonial South Australia as possible. Rob Foster and I are responsible for the project's archival research. We apply a broad understanding of violence that includes death, injury, confrontation, theft, the destruction of goods, rape, treatment of Aboriginal prisoners and witnesses, deaths in police custody and, if raised by interviewees, the destruction of Country. To date, we have unearthed hundreds of incidents of conflict, the vast majority of which did not end in fatalities and few of which have been remembered by either Aboriginal or settler communities. This research has illustrated the limitations of conceptualising frontier violence as primarily involving physical confrontation and resulting in deaths.

For decades now, the frontier has been widely understood to have been a place and time of accommodation as well as resistance, of intimacy as well as violence, of dynamic cross-cultural exchange and hybridity (see e.g. Clendinnen, 2003; Jones, 2007; Krichauff, 2011; Rose & Davis, 2005; Shellam, 2009). Twenty-first-century researchers are well placed to provide nuanced, comparative accounts that communicate advances in frontier scholarship and expand understandings of the colonial experience. Aboriginal responses to European occupation, and colonists and government officials' responses to frontier violence, were diverse and varied from colony to colony and region to region, depending on numerous factors. For example, primary sources relating to the Mount Bryan murders show that, in South Australia in 1844:

- highly ranked government officials determinedly sought to learn the truth of events in which Aboriginal people were injured or killed
- the protector was readily employed to make enquiries and provide the Aboriginal version of events
- Aboriginal people were typically employed to act as interpreters
- Europeans were imprisoned and tried for their involvement in crimes against Aboriginal people
- the colonial government spared no effort or expense to bring suspected guilty people to trial
- country magistrates could be severely reprimanded for failing to investigate crimes against Aboriginal people
- stockholders' status as gentlemen and holders of government positions could be gravely questioned if suspected of hiding information.

These responses were not unusual in early colonial South Australia. And while they in no way diminish the violence of colonial invasion in South Australia or the biases of the British legal system, they highlight the need to re-examine popularly held assumptions regarding government officials' responses to violence, settlers' treatment of Aboriginal people, Aboriginal responses to the occupation of their land and the role played by influential individuals (both non-Indigenous and Indigenous).

Accounts of frontier violence that focus on physical violence and emphasise the defencelessness of Aboriginal people provide a limited understanding of frontier life. The historical records contain countless examples of the dynamism and adaptability of Aboriginal culture and society, Aboriginal agency and cross-cultural communication. By drawing attention to the abundant and rich information contained in the primary sources describing Aboriginal people's actions, historians (and other frontier violence scholars) can expand knowledge of Aboriginal people's creative and proactive responses to the occupation of their Country, which can be a source of pride for current generations.

Rob Foster and I regularly come across examples of Aboriginal people's ingenuity and assuredness in outwitting the stockowners and settlers. For example, Aboriginal people had elaborate systems for taking sheep:

they tied sheep's legs together and came back for them when they were certain no Europeans were around, they constructed bush yards and moved sheep into inaccessible places (dense scrub or narrow rocky gorges that horses could not traverse). At times they took sheep in full view of the shepherds, taunting the shepherds to come and retrieve them. Their actions seriously impacted the ability of pastoralists to build up their fledgling flocks. Colonists' frustration regarding Aboriginal people's ability to derail the pastoral enterprise was real. I state this not to justify settler reprisals, but to better understand how and why both groups reacted to the other, and to show that there is ample evidence of Aboriginal people challenging Europeans and resisting dispossession.

In addition to containing information about Aboriginal people's responses to European occupation, primary sources describing incidents of frontier conflict often contain Aboriginal names for people and places, many of which have long fallen into disuse. For those groups whose lands were invaded early and intensively, much language and knowledge of precolonial and early colonial culture has been lost. From consultation with the 'South Australian Frontier and its Legacies' project's Aboriginal Reference Group and South Australia's Aboriginal Heritage Committee, and from informal discussions with representatives of diverse Aboriginal heritage and community groups (including Ngadjuri Elders), it is clear that information about Aboriginal nomenclature, personal names and early responses to Europeans is sought after and highly valued by Aboriginal communities, perhaps more so than information about violence and conflict. Such details are an important means through which current generations can deepen their reconnection with Country and ancestors, particularly groups such as the Ngadjuri, whose lengthy displacement led to the loss of language and knowledge of Country. If these details are not alluded to or referenced by those who are most confident and knowledgeable with regard to navigating the archives (historians), it is difficult for non-historians to find and access them.

Distancing current generations from their implication in the colonial process

Chris Healy, in this volume, questions whether the commemoration of colonial violence is, 'like "Aboriginal art", a "white thing"'. This is a pertinent observation. In conversations I have had with Aboriginal interviewees for the 'South Australian Frontier and its Legacies' project, it is clear that more recent episodes of violence are at the forefront of current generations' minds. The continued damage to Country, the prioritising of profit over the health of the natural environment, the Stolen Generations, the restrictions and injustices suffered on missions and government reserves – these are more readily referred to than the killings that occurred over a century ago. While stories of frontier violence are recognised as important and needing to be known, this is not at the expense of other injustices suffered under colonialism. Of equal significance is the possibility that focusing on physical violence during the frontier era hinders non-Aboriginal Australians' recognition of their implication in the colonial process.

Having grown up in post-WWII Germany, Gabriele Schwab insightfully notes that processes of taking responsibility, and working through guilt and shame, operate across generations. The dynamics of the process change if the acts of perpetration belong to earlier generations because it is easier to face one's historical legacy if it is not a personal legacy (Schwab, 2010, pp. 80–81). The revisionist Australian histories of the late 1960s onwards can be understood as a collective recognition – a desire and ability to confront non-Aboriginal Australia's shameful past – which is made possible (or easier) because of the significant length of time that has passed. As amateur historians, Stolte and Pope are to be commended for drawing attention to records contained in South Australian archives that document the colony's violent past and for raising awareness and beginning the process of coming to terms with the historical injustice of colonialism. Over the past three decades, more nuanced, contextualised and informed readings of the historical records have expanded the focus and, by demonstrating the complexity of the past, deepened successive generations' understandings of colonialism.

Scholars interested in understanding how Australians come to terms with historical injustices have pointed out that revisionist Australian historiography that has violence and bloodshed as its primary focus can distance current generations of settler descendants from their implication in the colonial process (Attwood, 2005, p. 248). Rather than facilitating a process of working through and taking responsibility, such historiography can be perceived as an act of condemnation – that is, as illustrative of a 'defensive mechanism' (Veracini, 2010, p. 89). Anthropologist Gillian Cowlishaw has observed that histories that draw attention to the violence of colonialism (the atrocities, the brutality, the genocides) work to distance this unpalatable and disturbing past from the present, where the violence of colonialism continues. She warns:

> The call to examine the colonial past is in danger of foundering on the complacency of an imagined distance from the spectacle of blood and violence. Continuity with the past is easily severed and the cultural source of these events is lost. Our disgust and horror at the violence and abusive racism means we are absolved. (Cowlishaw, 1992, p. 27)

Cowlishaw queries how it is, in reading these histories, that we 'position ourselves on the sides of the Aborigines and identify our forebears as the enemy?' She points out the hypocrisy of this imagined distancing, for our forebears – 'our grandfathers' – may well be the violent and racist men depicted in revisionist histories, and subsequent generations were surely left something by these men, 'if not the land they took or the wealth they made from it, then the culture they were developing' (p. 27).

In contrast, histories that demonstrate the multiplicity of positions occupied by settlers in the colonial era, the agency of Aboriginal people and the dynamism of Aboriginal culture are more likely to enable current generations of both cultural groups to recognise parallels with the present. Such histories are also more likely to enable settler descendants to recognise their own implication in the colonial process.

Subjective positioning

Regarding historians' (and other scholars) subjective positioning when researching and writing politically charged histories, it is worth bearing in mind Dominick LaCapra's point that, for people who were not present at the time and whose position has not been tested, it is easy to occupy a position of moral outrage and superiority, but such a position is not necessarily earned (LaCapra, 1998, p. 41). It is easy to judge others (particularly those long dead, or those far removed from us – physically, socially and in lifestyles and employment) as different from ourselves. For example, just as it is easy to judge Hallett's shepherds as brutal murderers, it would be easy to judge Marlene Richard's lack of reference to the Mount Bryan murders in her published history (*Hallett*) as illustrative of settler denial or disavowal. However, the full story is more enlightening.

Marlene was the only settler descendant I interviewed who referred to the conflict at Mount Bryan. Since publishing *Hallett* in 1977, retiring and moving closer to Adelaide and the archives, Marlene learned not only about the murders but also, to her astonishment, that her great-grandfather (Charles Spratt) was one of the shepherds present at Hallett's station in 1844, and that he was imprisoned for his involvement. When I met with Marlene in 2013, she, unprompted, expressed her anguish and regret that she had not known any of this when compiling her history. As Marlene pointed out, when conducting research for *Hallett* in the 1970s, there was no money to travel to Adelaide, and even if there had been, access to the archives was difficult. She had had limited time, and her brief had been to research the centenary of the local council (see Krichauff, 2017, pp. 196–203, for a full account of my interview with Marlene).

The newly learned information profoundly affected Marlene, who told me that if she had known about the murders, and, in particular, Spratt's involvement, writing and researching the history of Hallett would have 'been more meaningful'. Her personal connection brought the ethics of colonialism into the present for Marlene, and alerted her to the different responses settler descendants could display upon learning about historical injustices committed on Aboriginal people. For example, Marlene's cousin, who had authored a family history, whitewashed his account. According to Marlene, he 'anaesthetised, not anaesthetised but sanitised' the story of Spratt's involvement in the murders. Her cousin demonstrated a desire to repress or disavow his great-grandfather's action and to minimise his forebears' (and consequently his own) involvement. In stark contrast, Marlene's older brother saw the murders as very 'black and white'. He did not seek to understand the complexities of his forebear's situation, but instead judged his great-grandfather negatively and had little sympathy – or empathy – for him.

Marlene's reaction is interesting. On learning of her great-grandfather's crime, she did not repress the information; she did not seek to keep the story to herself or to distance herself from her great-grandfather. Rather, she sought to make sense of what she had learned; she wanted to know more, she wanted to *understand*. As French historian Marc Bloch (shot by Nazis in 1944) has poetically and aptly pointed out:

> 'Understanding,' in all honesty, is a word pregnant with difficulties, but also with hope. Moreover, it is a friendly word. Even in action we are too prone to judge. It is so easy to denounce. We are never sufficiently understanding. (Bloch, 1954, pp. 143–144)

Bernhard Schlink, who grew up in post-WWII Germany, points out that reconciliation differs from condemnation and forgiveness in that it requires understanding; reconciliation requires a truth that can be understood (Schlink, 2009, p. 81). And, although revisions to Australian history have been around for decades, it was the *personal connection* – to her great-grandfather, and to a place where she has spent much of her life and knows intimately – that made Marlene more deeply connect with the history of colonialism and dispossession.

As previously stated, when conducting interviews with mid-northern settler descendants, I noticed a distinct sense of disconnection between their own histories (and the histories of the places in which they live) and the histories of Aboriginal people. Rather than condemn or judge them for this disconnect, I argue that we need to fully understand this disconnect to genuinely disrupt it. For those who have not experienced growing up in a tight-knit rural community, surrounded by others who have likewise grown up on land occupied by successive generations of their family, in a district in which the Traditional Owners have not been physically present for over a century, this disconnect may appear illustrative of settler denial and repression – a refusal by those who have directly benefited from the occupation of Aboriginal land to recognise their own implication in the colonial process. However, such a judgement does not take into account the concrete workings of memory and the primacy of lived experience that fundamentally affects how the past is known and made sense of. Nor does it allow for the interest many settler-descended interviewees demonstrated on learning about the experiences of the original owners and welcoming Ngadjuri people's reconnection with their ancestral land, and/or the incredulity and regret they expressed at not having previously contemplated how their forebears originally came to 'own' the land in the first place (see Krichauff, 2017, pp. 204–208, 2020).

While it is easy for non-Aboriginal Australians to express disgust – to point the finger – at the brutal actions of nineteenth-century colonialists, it can be difficult to recognise that we all – no matter where we live, where we were born, how long our families have lived here – benefit from living on Aboriginal Country, and that we all live on unceded land for which the Traditional Owners can never be adequately compensated.

Conclusion

If people do not remain in place, if those present are forced or compelled to move away from a district or do not survive, stories of those people in those places can slip from living memory. Districts where no oral histories about Aboriginal people have been passed down through the generations (by either cultural group) signal great loss; the reasons for the physical absence of Aboriginal people in such places need to be understood. In places such as the Mount Bryan district, where there is a dearth of oral stories of historical Aboriginal presence, the experiences of Aboriginal people and the work of historians, linguists, geographers, anthropologists and archaeologists are key means through which hegemonic settler understandings of Aboriginal absence can be disrupted. For this reason, both the research and the information conveyed need to be comprehensive and informative.

For memory scholars who research the relationship between different ways the past is known and depicted, for sociologists and anthropologists looking at how current generations live with and come to terms with the past, and for historians seeking to more deeply understand what happened in the past and why events unfolded as they did, it is crucial to critically and thoroughly analyse a multitude of sources and to recognise the impact of the norms, assumptions and taken-for-granted understandings of the culture and society upon individuals when constructing their narratives – whether verbal, written or digital. In twenty-first-century Australia, a narrow fixation on physical violence in the colonial era can inadvertently distance current and future generations from the actions of their predecessors. Such perceptions do not expand knowledge; they do not facilitate understanding or truth-telling about a broader range of violence, past and present. Nuanced histories that show both the complexity of the past and parallels with the present are more likely to enable non-Aboriginal Australians to recognise the longevity of colonialism and their ongoing implication in the colonial process.

References

Unpublished sources: State Records of South Australia (SRSA)

Colonial Secretary's Office, incoming correspondence, Government Record Group (GRG) 24/6

Finniss, B. T. (1844, 21 August). Police Commissioner to Colonial Secretary, GRG 24/6/1844/932.

Finniss, B. T. (1845a, 20 February). Police Commissioner to Advocate General, enclosed in GRG 24/6/1845/143.

Finniss, B. T. (1845b, 6 October). Commissioner of Police to Colonial Secretary, GRG 24/6/1845/1197.

Grey, G. (1844a, 25 August). Governor's memo to Police Commissioner, GRG 24/6/1844/932.

Grey, G. (1844b, 19 September). Governor's memo to Protector, GRG 24/6/1844/1044.

Grey, G. (1844c, 11 October). Governor's memo to on Advocate General's letter, GRG 24/6/1844/1135.

Grey, G. (1844d, 3 November). Governor's memo, GRG 24/6/1844/1248.

Grey, G. (1845a, 19 March). Governor Grey memo to Police Commissioner, GRG 24/6/1845/256.

Grey, G. (1845b, 20 March). Governor Grey memo to Advocate General, GRG 24/6/1845/256.

Hawker, G. & Price, H. (1844, 26 October). George Hawker JP and Henry Price JP to Colonial Secretary, GRG 24/6/1844/1249.

Moorhouse, M. (1844a, 7 October) Protector to Colonial Secretary, GRG 24/6/1844/1120.

Moorhouse, M. (1844b, 6 December). Protector to Colonial Secretary, GRG 24/6/1844/1446.

Moorhouse, M. (1844c, 24 December). Protector to Colonial Secretary, GRG 24/6/1844/1528.

Price, H. (1844, 25 October). Price to Colonial Secretary, GRG 24/6/1844/1249½.

Smillie, G. (1844a, 9 October). Advocate General to Colonial Secretary, GRG 24/6/1844/1135.

Smillie, G. (1845a, 5 February). Advocate General to Colonial Secretary, GRG 24/6/1845/143.

Smillie, G. (1845b, 18 March). Advocate General report of convictions at the March Criminal Sessions, GRG 24/6/1845/256.

Colonial Secretary's Office, outgoing correspondence, GRG 24/4

Grey, G. (1844e, 25 August). Memo to the Police Commissioner, GRG 24/4/9, p. 164.

Grey, G. (1844f, 11 October). Colonial Secretary to Henry Price, GRG 24/4/9, p. 230.

Grey, G. (1845c, 25 March). Colonial Secretary to Advocate General, GRG 24/4/7, p. 777.

Grey, G. (1845d, 9 April). Colonial Secretary to the Superintendent of Police Port Phillip and to J Blair Esqr. JP, Police Magistrate, Portland, GRG 24/4/7, p. 801.

Grey, G. (1845e, 6 June). Colonial Secretary to Police Commissioner, GRG 24/4/7, p. 887.

Grey, G. (1845f, 11 June). Colonial Secretary to Police Commissioner, GRG 24/4/7, p. 894.

Grey, G. (1845g, 11 June). Colonial Secretary to the Colonial Secretary, Van Diemen's Land, GRG 24/4/7, p. 895.

Miscellaneous

Aboriginal population of South Australia, compiled from census papers taken 2 April 1871. (1871, 4 August). Commissioner of Crown Lands, GRG 52/1/1871/168.

1851 Pastoral lease diagram. (1850, 24 December). Vol. 1, p. 2, GRS 11677.

Published sources

Attwood, B. (2005). Unsettling pasts: Reconciliation and history in settler Australia. *Postcolonial Studies*, 8(3), 243–259. doi.org/10.1080/13688790500231012

Bloch, M. (1954). *The historian's craft* (Peter Putnam, Trans). Manchester University Press.

Clendinnen, I. (2003). *Dancing with strangers*. Text Publishing Company.

Copley, V. & McInerney, L. (2022). *The wonder of little things*. ABC Books.

Cowlishaw, G. (1992). Studying Aborigines: Changing canons in anthropology and history. In B. Attwood & J. Arnold (Eds.), *Power, knowledge and Aborigines* (pp. 2–31). La Trobe University Press.

Cubitt, G. (2007). *Memory and history*. Manchester University Press.

Foster, R. & Nettelbeck, A. (2012). *Out of the silence*. Wakefield Press.

Jones, P. (2007). *Ochre and rust*. Wakefield Press.

The killing times. (2022, 16 March). *The Guardian*. theguardian.com/australia-news/ng-interactive/2019/mar/04/massacre-map-australia-the-killing-times-frontier-wars

Krichauff, S. (2011). *Nharrungga Wargunni Bugi-buggillu*. Wakefield Press.

Krichauff, S. (2017). *Memory, place and Aboriginal–settler history*. Anthem Press. doi.org/10.2307/j.ctt1trkkdh

Krichauff, S. (2019). Squatter-cum-pastoralist or freeholder? Recognising differences in the experiences of nineteenth-century colonists. In P. Payton & A. Varnava (Eds.), *The immigration histories of Britain, Australasia and the empire* (pp. 93–118). Britain and the World series. Palgrave Macmillan. doi.org/10.1007/978-3-030-22389-2_5

Krichauff, S. (2020). Recognising Country: Tracing stories of wounded spaces in mid-northern South Australia. *History Australia*, *17*(3), 423–447. doi.org/10.1080/14490854.2020.1798793

LaCapra, D. (1998). *History and memory after Auschwitz*. Cornell University Press. doi.org/10.7591/9781501727450

Mattey, R. (1968). *Deceptive lands: A history of Terowie and surrounding hundreds in the mid-north of South Australia*. South Australian Country Women's Association, Terowie Branch.

Police commissioner's court: Tuesday, December 24. (1844, 27 December). *South Australian Register*, 3A.

Police commissioner's court: Monday, December 30. (1845, 1 January). *South Australian Register*, 3C.

Pope, A. (1989). *Resistance and retaliation: Aboriginal–European relations in early colonial South Australia*. Heritage Action.

Richards, M. (1977). *Hallett: A history of town and district*. Lutheran Publishing House.

Rose, D. B. & Davis, R. (2005). *Dislocating the frontier: Essaying the mystique of the outback*. ANU E Press. doi.org/10.22459/DF.03.2006

Ryan, L., Debenham, J., Pascoe, B., Smith, R., Owen, C., Richards, J., Gilbert, S., Anders, R. J., Usher, K., Price, D., Newley, J., Brown, M., Le, L. H. & Fairbairn, H. (2018). *Colonial frontiers massacres, Australia, 1788 to 1930* (Vol. 2.1) [Massacres map]. University of Newcastle. c21ch.newcastle.edu.au/colonialmassacres/map.php

Schlink, B. (2009). *Guilt about the past*. University of Queensland Press.

Schwab, G. (2010). *Haunting legacies: Violent histories and transgenerational trauma*. Columbia University Press.

Shellam, T. (2009). *Shaking hands on the fringe: Negotiating the Aboriginal world at King George's Sound*. UWA Press.

Stolte, R. (1985). *Razorback Range country: A history of the settlement and development of Mt Bryan District*. Mt Bryan Book Committee.

Supreme Court criminal side: Tuesday, 26 November. (1844, 29 November). *Southern Australian Register*, 3A.

Supreme Court criminal side: Friday, 29 November. (1844, 30 November). *South Australian Register*, 3CD.

Veracini, L. (2010). *Settler colonialism: A theoretical overview*. Palgrave Macmillan. doi.org/10.1057/9780230299191

Warrior, F., Knight, F., Anderson, S. & Pring, A. (2005). *Ngadjuri: Aboriginal people of the mid north region of South Australia*. SASOSE Council Inc.

Part II: Remembering and forgetting in heritage spaces

7

A stone in the park of empire: Reclaiming First Nations space through burial

Alexandra Roginski

In the manicured parkland just south of the heart of Melbourne, genteel signage guides visitors and history buffs to sites that include the Victorian-era Royal Botanic Gardens, monuments to King and empire, and the Shrine of Remembrance, built to commemorate Australians killed and wounded in World War I (Figure 7.1). These arrows of bottle green and gold mark the Domain parkland, which is home also to Government House and – in turn – the state governor, the representative of King Charles III. Both Victorian (Victorian Heritage Database, n.d.) and national (Department of Climate Change, Energy, the Environment and Water [DCCEEW], 2022) heritage apparatuses recognise this sprawling parkland for its historical, cultural and social value, and the arrows extend a sense of order and integration across these accretions of empire.

The signage also includes an arrow pointing to the 'Aboriginal Reburial Site', a contemplative hill nestled above Linlithgow Boulevard, marked by a granite boulder sourced from the plains west of Melbourne (Figure 7.2). The signs that point readers to the reburial site, among other places in the Domain parkland, literally embody what Michael Rothberg (2011) terms 'multidirectional memory' – a multiplication of possibilities for engagement with public remembrance from the collision of different memory regimes. The rock marks the keeping place for the remains of 38 unknown Aboriginal

Victorians who, in the mid-1980s, became the symbolic centre of Aboriginal campaigning in the state for custody and respectful care of ancestors long held in museum collections. Although this site is tucked away, and the rock appears humble in size compared to the soaring monuments of Victorian-era ambition (despite its 7 tonnes; Berg, 2010, p. 22), it exerts a disruptive force in this landscape by anchoring continued renegotiations of power and identity within the settler-colonial state. In key actions since 1985, including dawn services held on Invasion Day (Australia Day) since 2019, Victorian activists from a number of First Nations groups have staged actions here that challenge the sovereignty of the European state and the celebratory narratives of its foundation.

This chapter begins with the Aboriginal history of this site, an area of lush, low-lying land and gentle slopes on the opposite side of the Yarra River[1] from the iconic grid of Melbourne's central business district. It establishes how, in the early years of invasion, members of the Kulin nation inhabiting and visiting the encampments on the south bank of the river repeatedly frustrated European attempts to order the space and their behaviour in line with settler-colonial desires for absence or compliance. It then outlines the events of the mid-1980s that led to the interment of ancestral remains here, situating this critical moment for cultural heritage and museum practice within broader repatriation history. This set the stage for a series of subsequent actions that challenged the foundational narrative of peaceable settler-colonial occupation, and I explore this by drawing on sources that include commemorative works by Indigenous historians and cultural heritage practitioners, Hansard and news coverage. These actions have altered the meanings originally inscribed in the site in the 1980s from a story of transfer of power over material remains and cultural revival, to political contest over sovereignty, and, more recently, to calls for truth-telling and re-narration of histories of frontier violence. Far from being silent witnesses of the modern city, the reburied remains work to create a space for campaigning and refusal, and, in fact, invoke the cross-cutting tensions from the late 1830s between Kulin, European settlers focused on pastoralism and trade, and the evangelical forces personified by the protectors of Aborigines.

---

1   See Gibson et al. (2018) for a discussion of the possible names of this river in Kulin language.

Figure 7.1. Signage in the Domain parkland.
The signage in the Domain parkland gestures towards an integrated regime of diverse heritages, yet the events at the burial site since the 1980s point towards a contest over memory and history in the Yarra parkland that disrupts settler-colonial dreams of possession. Photograph: Alexandra Roginski.

Figure 7.2. Kings Domain Resting Place.
Sourced from the You Yangs, west of Melbourne, the burial rock marks the resting place of the remains of 38 Aboriginal people. Photograph: Alexandra Roginski.

The site, therefore, illustrates multiple orders of dispute within the city. What counts as an acceptable or unacceptable use of public space, and what interpretations of First Nations and contact histories are acceptable? How does static heritage, embodied in instruments such as heritage listings, come to life in actions such as marches and encampments? These actions have invoked criticism and even panic from conservative commentators and politicians, along with members of the public peddling white settler-nationalism. Especially in 2006, when protesters established the 'Camp Sovereignty' encampment close to the rock, comments from conservative politicians echoed historical anxieties about an overflow of collective Aboriginal presence, and the idea of 'acceptable' and 'unacceptable' forms of First Nations identity and claim-making. As the historian Sarah Pinto (2021, pp. 197–199) observes, commemorations of First Nations history and frontier violence in settler-colonial Melbourne often take place in marginal spaces and seem small compared to monuments such as the Shrine of Remembrance, but they can also 'push the settler city into the background'. The Kings Domain burial ground demonstrates how a marginalised spatial position in a city can invite challenges to government power. With time, a site of dispossession becomes a place of repossession.

Unstable relations on the south bank

Somewhere between '1.2 million years ago and about 820,000 years ago', according to historian Gary Presland (2012, pp. 19–20), lava flowed through the Yarra River valley, eventually settling into the formation that became known as the 'the falls' – a rock ledge close to where Queen's Bridge traverses the Yarra River in modern Melbourne today. Far along this timeline, but still many thousands of years prior to the arrival of Europeans, unfolded the many sequential lives of the Kulin – a confederation (Broome, 2005, p. xxi) comprising groups that are today often referred to as the Wurundjeri, Bunurong, Wadawurrung, Taungurung and Dja Dja Wurrung.[2] Europeans poured into this history late in the timeline like a swirling flood and,

---

2 As the orthography of group names remains under debate, I adopt the spellings preferred by the Registered Aboriginal Parties recognised under the framework of the Victorian Aboriginal Heritage Council at the time of writing (aboriginalheritagecouncil.vic.gov.au/). The European scribes who wrote about Kulin life at the time of invasion adopted varying designations for the individuals they encountered. Where possible, I indicate, in brackets, likely group membership as it is understood in terms of contemporary traditional ownership.

as Diane Barwick (1984, p. 108) observed: 'Within six years almost 12,000 Europeans had appropriated the estates of most Kulin clans and dispossessed the owners.'

The official establishment of the settler-colonial city of Melbourne, the capital of today's state of Victoria, took place in 1836. As Ian D Clark and Toby Heydon write (2004, p. 13), settlers often chose sites for pastoral stations and towns that Traditional Owners valued for their richness of resources. The Melbourne settlement resulted from a process driven by a group of pastoralists from Van Diemen's Land (Tasmania) who, working together as the Port Phillip Association, in 1835 made a treaty with Kulin *ngurungaeta* (headmen) in an attempt to convince colonial powers of their right to ownership (Attwood, 2009; Barwick, 1984, p. 107). The British Government eventually intervened to govern the sale and granting of land in this locality. Although the violence of the pastoral frontier today dominates the public imagination, settler-colonial cities such as Melbourne also presented a patchwork of ongoing negotiations and intimate violence. Moreover, for at least 15 years following the arrival of Europeans, Traditional Owners secured habitation, often in 'unallotted' spaces such as riverbanks and swamp areas, and turned to bartering and labouring as food resources dwindled (Edmonds, 2010, pp. 130, 134). The Victorian-era edifice of Government House that today marks the parkland as a site of royal dominion only reared its neck to gaze over the terrain during the 1870s (Dunstan, n.d.). The land for the nearby Botanic Garden was carved out in 1846 (Maroske, n.d.). These structures of power and European knowledge in the area south of the Yarra followed an earlier period of intense negotiation.

For the first few years following the establishment of Melbourne, Kulin camped at a series of significant sites around the European settlements (Edmonds, 2010, p. 137), and the Europeans lived alongside them in a transcultural 'contact zone' (per Pratt, 2008) of misunderstanding and thwarted plans. The power structures already leaned heavily on the Kulin Traditional Owners. But what we might think of as an 'encampment zone' contained levelling elements – the shared vagaries of life exposed to the elements, the active exclusion of Europeans from insider Kulin information, and the gatherings and conflicts that they could not parse. In the encampment environment close to town – space that Penny Edmonds (2010) compellingly terms an 'intimate, urbanising frontier' – power, friction and friendship played out at an interpersonal level that could shift by the hour.

The Port Phillip Association's land grab of the 1830s coincided with an evangelical movement in the British Empire that both drew attention to settler atrocities committed against Indigenous peoples in the colonies and attempted to stem these practices (see Elbourne, 2003). In this climate, Governor of New South Wales Richard Bourke appointed Anglican catechist George Langhorne to serve as missionary to the Kulin under a plan that centred on establishing 'native villages', modelled in part on the scientific social plans of the Welsh reformer Robert Owen. At the end of 1836, Langhorne received instructions to 'protect the aboriginal natives of the District from any manner of wrong, and to endeavour to conciliate them by kind treatment and presents' (Cannon, 1982, p. 153; Langhorne, 1836; Colonial Secretary, 1836). When sawn timber became available, mission buildings were constructed in the hilly space by the present-day ornamental lake in the Botanic Gardens, part of a vast mission reserve of 895 acres (Cannon, 1982, p. 153).

Kulin who lived in and frequented the region made use of the mission station as part of their circuits for congregating, practising ceremony and obtaining food. While Langhorne (1837–39) found some success in educating children, with '20 children and youths resident' at the mission in late 1837 (30 November 1837), he bemoaned that 'no inducement' could prevent the Kulin from 'undergoing certain rites or assisting at certain ceremonies at particular times' (31 December 1838). Kulin ventured to work in the town, where they laboured as wood cutters and water carriers in exchange for money, rather than for the rations offered at the mission (30 November 1838), and often avoided the mission altogether because – some reported – Langhorne hindered a newfound 'passion for shooting' (31 January 1839). Langhorne's own tensions with Police Magistrate William Lonsdale came to a head in May 1838, when Lonsdale, associate Captain de Villiers and three mounted police stormed the mission station in search of the supposed culprits of sheep killing. Langhorne reported that 'the conduct of some of the police on this occasion was brutal in the extreme' and converted 'the Mission into a scene of bloodshed and confusion' (31 May 1838). By February of the following year, only three children lived at the mission and the missionary concluded that the mission had failed in terms of employment and education. In fact, espousing a goal of disconnecting people from culture and kinship networks, he wrote that he doubted that it was possible to 'settle' people in their own districts, especially in proximity to a town such as Melbourne (Langhorne, 1837–39, 28 February 1839, 31 March 1839; Langhorne, 1839).

New efforts to offer 'protection' to the resident Kulin – against both wanton European settlers and from the First Nations lifeways deemed inappropriate by British evangelicals – arrived in the forms of Chief Protector of Aborigines George Augustus Robinson and assistant protectors William Thomas, Edward Stone Parker, William Dredge and Charles Sievwright. The assistant protectors – all Wesleyan Methodists, except for Sievwright – sailed into Melbourne in the early days of 1839, pitching tents on a hill by the south bank of the Yarra (Thomas, 1839–43, January 1839, p. 3). The Kulin sometimes camped close to them – with the 'Wa Woo rong & Port Phillip Tribes' (the Wurundjeri and Bunurong) camping between the protectors and the falls (Thomas, 1839–43, 12 February 1839, p. 5). The encampments around Melbourne could swell to include hundreds of people, especially when other members of the confederation, such as the Taungurung, visited, with Robinson recording 500 people at one gathering in the autumn of 1839 (Robinson, 1839a).

The canvas offered the protectors but a flimsy barrier between their counterfeit European domesticity and life on Kulin land. The climate buffeted them (Dredge, 1839, 29 January, 9 May, p. 428). They often misinterpreted Kulin intention. In early February, for example, 'four fine young' Waworong (Wurundjeri) arrived at the camp 'just as the evening shades closed in'. Dredge and Thomas and their parties became anxious at the sight of these men, three of whom stood nearly 6 feet high, armed with spears, shields, waddies and a musket. They determined that two men should keep watch all night, and that they must seize the firearm. But they soon found that the men only wished to make camp. The Waworong stayed for four days, venturing to Melbourne during the day after feasting on protector-supplied breakfasts (Dredge, 1839, 4 February; Thomas, 1839–43, 5 February 1839). Meanwhile, the failures of the protectors to properly understand Kulin culture became evident when Thomas observed a corroboree, early during his tenure, that was performed at the time of a visit from a rival group. He could not grasp the shift between battle and dance – the ritualised combat and resolution of Kulin law – and the ways that these cultural forms nested together. 'The transition from fighting to dancing so quick, in but a few hours … I thought that anger or play must be one or the other artificial', he wrote (Thomas, 1839–43, 23 March 1839).

The administrative tasks of empire also became a negotiation. When Thomas attempted to take a census of the 'Yarra and Western Port people and those who claim the country a few miles around the Town' (Wurundjeri and Bunurong) who camped close to his tent, behind the brickfields south of the Yarra, some shifted from miam (temporary shelter) to miam to trick him into recording their names multiple times. First wary, then amused, he communed with curious onlookers over the foundations of writing, guiding them as they put pencil to paper while small boys followed him and attempted to snatch his pencil (Thomas, 1839–43, 9 March 1839).

Thomas remained in the district once Dredge, Parker and Sievwright fanned out to their allocated parts of Victoria. He travelled between his new station, Tubberubbabel (a site selected by Bunurong close to Arthur's Seat), and back to the Melbourne encampments when summoned by Robinson for supervisory duties (Fels, 2011, p. 124). Robinson and Superintendent Charles La Trobe were both eager for the Kulin to vacate Melbourne. 'I by no means want you in or near Melbourne', barked Robinson (1839b) to Thomas in a letter: 'But so long as the natives are on its confines it will be necessary, ere you entirely absent yourself, to first get them away.' La Trobe (1839) described Kulin encampments close to town as 'the source of great disorder', instructing Robinson to exert 'sufficient influence to persuade the parties to keep to their promise of an early retirement to their several districts'. However, the Europeans could not predict Kulin use of the encampments, although they at times believed that they could, and attempts to intervene in cultural conflict often failed. In early 1840, Thomas insisted to Robinson that his reports about the movements of Kulin from the camps were faithful but frustrated by what he called the 'vacillating manners and sentiments of these people' (Thomas, 1840).

The reports, letters and diaries of the protectors demonstrate the close habitation of the area south of the Yarra by Bunurong and Wurundjeri and other Kulin groups visiting for cultural business or combat. Even as the settler-colonial town expanded on the northern side of the Yarra, filling into its newly laid grid, Kulin married according to custom, raised families, performed corroborees and buried their dead. Some engaged in labour for Europeans, with a number joining the Native Police Corps (Clark & Heydon, 2004, p. 15). For the Kulin camping south of the Yarra, the protectors personified both an ever-expanding list of hindrances and a source of material goods such as tea, tobacco and food. They sometimes tolerated earnest European audiences, including those from the elite who visited to observe ceremony (Thomas, 1839–43, 18 November 1839). At other times, the enquiries and presence of the protectors created consternation. For example, in September 1839, a group of 14 Kulin returned with raised spears from a journey to the inland. Thomas observed them carefully, suspicious that the mission had been one of violence. He built a fire to feign solidarity and try to sneak an insight into the events of their journey. 'I could not refrain from watching their actions. They as assiduously watched mine,' wrote Thomas. Eventually, the Kulin dismissed the assistant protector: 'You go home, black fellow want to talk no we kill Black fellows, no find any' (Thomas, 1839–43, 9 September 1839).

The period during which Thomas and the other protectors camped alongside the Kulin offered moments of levelling, although it also highlighted different interpretations of how encampment should function. For Europeans, encampment was part of a teleology of settlement in which canvas eventually made way to fixed buildings: encampments ended. Meanwhile, the Kulin utilised encampments for structured purposes of ceremony and for seeking food and shelter. Encampment symbolised persistence of culture, even as the Kulin incorporated European technologies and engaged with the settler economy, and even as the superintendent yearned to move them on. Nevertheless, the Kulin faced persistent ravages of settler colonialism: European violence; a legal system that favoured white perpetrators because it did not allow Aboriginal testimony; European diseases (Edmonds, 2010, 140–141; Thomas, 1839–43, 6 May 1839); and – as the century crept on – the appeal of Aboriginal bodies for Western science.

1985: Care through reburial

At the same time as Kulin inhabited their encampments south of the Yarra, the disciplines of ethnography, comparative anatomy, and – by century's end – anthropology, together with antiquarianism and the science of phrenology, fuelled an acquisitive hunger for human remains. First Nations Australians became prized components of such collections, their remains stolen from graves, obtained postmortem from hospitals, or collected in the aftermath of frontier violence (Turnbull, 2017). With the appointment of renowned naturalist and ethnographer Walter Baldwin Spencer in 1899 as the honorary director of the National Museum of Victoria, several kilometres north of the Yarra, the institution expanded its collecting practices and networks, including through a relationship with Victoria Police for the transfer of Indigenous remains to the museum (Mulvaney, 1990; Spencer, 1902). This led to a collection at the museum containing the remains of more than 3,000 Indigenous people, with a particular focus on skulls – the result of the rise of craniometric methods such as phrenology that deduced racial hierarchies from differences in human morphology.[3] In the mid-twentieth century, Indigenous activists around the world began campaigning for museums and other collecting institutions to disclose and return Indigenous ancestral remains stolen through scientific processes in order to enable appropriate Indigenous custody and care. This new repatriation movement spurred crucial transfers such as the handover of Truganini's remains from the Tasmanian Museum during the 1970s following years of campaigning, a process that enabled her cremation and the scattering of her ashes in the D'Entrecasteaux Channel in 1976 (Fforde, 2004, pp. 97–100).

Repatriations today occur regularly across Australia and include the return of ancestral remains from overseas and locally based institutions (for an overview of the movement internationally, see Fforde et al., 2020). Olivia Robinson, a Bidjara Aboriginal woman who leads collection engagement at the State Library of Queensland, reflects on repatriation in this volume. She explains that:

> there's really nothing like it in [the] sense of spiritual connection that people have, and it transcends sort of everything ... To take a person who has been sitting in a museum storeroom or something like that, for 100 years or so, and take them back home and then lay them on Country – how good is that?

In Victoria during the 1980s, Gunditjmara heritage worker and employee of the Victorian Aboriginal Legal Service (VALS) Jim Berg began challenging the powers of non-Indigenous individuals and institutions – public and private – to control and dispose of cultural heritage. A major commemorative project published in 2010 and led by Indigenous studies scholar Shannon Faulkhead and Berg captures the historical impact of the thicket of legal and processual changes that resulted from this revolutionising of First Nations control over cultural heritage and ancestral remains at the state level. Between late 1983 and 1984, Berg, in his overlapping roles as CEO of VALS, inspector under the *Archaeological and Aboriginal Relics Preservation Act 1972* and deputy chairperson of the advisory committee established by the legislation, instigated legal proceedings against Leonard Joel, an auction house in Melbourne, to try to block the sale of a private collection of Victorian Indigenous material culture in contravention of the legislation. The case, although unsuccessful, prompted amendments to the Act regarding ancestral remains, and this enabled Berg to step in when

---

3 By 2014, Museums Victoria had handed back the remains of more than 1,700 people, with further remains awaiting reburial or claiming by relevant Indigenous groups. See Allen (2014).

Museums Victoria attempted to send remains of great antiquity to New York for an exhibition (Berg, 2010, pp. 8–12). Berg also instigated legal action against the University of Melbourne for the transfer of the so-called Murray Black Collection (named after a collector who, during the mid-twentieth century, collected the remains of about 1,600 Aboriginal people) to Museums Victoria for appropriate custody (Berg, 2010, pp. 14–18; Russell, 2010). During this time, Berg came to lead discussions about how the remains of 38 Indigenous people in the museum deemed to be of unknown provenance should be cared for (Berg, 2010, pp. 21–22). This care for long-passed ancestors, and attendant sadness, reflected aspects of his early work during the 1970s with VALS when, as a field officer, he transported eight different Indigenous people who had passed away in Melbourne back to Country (Berg, 2010, pp. 5–7).

In 1985, Melbourne City Council immediately supported Berg's request for the designation of a site in the parkland for the remains of 38 Victorian Aboriginal people whose provenance was unknown, and a burial date was set for 22 November 1985. The granite boulder came from the You Yangs west of Melbourne, and the night before the reburial ceremony, Jim Berg and others met at the museum – then located with the State Library in Melbourne's CBD – to wrap the remains in bark. As often occurs with repatriation events even today, a level of uncertainty permeated the morning, with Berg's nervousness building after he and Soulmate Kylie Mim prepared tea, coffee and biscuits and waited to see who would turn up (Berg, 2010, p. 24). The moment broke when 'people began to arrive by bus from the country areas, and also on foot'. He recounts that 'there were about 200 Koories and non-Koories gathered together in the courtyard, with warm drinks in hand, getting to know each other'. Eventually, these conversations quietened as Berg asked for volunteers to carry the bark parcels, and 38 people came forward for the task, the youngest of whom, Nicole Cassar, was just eight years old (Cassar, 2009). Berg (2010, p. 26) recalls that:

> the walk down Swanston Street was really quiet and peaceful. When members of the public asked us what was the purpose of the march, we told them about the reburial and they wished us well.

After the parcels were placed in the grave, the participants filled it with soil and a crane lodged the protective granite boulder, which included a plaque with a poem:

> Rise from this grave
> Release your anger and pain
> As you soar with the winds
> Back to your homelands.
> There find peace with our
> Spiritual Mother the Land
> Before drifting off into the
> 'Dreamtime'.

Accompanying this epitaph, drafted by Berg, was a list of Victorian Aboriginal groups.

Oral histories regarding the reburial reflect the 'mixed emotions' and difficult conversations that can circle around such events, with some people expressing concern that these ancestral remains would be buried away from Country, and others criticising the site as too public (Berg, 2010; Dugay-Grist, 2009; Mullett, 2009–10; Thorpe, 2009). These debates reflect the diverse approaches to memorialisation and sovereignty among First Nations Australians. Nevertheless, the Kings Domain keeping place has since been recognised by various First Nations activists as holding spiritual or sacred value (Berg, 2010, p. 26).[4]

Concurrently, the keeping place has also been recognised for its heritage value as part of state and national apparatuses, itemised within the plethora of monuments that comprise the Domain parkland. The Victorian Heritage Database (n.d.) notes its 'social significance' and potential spiritual significance, while the DCCEEW (2022) recognises the central role that the burial site plays in Australia's history of repatriation. This confluence of recognitions – by First Nations historians and cultural heritage workers, and by the mechanisms of settler-colonial government – implies a cohesive integration of the reburial site into landscapes of governance, both material and symbolic.

Yet the gatherings that the site has attracted during this century, moments that contribute to the social value celebrated in the Victorian heritage listing, complicate these narratives. The stories of these events reflect periodic debates about what are considered 'acceptable' forms of political challenge. It is the action that the rock generates, a persistence of forms

---

4   *Returning our ancestors*, a recent documentary about the 1985 reburial and repatriation in Victoria today more generally, can be viewed online on the website of the Victorian Aboriginal Heritage Council (www.aboriginalheritagecouncil.vic.gov.au/media/44826).

such as encampment, that most challenges the settler-colonial narratives, and that draws out the tensions between different levels of government and the different approaches of settler-colonial politicians.

2006: 'Stolenwealth' and sacred fires

One of the strongest challenges to the cohesion of the Domain parkland as a 'settled' site occurred in 2006, in the lead-up to Melbourne's Commonwealth Games. On 12 March 2006, in anticipation of international media attention surrounding the 'Stolenwealth' Games, Indigenous activists calling themselves the Black GST ('Genocide to be stopped, Sovereignty to be restored, Treaty to be made') began an occupation of a clearing close to the site of the 1985 reburial. The group – led by senior Indigenous figures Marg Thorpe, Gary Foley and Robbie Thorpe, as well as younger activists – argued that 'Australia's "unfinished business"' could only be resolved through their three-pronged approach. The protesters built on political actions performed at previous Commonwealth Games and adapted their encampment model from the Aboriginal Tent Embassy (established in 1972 outside what is now Old Parliament House in Canberra), with the sacred flame at the centre of this Melbourne site echoing that iconic resistance site (Birch, 2018; Holroyd, 2006b; Mansell, 2006).

What the Black GST called 'Camp Sovereignty' became the focus of international media attention, a legal challenge and even censure from conservative Prime Minister John Howard. Author and historian Tony Birch (2018, p. 3), in his razor-sharp essay about the protests, observes how 'what began as a two-week occupation soon morphed into a contest over place and memory'. In April 2006, the group obtained a 30-day cultural protection order through Wurundjeri heritage officer Vicki Nicholson-Brown, under the *Aboriginal and Torres Strait Islander Heritage Protection Act 1984*, to protect the site from interference by the City of Melbourne (Holroyd, 2006a). This order protecting the fire was later upheld by the Victorian Supreme Court (although camping gear had to be removed). Nevertheless, acting Premier John Thwaites, of the Labor party, stressed that 'the government doesn't support it … We don't believe it's appropriate for that place' (Holroyd, 2006b). In this instance, both sides of politics were united, with Prime Minister John Howard, leader of the Coalition, warning that the camp shouldn't become 'entrenched' like the Canberra tent embassy: 'The Canberra tent embassy was left for years and then the longer it's left the harder and harder it becomes to do anything about it' ('Uproot camp', 2006). This white panic about encampment echoed concerns dating back to La Trobe–era Melbourne.

Leading up to Anzac Day in 2006, calls for dousing the fire led to a contest between this flame and the one burning in front of the Shrine of Remembrance. Spokesperson Robert Corowa pointed out that Indigenous ceremonial fires had burned long before World War I: 'Anzacs are newcomers to Australia. The British are not really the custodians of this country' (Holroyd, 2006b). His argument was particularly cutting considering that, as the *Herald* reported on 12 November 1929, Aboriginal ancestral remains were unearthed by a 'steam shovel excavating' the site as part of the shrine's construction ('Shovel unearths human bones', 1929, p. 4).[5] As Birch (2018, p. 8) notes, the press in 2006 came to recognise that the great-grandfather of activist Robbie Thorpe had served during WWI – a layer of inherited memory. On Anzac Day itself, a contest framed by sensationalist media reports as a simple binary between two sacred flames – Koorie and Anzac – took on new angles as Vietnam veterans also attended the Camp Sovereignty flame in a gesture of reciprocal commemoration.

Part of an established history of reoccupation, the actions of the Black GST demonstrated a different approach from the engagement with settler-colonial laws that characterised the repatriation to the Kings Domain two decades earlier. For Berg, his power – emphasised in the title of his and Shannon Faulkhead's history project, *Power and the Passion* (2010) – derived from new possibilities afforded by changes to heritage legislation, his position as inspector and the influence of VALS, of which he was a pillar with non-Indigenous lawyers Ron Merkel and Ron Castan. While the Black GST protesters drew on the power of settler-colonial law, with Nicholson-Brown's role central to the longevity of the camp, the protest also represented a radical politics of refusal that challenged European occupation.

These tactics ruffled the Victorian Labor government. At the time, it was close to passing the Aboriginal Heritage Bill following two-and-a-half years of consultation, debate and drafting (Jennings, 2006, p. 1533). The Bill established the Victorian Aboriginal Heritage Council and Register and created powers for recognised Aboriginal parties and officers (*Aboriginal Heritage Act 2006*). While this legislation is today a business-as-usual component of government bureaucracy – and has even been criticised for

---

5   I thank David Tutchener of the Bunurong Land Council Aboriginal Corporation for alerting me to these events. See also Birch (2018, p. 9), citing Francesco Vitelli, on disinterment history at the shrine.

legitimising destruction of cultural heritage while simultaneously conferring greater powers on First Nations groups (see Tutchener et al., 2021, p. 1315) – in 2006 the government faced attacks from the Coalition, the property development lobby and conservative media about perceived threats to development and property rights (Asher, 2006; Giles & McRae, 2005). During the Bill's second reading in early May 2006, opposition members of parliament (Thompson, 2006) latched onto differing opinions within the Aboriginal community about the legislation to argue that the Bill was flawed. Meanwhile, according to Liberal politicians such as Member for Brighton Louise Asher (2006, p. 1134), the occupation showed that 'the government is incapable of dealing with the sensitivity and the rights of property owners in this particular example', and that Aboriginal Affairs Minister Gavin Jennings 'did himself and the government no credit at all' in his dealings with protesters at the Kings Domain. A month earlier, the Coalition had tried to embarrass Minister for the Commonwealth Games John Madden by asking what agreements the government had made with the activists regarding their presence and ultimate withdrawal from the site at the end of the games. In response, Madden (2006) highlighted the success of the games and the extensive engagement with members of other Indigenous groups for the event, which resulted, in his view, in the successful presentation of Aboriginal culture to 'the rest of the world', including through 'the opening ceremony, but also in the Koori business showcasing that took place in and around Federation Square and a number of other elements of the cultural festivities'. Madden stressed that he had not made any agreement with the activists, leaving the matter of occupation up to the police. In doing so, he attempted to distance the government from the action by placing the protesters outside the framework of negotiation, relegating their claims to those of disorder – that is, something that should be addressed through policing – rather than as a challenge to state authority.

The encampment ended on 11 May 2006 when – following the expiry of the 30-day protection order – security guards and police entered the site and extinguished the flame (Birch, 2018, p. 9). In its two-month lifespan, Camp Sovereignty highlighted debates about what constituted an 'acceptable' expression of First Nations identity and claims. For Prime Minister Howard, the process represented:

> the unacceptable face, in a way, of reconciliation … The sensible face is where you cooperate to try to remedy wrongs and help people become part of the community in the fullest possible sense. ('Uproot camp', 2006)

The events of state politics echoed the paternalism of the colonial period, with the conservative state opposition attacking the government's credentials in Aboriginal affairs by pointing to failures to 'manage' the problem of non-compliant First Nations people.

In addition to highlighting what Birch (2018, p. 8) calls 'the fragility of landscapes overburdened with meaning', the protests highlighted the multi-party configurations of power in the settler-colonial context. The Labor ministers, like the protectors of the 1830s, were seen as posing a threat to settler enjoyment of land. Yet, through these negotiations of the right and wrong forms of commemoration, the protests added another layer to a history of First Nations land use in the Kings Domain that would add to its weight as a political site.

2019–2021: Commemorating the frontier wars

On Australia Day in 2019, First Nations activists and allies gathered on the lawn above the memorial stone and keeping place for the inaugural Invasion Day dawn service. A complement to the Invasion Day march in the centre of Melbourne, the event represented a fusion of Aboriginal cultural practices, including smoking ceremonies, with the dawn service adapted from Anzac commemoration culture.

DjabWurrung-Gunnai-Gunditjmara activist and politician Lidia Thorpe (since 2020 a senator for Victoria in the federal parliament) organised the first dawn service in 2019 as a complement to the march on a day that she says fills every Aboriginal person with anxiety (Wahlquist, 2019). The success of the event saw it repeated on 26 January 2020 and again in 2021. The dawn service now brings together the affective power of mourning with a ritual of truth-telling about the violence of historical dispossession, and a political message of responding to the current ecological crisis by recognising First Nations landcare practices and connection to Country (Tungandame, 2020). (In this, it partly reflects a discourse of 'truth-telling' central to Australian politics today, as seen in the Victorian Yoorrook Justice Commission.) As with the Kings Domain reburial when volunteers came forward to carry remains, the event is highly participatory, and Thorpe invites members of the audience to come forward to read the details of massacres that took place during the Victorian colonial period (Wahlquist,

2019). And, as with Camp Sovereignty, the focus on truth-telling about frontier violence challenges a national narrative of peaceful conquest and the foundations of governance. In the lead-up to the 2020 event, Thorpe integrated the symbolic force of truth-telling with a material component, aligning it with a 'Pay the Rent' campaign that she and other Indigenous leaders coordinate ('Lidia Thorpe announces', 2020).

Sanctioned by the Melbourne City Council, the dawn service nevertheless still highlights the uneasy cohabitation of First Nations culture and political aims within a settler-colonial city. In 2019, Lidia Thorpe began preparations for the dawn service by caring for the boulder that crowns the Aboriginal reburial site. 'We cleaned off bottles of beer that were smashed over that rock yesterday', she recounted (Wahlquist, 2019). In 2021, in the midst of tensions over management of COVID-19 and social distancing, the dawn service went ahead, even while events such as the Australia Day parade were cancelled. This latter cancellation became a source of attacks from right-wing commentators. Steve Price (2021) of the *Herald Sun* lambasted:

> the Andrews government and the impossibly politically correct Melbourne City Council … [H]ow dare the council support an 'Invasion Day' dawn service but cancel the annual multi-cultural Australia Day parade through our city.

In the daylight hours of Invasion Day 2021, a group of far-right activists marched down Melbourne's St Kilda Road, past the parkland and towards the suburb of St Kilda. 'Australia is a proud Western nation, and we should not apologise for building the society that we live in', declared one speaker. Ten of the hundred-or-so participants wore t-shirts that identified them as 'Proud Boys' – the US white nationalist militant group (Vinall, 2021). One of these men, draped also in an Australian flag, later attempted to disrupt the Invasion Day rally taking place in Melbourne's central business district ('Invasion Day rally', 2021).

In contrast to the disruption to Australian nationalism that commentators such as Price feared, the dawn service of 2021 unfolded in a contemplative, peaceful manner behind a white picket fence (a biosecurity measure for containing crowd numbers). Participants, who included councillors and members of parliament, pre-registered, and each person received a mask and hand sanitiser at the entrance, along with a battery-operated candle. The proceedings, captured by cameras from multiple news organisations, took place in a summer rain shower. Jim Berg and his Soulmate Kylie Mim were acknowledged at the start of the service as guests of honour.

An official breakfast followed in a nearby marquee. Nevertheless, despite this orderliness and growing role in the civic calendar, the dawn service was perceived by some to be just as destabilising as the encampment of 2006. Although the rock rests at this site for the entire year, largely overlooked, the action that it ignites and invites at particular times of the year poses a challenge to celebratory Australian nationhood.

Culture and history reinscribed

Jim Berg's exhortation to the 38 people whose remains lie in the Kings Domain to 'rise from this grave' marked a turning point for First Nations Victorians and their stewardship of cultural heritage. In the decades since the reburial, these remains have summoned crowds of activists and their allies to the telling of stories of violence and dispossession that unsettle settler-colonial narratives, with the annual dawn service now lodging these enactments in the civic calendar.

The rock now serves as one piece in the heritage apparatus for the Kings Domain parkland at both a state and federal level, listed alongside the Botanic Gardens and various memorials to monarchs, wars and the British Empire. The Victorian Heritage Database (n.d.) recognises the 'social significance' of the burial site for Aboriginal Victorians and its role in 'continuing and developing cultural traditions'. Along with heritage criteria focused on historical, architectural or environmental aspects of cultural history, the 'social value' heritage criterion represents the currents of human gatherings through time, allowing – as practitioner Chris Johnston (1992, p. 17) notes – for the meanings of a site to be 'constantly redefined, reviewed and reiterated' by a community or group.

Repatriation itself – among its crucial healing and restorative purposes – has come to serve as a compelling performance of reconciliation for both sides of politics, with even conservative politicians bundling it into a politics of nation-building forged from the supposed consensus between First Nations people and settlers (e.g. see Pyne, 2015). Yet, it is the actions that sites of reburial invite – calls for sovereignty, reparations, truth-telling and rebellious encampment – that carry the potential to disorient, disturb and embarrass settler governments. The rock at the reburial site is dwarfed by Government House and the King George V memorial. Visitors must seek it out in the rolling mounds of the area. But its comparatively small size leaves space in the grassland for culture and story to pour back in.

Acknowledgements

I wish to thank Jim Berg for reading and commenting on this draft, Lidia Thorpe for a conversation in relation to this piece in 2020, and Deakin colleagues Billy Griffiths, Jason Gibson, Sarah Hayes and Steven Cooke, as well as other participants in the 2020 workshop that shaped this work. I also thank Cameo Dalley and Ash Barnwell for including me in this conversation, and for their thoughtful advice.

References

Primary sources

Asher, L. (2006, 2 May). In Victoria, *Parliamentary Debates (Hansard), Legislative Assembly*, pp. 1133–1134.

Berg, J. (2010). Jim's story. In S. Faulkhead & J. Berg (Eds.), *Power and the passion: Our ancestors return home* (pp. 3–30). Koorie Heritage Trust.

Cannon, M. (Ed.). (1982). *Historical records of Victoria. Vol. 2A. The Aborigines of Port Phillip, 1835–1839*. Victorian Government Printing Office.

Cassar, N. (2009). Interview. In S. Faulkhead & J. Berg (Eds.) (2010), *Power and the passion: Our ancestors return home* (pp. 38–39). Koorie Heritage Trust.

Colonial Secretary. (1836, 9 December). [Final draft of instructions to Langhorne.] In M. Cannon (Ed.) (1982), *Historical records of Victoria. Vol. 2A. The Aborigines of Port Phillip, 1835–1839* (pp. 161–163). Victorian Government Printing Office.

Dredge, J. (1839). [Journal: 29 January, 4 February.] In M. Cannon (Ed.) (1983), *Historical records of Victoria. Vol. 2B. Aborigines and protectors, 1838–1839* (pp. 421–423). Victorian Government Printing Office.

Dugay-Grist, M. (2009). Interview. In S. Faulkhead & J. Berg (Eds.) (2010), *Power and the passion: Our ancestors return home* (p. 35). Koorie Heritage Trust.

Jennings, G. (2006, 13 April). In Victoria, *Legislative Council Legislation Committee, Disability Bill*, p. 1533.

La Trobe, C. (1839, 18 December). [Letter to George Augustus Robinson.] In M. Cannon (Ed.) (1983), *Historical records of Victoria. Vol. 2B. Aborigines and protectors, 1838–1839* (pp. 610–611). Victorian Government Printing Office.

Langhorne, G. M. (1836, 26 November). [Letter to Sir Richard Bourke.] In M. Cannon (Ed.) (1982), *Historical records of Victoria. Vol. 2A. The Aborigines of Port Phillip, 1835–1839* (pp. 157–160). Victorian Government Printing Office.

Langhorne, G. M. (1837–39). [Mission reports: 30 November 1837, 31 December 1838, 31 May 1838, 30 November 1838, 31 January 1839, 28 February 1839.] In M. Cannon (Ed.) (1982), *Historical records of Victoria. Vol. 2A. The Aborigines of Port Phillip, 1835–1839* (pp. 208–209, 220–222, 233–236). Victorian Government Printing Office.

Langhorne, G. M. (1839, 15 October). [Letter to Charles La Trobe.] In M. Cannon (Ed.) (1983), *Historical records of Victoria. Vol. 2B. Aborigines and protectors, 1838–1839* (pp. 507–510). Victorian Government Printing Office.

Madden, J. (2006, 6 April). In Victoria, *Parliamentary Debates (Hansard), Legislative Assembly* (pp. 1349–1350).

Mullett, R. (2009–10). Interview. In S. Faulkhead & J. Berg (Eds.) (2010), *Power and the passion: Our ancestors return home* (pp. 102–104). Koorie Heritage Trust.

Robinson, G. A. (1839a, 26 March). [Gathering of tribes on the Yarra.] In M. Cannon (Ed.) (1983), *Historical records of Victoria. Vol. 2B. Aborigines and protectors, 1838–1839* (pp. 448–449). Victorian Government Printing Office.

Robinson, G. A. (1839b, 3 September). [Letter to William Thomas.] In M. Cannon (Ed.) (1983), *Historical records of Victoria. Vol. 2B. Aborigines and protectors, 1838–1839* (pp. 577–582). Victorian Government Printing Office.

Robinson, G. A. (1839c, 28 October). [Letter to Charles La Trobe.] In M. Cannon (Ed.) (1983), *Historical records of Victoria. Vol. 2B. Aborigines and protectors, 1838–1839* (pp. 599–600). Victorian Government Printing Office.

Shovel unearths human bones. (1929, 12 November). *The Herald*, 4.

Spencer, W. B. (1902, 2 July). [Letter to Chief Commissioner of Police Thomas O'Callaghan.] Department of Humanities, Museum Victoria (Correspondence file regarding acquisition of ancestral remains through Victoria Police), Melbourne.

Thomas, W. (1839–43). In M. Stephens (Ed.) (2014), *The journal of William Thomas: Assistant protector of the Aborigines of Port Phillip & guardian of the Aborigines of Victoria 1839–1843*. Victorian Aboriginal Corporation for Languages.

Thomas, W. (1839, 30 December). [Letter to George Augustus Robinson.] In M. Cannon (Ed.) (1983), *Historical records of Victoria. Vol. 2B. Aborigines and Protectors, 1838–1839* (p. 612). Victorian Government Printing Office.

Thomas, W. (1840, 6 January). [Letter to George Augustus Robinson.] In M. Cannon (Ed.) (1983), *Historical records of Victoria. Vol. 2B. Aborigines and Protectors, 1838–1839* (p. 614). Victorian Government Printing Office.

Thompson, M. (2006). In Victoria, *Parliamentary Debates (Hansard), Legislative Assembly*, pp. 1122–1128.

Thorpe, W. (2009). Interview. In S. Faulkhead & J. Berg (Eds.) (2010), *Power and the passion: Our ancestors return home* (pp. 43–47). Koorie Heritage Trust.

Secondary sources

Aboriginal Heritage Act 2006. legislation.vic.gov.au/in-force/acts/aboriginal-heritage-act-2006/024

Allen, L. (2014). The never ending story: The repatriation of ancestral remains from museums. *Melbourne Historical Journal, 42*(2), 21–28.

Attwood, B. (2009). *Possession: Batman's treaty and the matter of history*. Melbourne University Publishing.

Barwick, D. (1984). Mapping the past: an atlas of Victorian clans 1835–1904: Part 1. *Aboriginal History, 8*(1/2), 100–131. doi.org/10.22459/ah.08.2011.08

Birch, T. (2018). Rise from this grave. *Overland, 230*(Autumn). overland.org.au/previous-issues/issue-230/essay-tony-birch

Broome, R. (2005). *Aboriginal Victorians: A history since 1800*. Allen & Unwin.

Clark, I. D. & Heydon, T. (2004). *A bend in the Yarra: A history of the Merri Creek protectorate station and Merri Creek Aboriginal School 1841–1851*. Aboriginal Studies Press.

Department of Climate Change, Energy, the Environment and Water. (2022). National heritage places – Melbourne's domain parkland and memorial precinct. www.dcceew.gov.au/parks-heritage/heritage/places/national/melbourne-domain-parkland-memorial-precinct

Dunstan, D. (n.d.). Government House. *eMelbourne: The city past and present*. www.emelbourne.net.au/biogs/EM00658b.htm

Edmonds, P. (2010). The intimate, urbanising frontier: Native camps and settler colonialism's violent array of spaces around early Melbourne. In T. Banivanua Mar & P. Edmonds (Eds.), *Making settler colonial space: Perspectives on race, place and identity* (pp. 129–154). Palgrave Macmillan. doi.org/10.1057/9780230277946_9

Elbourne, E. (2003). The sin of the settler: The 1835–36 Select Committee on Aborigines and debates over virtue and conquest in the early nineteenth-century British white settler empire. *Journal of Colonialism and Colonial History, 4*(3). doi.org/10.1353/cch.2004.0003

Faulkhead, S. & Berg, J. (Eds.) (2010). *Power and the passion: Our ancestors return home.* Koorie Heritage Trust.

Fels, M. H. (2011). *'I succeeded once': The Aboriginal protectorate on the Mornington Peninsula, 1839–1840.* ANU E Press. doi.org/10.22459/iso.05.2011

Fforde, C. (2004). *Collecting the dead: Archaeology and the reburial issue.* Duckworth Books.

Fforde, C., McKeown, C. T. & Keeler, H. (2020). *The Routledge companion to Indigenous repatriation: Return, reconcile, renew.* Routledge, Taylor & Francis Group. doi.org/10.4324/9780203730966

Gibson, J., Gardner, H. & Morey, S. (2018, 10 July). Rediscovered: The Aboriginal names for ten Melbourne suburbs. *The Conversation.* theconversation.com/rediscovered-the-aboriginal-names-for-ten-melbourne-suburbs-99139

Giles, T. & McRae, S. (2005, 20 October). Builders fear cost of history. *The Herald Sun.*

Holroyd, J. (2006a, 12 April). Decamp by Thursday, judge orders. *The Age.* theage.com.au/national/decamp-by-Thursday-judge-orders-20060412-ge246k.html

Holroyd, J. (2006b, 20 April). Protesters won't douse sacred fire. *The Age.* theage.com.au/national/protesters-wont-douse-sacred-fire-20060420-ge25qd.html

Invasion Day rally sees thousands take to Melbourne streets, two men detained by police. (2021, 26 January). *ABC News.* abc.net.au/news/2021-01-26/australia-day-melbourne-invasion-day-protest-rally/13092528

Johnston, C. (1992). *What is social value?* Australian Heritage Commission, Technical Publications, Series Number 3.

Lidia Thorpe announces Invasion Day 2020 under the banner of 'pay the rent'. (2020, 24 January). NITV Radio. sbs.com.au/language/english/audio/lidia-thorpe-announces-invasion-day-2020-under-the-banner-of-pay-the-rent

Mansell, M. (2006). The black GST: A proposition for all Indigenous people and supporters. *Indigenous Law Bulletin, 1.* www5.austlii.edu.au/au/journals/IndigLawB/2006/1.html

Maroske, S. (n.d.). Royal Botanic Gardens. *eMelbourne: The city past and present.* www.emelbourne.net.au/biogs/EM01270b.htm

Mulvaney, J. (1990). Sir Walter Baldwin Spencer (1860–1929). *Australian Dictionary of Biography.* adb.anu.edu.au/biography/spencer-sir-walter-baldwin-8606

Pinto, S. (2021). *Places of reconciliation: Commemorating Indigenous history in the heart of Melbourne.* Melbourne University Press.

Pratt, M. L. (2008). *Imperial eyes: travel writing and transculturation*. (2nd ed.). Routledge, Taylor & Francis Group.

Presland, P. (2012). *The place for a village: How nature has shaped the city of Melbourne*. Museum Victoria.

Price, S. (2021, 15 January). Anzac Day should change to honour new era of heroes. *The Herald Sun*.

Pyne, C. (2015). *A letter to my children*. Melbourne University Press.

Rothberg, M. (2011). From Gaza to Warsaw: Mapping multidirectional memory. *Criticism, 53*(4), 523–548. doi.org/10.1353/crt.2011.0032

Russell, L. (2010). Reflections on Murray Black's writings. In S. Faulkhead & J. Berg (Eds.) (2010), *Power and the passion: Our ancestors return home* (pp. 56–60). Koorie Heritage Trust.

Tungandame, B. (2020, 26 January). '2020 Invasion Day dawn service marks 250 years of warfare against Aboriginal people' – Lidia Thorpe. NITV Radio. sbs.com.au/language/english/audio/2020-invasion-day-dawn-service-marks-250-years-of-warfare-against-aboriginal-people-lidia-thorpe

Turnbull, P. (2017). *Science, museums and collecting the Indigenous dead in colonial Australia*. Palgrave Macmillan. doi.org/10.1007/978-3-319-51874-9

Tutchener, D., Kurpiel, R., Smith, A. & Ogden, R. (2021). Taking control of the production of heritage: Country and cultural values in the assessment of Aboriginal cultural heritage significance. *International Journal of Heritage Studies, 27*(12), 1310–1323. doi.org/10.1080/13527258.2021.1969984

Uproot camp, PM urges. (2006, 7 April). *The Age*. theage.com.au/national/uproot-camp-pm-urges-20060407-ge23ds.html

Victorian Heritage Database. (n.d.). *Domain parklands*. Victorian Heritage Register (Number H2304). vhd.heritagecouncil.vic.gov.au/places/165951

Vinall, F. (2021, 26 January). Far-right protesters hold rally in Melbourne to 'restore' traditional Australia Day parade. *news.com.au*. news.com.au/national/victoria/news/farright-protesters-hold-rally-in-melbourne-to-restore-traditional-australia-day-parade/news-story/d1122cd10be5510f9bfd1bd16e841692

Wahlquist, C. (2019, 26 January). 'Overwhelmed': Hundreds attend first dawn service to be held on Australia Day. *The Guardian*. theguardian.com/australia-news/2019/jan/26/overwhelmed-hundreds-attend-first-dawn-service-to-be-held-on-australia-day

8

Place as archive: The heritage of children's homes and the legacies of colonial violence

Sarah Hayes, Steven Cooke, Edwina Kay and Antony Catrice

Introduction

A set of white cricket stumps (Figure 8.1), roughly painted on a red brick wall, is an iconic image of an Australian summer, evoking a series of contradictory multi-sensory memories of childhood. These contradictions become dissonant through the interaction between this perhaps sanctioned graffiti and the history of the building on which it is located, now part of Deakin University's Burwood campus. From the 1930s until 1990, the building functioned as part of a network of institutional children's homes in Australia. From 1937, it went under the name of Kildonan and from the 1960s as Allambie, it was Victoria's main reception centre for children requiring out-of-home care. The site was just one of 800 such orphanages and children's homes in Australia that operated during the twentieth century, housing approximately 500,000 children who experienced institutionalised care (the 'Forgotten Australians'), 50,000 Aboriginal or Torres Strait Islander children ('the Stolen Generations') and 10,000 child migrants from Britain or Malta. The significance of the connections of these places to histories of dispossession as a form of colonial violence for the Stolen Generations and First Nations communities, to the trauma associated with child migration schemes and to the suffering of others who experienced out-of-home care

MEMORY IN PLACE

cannot be overestimated. Indeed, one could argue that these difficult histories are central to the Australian historical experience. As such, the aftermath of these histories has ongoing contemporary echoes in the lives of care leavers and their children, and in current debates over healing and reconciliation within the context of the National Apology to the Forgotten Australians and Former Child Migrants (2009), the National Apology to the Stolen Generations (2008), and processes of truth and reconciliation, or what Carr (2009) calls the 'politics of regret'.

Figure 8.1. Cricket stumps painted on an exterior brick wall at the former Kildonan/Allambie Children's Home.
Source: A Catrice.

The presence of material fragments of the past such as painted cricket stumps raises questions about how the conservation of such sites and their associated artefacts might disrupt consensus histories and allow an acknowledgement of the complexities of experience. Given current debates over the use and reuse of sites associated with children's homes (Chynoweth, 2014; Cooke et al., 2020; Wilson, 2014; and see 'Places of trauma and healing', 2020), including those implicated in colonial violence in Australia, this chapter draws on literature on children's heritage, aftermath studies and archaeological approaches to the study of material culture to creatively explore the affective potential of the material remains of Kildonan/Allambie[1] to reanimate memory in place. The traditional archive is notoriously scant when it comes to children's experiences in such places, so we seek to view the Kildonan/Allambie site as an archive in its own right. From the buildings themselves to the fittings and artefacts that were left behind when the site closed as a children's home and Deakin University acquired the property, there is a rich archive that can reanimate childhood experiences in such places and might provide some opening to other forms of acknowledgement that complement formal processes of redress.

Kildonan and Allambie

Kildonan was a children's home run by the Presbyterian Church of Victoria from 1937, housing children between the ages of two and 15 (Figure 8.2). In 1961, the government-run Allambie Reception Centre opened on the site, after Kildonan shifted to a group-home model. This was the Victorian Government's main reception centre for children who had been removed from parents, given over by parents or were orphans. Allambie could accommodate up to 90 children, including (from 1964) babies and toddlers, and by the 1970s its capacity had grown to 228 children. Allambie closed in 1990. The children included members of what would become known as the Stolen Generations – First Nations children who were forcibly removed from their families as part of federal and state government initiatives to 'absorb' First Nations Australians into the white population and thus cause them to vanish as a people (Moses, 2004), policies that the *Bringing Them Home Report* (Human Rights and Equal Opportunity Commission, 1997) classified as genocide.

---

1   In this chapter we will use Kildonan/Allambie as conscious terminology as a way of foregrounding the long-entangled histories of the site and the complexities of provenance of these traces.

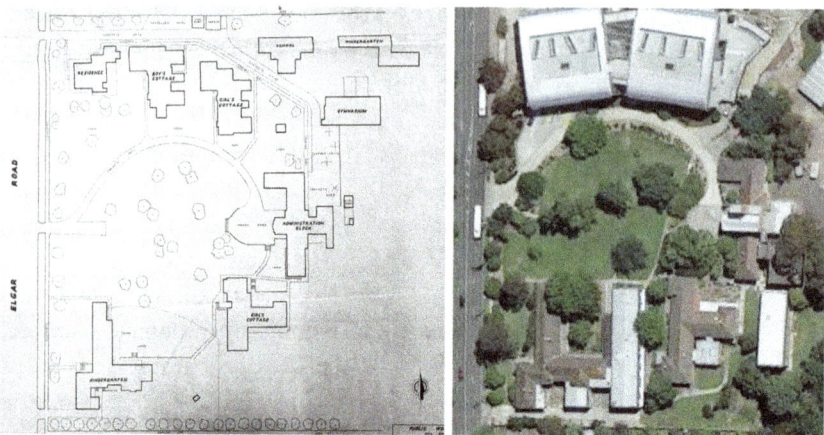

Figure 8.2. Left: Plan of the Allambie site, 1962, showing location of main buildings. Right: Aerial photograph of the current Deakin University campus.
Source: Public Record Office Victoria, VPRS 3686/P20 3182; Google Maps, 5 May 2020.

Places like Kildonan/Allambie often fall into a gap that is overlooked by both heritage and archaeology. Archaeology has made significant inroads into understanding the built environment of institutions, including prisons, migration centres, mission stations and convents, particularly in the nineteenth century, but orphanages and children's homes have received less attention (Hayes et al., 2020; but also see Wilson, 2014). In the archaeological context, this is likely because of a lack of development of such sites and, therefore, a lack of triggered cultural heritage-management excavations. Within the 'Authorised Heritage Discourse' (Smith, 2006) inclusion on a heritage register is often based on perceived architectural and historical significance. Adaptive reuse of such places frequently retains the fabric of the buildings and, in many cases, such places are open to the public. However, the need to create appealing public space sometimes obscures the difficult and often painful histories of such places, marginalising the experiences of care leavers within statements of significance that guide conservation practices (Cooke et al., 2020).

Debates about the memorialisation of colonial violence are often centred around sites of massacres (Batten, 2009; Gibson & Green, this volume; Griffiths, this volume; Ryan et al., 2018) or arguments over whether to include 'frontier wars' in displays at museums and memorials ('Victoria says "no"', 2018; Ashenden, 2019; Pooley, 2013; Rogers, this volume). Although largely overlooked, former orphanages and children's homes are vitally important in understanding the memory of colonialism and colonial violence in Australia. As Kate Darian-Smith and others have argued, the histories and experiences of Forgotten Australians, child migrants and the Stolen Generations in institutionalised care are discrete, yet they intersect in particular and significant ways (Darian-Smith, 2012; Swain, 2016). For Darian-Smith (2012, pp. 159–160):

> The emerging historiography of children and childhood in Australia has highlighted that although white children were positioned as immigrants and colonizers, and Indigenous children were subjected to the destructive forces of colonization, all children in Australia had limited agency in comparison to adults. Moreover, children's experiences were dictated, in varying degrees and at different historical moments, by state policies and regulations in accordance with their class and, most importantly, their race.

Thus, the complexities of conserving Kildonan/Allambie illustrate 'the wider historical and political context framing the rights of children and what this means in terms of cultural heritage' (Darian-Smith, 2012, p. 170), embodying both the physical and emotional violence of institutionalisation and the 'violence of organised forgetting' (Giroux, 2014).

The archaeology and heritage of orphanages and children's homes

In spite of an ever-growing body of research on Australian prisons (Casella, 2000; Davies et al., 2013; Dewar & Frederickson, 2003), asylums (Longhurst, 2017; Piddock, 2007), missions (Lydon, 2009), quarantine stations (Clarke et al., 2017; Longhurst, 2016) and laundries (Kay, 2015), there are very few archaeological or material culture studies on orphanages or children's homes, one notable exception being Rhian Jones's (2018) study of the Parramatta Industrial School for Girls. The situation is not that different globally, with only a small number of studies to date (e.g. Feister, 2009; Hughes, 1992). Given contemporary debates around the role of orphanages and children's homes in Australian society and attempts to come to terms with the legacies of sexual abuse and the Stolen Generations, there is a need for research to understand the lived experience of these places. Previous work on institutions highlights the potential of an archaeological approach to places that are hidden from public view. This is just as true for a twentieth-century children's home as for a nineteenth-century institution.

Former residents or inmates of institutions rarely leave detailed accounts of their time inside the institution, especially in the case of institutions operating in the nineteenth and early twentieth centuries. Archaeology has a role to play in understanding and highlighting the experiences of institutionalised children, and the role such institutions played in Australian society and history. One way this can be achieved is through an analysis of institutional buildings. Treating extant buildings as material culture is an established approach in historical archaeology and is particularly useful for the analysis of former institutional buildings. In addition to examining extant buildings, archaeologists utilise historic plans, photographs and written descriptions to analyse the use of buildings and rooms, the arrangement of space and change over time. Buildings are analysed to generate information about inmate experiences (Newman, 2013), the role of institutions (Kay, 2015), the ideology imbued in the physical structures (Piddock, 2007, 2011) and the role of material culture in achieving the aims of the institution (De Cunzo, 1995). In the case of more recent institutions, such as Kildonan/Allambie, analysis of the buildings can complement oral histories and provide information about how the spaces were used, how they changed over time and what ideology was conveyed by the physical structures.

Ideology versus reality is an important consideration. For example, mission buildings, according to Flexner et al. (2015, p. 265):

> are seen as material statements about the aspirations of the builders as well as colonial ideals concerning order and hierarchy, though these are often contested statements that are undermined by the realities of everyday life.

Architectural features could carry religious symbolism and play a role in establishing discipline, righteousness and order; however, a tension exists between the intention of a building or set of buildings and how those intentions are received by users of the space. This is pertinent for our study of Kildonan/Allambie. There may have been, for example, a desire to create a 'homely' environment, but how was this experienced by the children living there? It is possible to see the Kildonan/Allambie buildings as evidence not just of their operation as a children's home, but also of subsequent attitudes to the home as the buildings ceased to be a mere backdrop and became an integral part of the history and legacy of the institution.

Turning from buildings to artefacts, a common thread in studies of artefacts from institutions are themes of resistance, personal expression, adaptation and survival. As Starr (2015, p. 37) points out in her study of clothing and personal items belonging to inmates at the Hyde Park Barracks: 'Improvisation allowed them to adapt and respond to their human needs, minimise the impact of the penal system, and make-do in their situation of confinement and segregation from society.' It is reasonable to expect that the children at Kildonan/Allambie were doing something similar. Artefacts can also provide evocative insights into the daily operations of the home and create empathy for those who lived there.

Within critical heritage studies, there is a growing body of literature related to places of 'pain and shame' (Logan & Reeves, 2009), including orphanages and children's homes. This literature has covered a variety of responses, including collaborative approaches to heritage management (Tiwari & Stephens, 2020), memorialisation (Atkinson-Phillips, 2020; Wilson, 2014), recognition of the potential for former sites to be places of reconciliation (Carr, 2009) and explorations of the opportunities afforded by 'extended reality' to create affective experiences that 'embody empathy' (Woolford et al., 2019). Given the ubiquity of sites in Australia (Find & Connect, 2011), and the variety of states of conservation, we argue that paying attention to the traces that remain (McGeachan, 2018) allows us to examine not only the ghostly presence and hauntings of sites of absence, but also those sites that have been adaptively reused. Our purpose in this chapter, therefore, is to critically examine the work that these traces do to disrupt consensus histories (Chynoweth, 2014) and their potential to speak to the present.

Understanding the affective potential of archival traces

To 'trace' has a double meaning, signifying both a process of discovery and an object, an indication of existence or a passing. Thus, material remains constitute an archive of the past but are also potentially useful for recovering multi-vocal, heterogeneous stories (McGeachan, 2018). We should not regard traces in the built environment as something distinct from archives in state-sanctioned collecting institutions but as constituent parts of a broader historical and contemporary archive. The potential of archives to speak to the present has long been recognised. As Stuart Hall argued in 2001:

> Archives are not inert historical collections. They always stand in an active, dialogic, relation to the questions which the present put to the past; and the present always puts its questions differently from one generation to another. (p. 92)

Hall draws on the work of Walter Benjamin to suggest that archives thus have the potential to disrupt settled imaginations in which the past 'flashes up before us as a *moment of danger*' (Hall, 2001, p. 92, original emphasis). Seen from this viewpoint, the archive functions as a form of testimony – in Roger Simon's terms, a 'terrible gift' (Simon, 2005) with the ability to ask something of us in the present.

Therefore, within the context of the archival traces of former orphanages and children's homes, we are interested in how the concept of 'object-mediated empathy' (Byrne, 2013; Auld et al., 2019) might play a role in the remembering of places like Kildonan/Allambie and in the empathetic handling of the awareness-raising process surrounding their painful legacy. As Auld et al. (2019, p. 361) argue, objects have an 'affective capacity … to trigger an experience of the humanity of others and to potentially alter ingrained community perceptions'.

However, as McGeachan (2018) argues, the ethics of recovering traces of the past is fraught and raises questions about whether every story can or should be told. We suggest that combining work on the affective potential of things with Trish Luker's (2017) decolonising approach to archival studies provides a way of engaging with the material traces of a site's past. This affords an approach to engaging with a site's difficult histories and with the care leavers who experienced them.

Archival traces of Kildonan/Allambie

As Stuart Hall (2001, p. 89) has argued, 'no archive arises out of thin air'. The serendipity of a university's formal institutional archives being relocated to a former children's home in the 1990s meant that Antony Catrice, Deakin University's archivist, became aware of the difficult histories of the Kildonan/Allambie site. As part of the process, Antony witnessed the clearing out of many objects and ephemera related to the institutions. He documented and retained as much as possible while the retrofitting of the buildings for university use took place. But the true importance of this material was not fully realised until Antony hosted reunions for care leavers at the site in August 2015 and October 2017 and started to receive their testimony about the role that the Kildonan/Allambie buildings and associated objects had for them. One former resident wrote:

> One of the reasons those things [the Allambie artefacts] are so important is that somebody cared enough … When I came here and Antony had collected all those beautiful little trinkets, it meant that someone had cared enough to put them aside, that our existence hadn't just … The one theme through all of our lives is just the lack of care or compassion. Now when you got those objects and you say these are a part of this history and they're valid, somehow it makes us feel valid. I was moved when Antony came out [when Biddy first visited the Allambie site], that he spotted me crying out of this huge place, just standing at the plaque having a little tear, and then he offered to take us around and show us what he had. Time out of his day. Love isn't what you say. Love is what you do … What Antony did was an action, and it validated our existence, and it meant that someone actually thought about what happened here. (Binny, personal communication, 2 March 2018)

In the remainder of this chapter, we use Kildonan/Allambie as a case study to critically examine the affective potential of archival traces. These traces come from the official, state-sanctioned archives of collecting institutions, as well as the more intimate traces of graffiti and objects left behind when Allambie closed. The archive, therefore, comprises the material culture that constituted the institution, the internal fittings and furnishings of the buildings, graffiti, artwork and objects. All these things shaped the experience of the place. The fabric of the buildings, their design, layout and aesthetics, will be discussed separately for an understanding of how they structured space, movement, daily operations and the lived experience of Kildonan/Allambie.

Archive part 1: Buildings and the structuring of experience at Kildonan/Allambie

Architectural plans of former institutions can provide information about the intended uses of buildings and rooms, change over time and the organisation of space. These, in turn, can contribute to knowledge of the operation and role of the institution, and if and how it changed. It should be noted that such plans represent the *intended* use of the space, which is not necessarily how it was built or used in practice. Ideally, this type of information would complement oral histories of the site that could provide detailed information about official and unofficial uses of the space. Public Record Office Victoria (PROV) holds a number of architectural and site plans of Kildonan/Allambie. These plans provide information about how the space was organised and how Kildonan changed as attitudes towards institutional care for children changed in the mid-twentieth century.

1930s

Two architectural plans dated 1936, for buildings named 'House No.1' and 'House No.2', depict the boys' cottage and the girls' cottage (PROV, VPRS 3868/P19 Unit 2995). These plans provide information about the initial Kildonan buildings. The cottages are very similar, with separate spaces for staff within them, and no dining or laundry facilities, as these activities happened in separate buildings. The staff area appears quite domestic, with a sitting room, bedroom and bathroom, and a door enabling this section to be shut off from the rest of the cottage. In the boys' cottage, House No.1, there were two large dormitories, a common room, a bathroom and a storeroom. There are two baths in the plan, inside one smaller room within the bathroom, suggesting that the boys did not have privacy while bathing.

House No.2, the girls' cottage, differs slightly from the boys' cottage. It has four dormitories, two occupying the same space that one dormitory occupied in the boys' cottage. In the bathroom, there are two (rather than four) toilets, and the two baths are in separate rooms with doors, suggesting that the girls were to be given privacy in the bath. In both cottages, the rooms were accessed via a wide corridor labelled 'Dressing Room' on the plan, which has bench seats along one side and what appear to be lockers along the other. Apart from the dormitories and communal bathing area, this corridor/dressing room stands out as being significantly different from a domestic cottage and marks the building very clearly as an institutional structure.

1940s

Architectural drawings of the 'New Girls' Cottage', dated 28 March 1946, depict a shift in ideology, moving away from the large institution and towards a more home-like environment. Instead of dormitories, the plan has bedrooms, containing a maximum of four beds. The plans show the rooms were fitted with enough wardrobes and dressing tables for each child to have their own. Unlike the 1936 plans, this building contains a kitchen and dining room on the lower ground floor, as well as a utility room (laundry), and a large recreation room and a reading room on the ground floor. The plan shows two staff bedrooms, a staff bathroom and a staff sitting room, but, unlike the 1936 plan with its staff 'zone', the rooms are spread throughout the building.

1960s

Architectural plans of Kildonan in the 1960s indicate a further shift away from the institutional system. The plans show proposed changes to the cottages to make them more domestic and suggest a greater focus on teaching the children how to live in a house, rather than housing them in an institution where cooking, laundering and sleeping all happen separately in separate buildings. Kildonan was closed and sold in 1961, so it seems unlikely that the proposed changes were ever completed; however, they remain useful for the insights they provide into the changing ideology. PROV holds negatives of architectural plans in their collection, one of which is labelled 'Proposed Alterations to House No. 2' and dated 10 February 1960 (PROV, VPRS 10516/P5 Unit 1). The plan shows the 1930s cottage divided into two separate 'homes', each with their own bathroom, bedrooms, kitchen, dining room, laundry and staff bedroom. The large dormitories from the 1930s are shown divided into bedrooms, containing two or three beds, a wardrobe and a dressing table. The single large bathroom is shown divided down the centre, making two smaller bathrooms, one for each half of the cottage. Two laundries occupy part of the space that was the corridor/dressing room. The division between staff and children is less obvious than in the 1930s plan, with each half of the building having only one sitting room, rather than one for the staff and one for the children.

A second plan entitled 'Proposed Alterations to House No. 1', dated 10 February 1960, appears to show planned alterations to the boys' cottage, also known as Buchanan Cottage, which had been called House No. 1 in the 1936 plan. Featuring handwritten annotations and walls crossed out, this plan is more difficult to understand than the 'Proposed Alterations to House No. 2'. It is possible the annotations depict changes the architect made following consultation with the client, or changes someone at Kildonan made after seeing the plans. For example, a room that was a large dormitory in the 1936 plan is shown divided into three bedrooms, two with two beds and one with four beds. Someone has scribbled over the proposed new dividing walls and written a note saying, 'Dormitory No.1'. The line dividing the original bathroom in two has been scribbled out, but the two separate baths in separate rooms have been given a tick each. Later plans show both the girls' and boys' cottages with different footprints from those of the original plans; however, it is unclear if they were indeed divided into smaller 'houses' with bedrooms rather than dormitories.

The architectural plans showing the changes at Kildonan are particularly poignant when we consider that, following Kildonan's closure, in a final move away from the institutional system, the government-operated Allambie opened at the site. The changes that took place at Kildonan were gradual, and the changes proposed in the 1960s indicate a level of consideration being undertaken before selling. One can imagine the relevant authorities asking – do we alter the existing buildings to make a more homely place, or sell up and have group homes scattered in the community? The decisions made by the Kildonan management were clearly well considered, and the opening of Allambie in buildings that had been rejected by Kildonan is an indication of the complexity and inconsistency of the Victorian child welfare system. It was widely understood that institutions were not ideal, yet the government continued to operate them, struggling to establish a system that did not rely on institutions to house children who needed out-of-home care but were difficult to place in foster homes.

The traces contained within state-sanctioned archives provide useful information about the institutional histories of Kildonan/Allambie and how the architectural geographies of the buildings changed over time in response to changes in approach and governance. However, this context is nowhere made visible on the present-day Deakin University campus. Students and staff have no sense of the history as they move through the buildings. Yet, visiting a place has the power to inform and enliven in ways that archives alone cannot (see Judd & Ellinghaus, this volume). Drawing on recent developments in exhibitions practice to display difficult histories (see Dalley & Barnwell, this volume), the potential exists to meld traces from the state archive with the physical location in an interpretation that better utilises the site for raising awareness among students, staff and visitors. There is also an opportunity to provide an interpretation that enters into dialogue with care leavers who visit the physical buildings, either individually for a tour with the university archivist or for a reunion, that acknowledges the complex and varied responses of those who experienced care. Yet, what is missing is the traces of the care leavers themselves. The next section will, therefore, examine these material archival traces at Kildonan/Allambie itself.

Archive part 2: Artefacts of childhoods in care

At Kildonan/Allambie, due to the work of Antony Catrice, the university archivist, we are lucky to have a physical collection of artefacts from the home and a photographic record of others. Most of the artefacts relate to the Allambie phase of the site's history, but there are a small number of items dating to the Kildonan period. In this chapter, we diverge somewhat from prior studies of recovered (rather than excavated) archaeology, as the artefacts we discuss were opportunistically collected (i.e. they were not collected in response to a cultural heritage-management program) and date to the twentieth century.

Catrice's photographic documentation of the artefacts was used as the basis for generating a catalogue. The catalogue included many elements of a traditional historical archaeology catalogue, such as object description, date, phase, location found, activity, function and sub-function. The decision was made not to re-photograph the retained artefacts with scale bars and a blank white background, as the context provided in the originals evokes much more of the sense of the place and the context of the discovery of the items. The catalogue forms the basis of the analysis and interpretation presented below. There is scope to take the project further by creating an archive of oral testimonies of experiences and recollections of material culture; this is something we will be pursuing in the future after careful consideration and ethics approval processes.

The 34 artefacts recorded in the catalogue create an evocative sense of the experience of living in a children's home. The key themes that emerged were the creation of the environment, daily operations and activities, and children's responses and experiences. While the sense of the place created by these things is still distanced from the lived experience of the place, the analysis of the things does create a degree of empathy and understanding. It was the objects and graffiti, more so than the extant buildings, that had the most powerful affective impact on the authors. Following Auld et al. (2019, p. 376), we believe that the objects and graffiti discussed below could 'become a vehicle for object-mediated empathy' and bridge gaps between the archival accounts of children's homes and the lived experience of them.

MEMORY IN PLACE

Figure 8.3a. Print by Hal Thorpe of a 'gypsy' caravan, gifted to the Children's Health Bureau by Dr Apderham in October 1934.
Photograph: A Catrice.

Figure 8.3b. Label on the back of Figure 8.3a.
Photograph: A Catrice.

8. PLACE AS ARCHIVE

Figure 8.4. Floral paintings.
Photograph: A Catrice.

The collection of artefacts gives a curious insight into the nature of the environment at Kildonan/Allambie, and of the varied, and at times competing, agendas for the place. The material culture suggests an uneasy hybrid of home, school and institution. The first notable group of artefacts in the collection are paintings and a poster. The earliest of these was a painting of a caravan (Figure 8.3a), with a label stating that it was gifted to the Children's Health Bureau by Dr Apderham in October 1934 (Figure 8.3b). There are a further two floral paintings also most probably dating to the Kildonan phase (Figure 8.4). Finally, there is a poster titled 'Space Age' (Figure 8.5). Public excitement around space exploration created a high

MEMORY IN PLACE

demand for merchandise in the late 1950s and 1960s. This example was produced in 1959 and likely graced many children's bedrooms. Incidentally, this poster is now a rare collector's item. The paintings and poster reflect twentieth-century values around creating a homely environment in institutions. But just how far did such items go towards mediating the often painful experience of being at Kildonan?

Figure 8.5. 'Space Age' poster.
Photograph: A Catrice.

8. PLACE AS ARCHIVE

Figure 8.6. Wicker basket full of brightly coloured key tags and keys.
Photograph: A Catrice.

A basket of keys and brightly coloured tags were handed over when Deakin University acquired the site (Figure 8.6). The large number of keys suggests that children were given their own key to a bedroom, storage space or locker during the Allambie period. A space of their own presumably gave the children some small sense of ownership and privacy in a place that would have offered very little in that regard.

Two other items give slightly different insights into the environment. The first, a ubiquitous child-sized plastic chair (Figure 8.7), brings to mind a primary school room and suggests school-like elements to some of the space. The second is a small plinth shelf (Figure 8.8), usually associated with the display of religious items in churches. It was found in the laundry. The shelf echoes the previous use of the building as a church. Its presence suggests a decision not to remove it when the building changed in use, or perhaps it was overlooked. In either case, its presence may have contributed to creating a Christianising/colonising aesthetic or atmosphere. Such symbolism may not have gone unnoticed by children at the home and, along with other elements of the built structure, may have communicated a certain alienation to children from different faith backgrounds, and First Nations children.

MEMORY IN PLACE

Figure 8.7. Child-sized plastic chair.
Photograph: A Catrice.

Figure 8.8. Plinth in laundry.
Photograph: A Catrice.

8. PLACE AS ARCHIVE

Figure 8.9a. Laundry chutes.
Photograph: A Catrice.

Figure 8.9b. Laundry chutes.
Photograph: A Catrice.

MEMORY IN PLACE

In spite of these elements of home, school or church, the fact remains that Kildonan/Allambie *was* an institution, and signage was a strong communicator of this fact. These include an 'ALLAMBIE' sign, a map of the layout of the site and a 'NIGHT BELL' sign. The night bell sign, in particular, is evocative of regimented routines associated with an institution.

The predominate association within the artefact collection is, somewhat surprisingly, laundry. When looked at collectively, the large laundry trolleys, four laundry chutes, laundry tables and shelving for storing blankets, doonas, pillows and bedspreads (Figures 8.9a, 8.9b, 8.10a, 8.10b and 8.11) give a strong sense of the sheer amount of work involved in operating a place like Kildonan/Allambie, and the numbers of children living there. One of the more evocative pieces of graffiti (also discussed below) reads 'GOOD BY [sic]// LAUNDRY' (Figure 8.12). In paint (or maybe liquid paper), a child captured their thrill at leaving all that laundry behind before, presumably, moving on from the home. There is a certain charm in that moment of celebration and in the misspelling. This graffito also highlights that the children were involved in the labour of daily operations at the site.

Figure 8.10a. Laundry trolleys.
Photograph: A Catrice.

Figure 8.10b. Laundry trolleys.
Photograph: A Catrice.

Figure 8.11. Laundry shelving.
Photograph: A Catrice.

Figure 8.12. Graffito on laundry floor.
Photograph: A Catrice.

In-built timber shelving with masking-tape labels bearing words in texta provide insight into the provision of food at Allambie. Labels read 'VEGEMITE', 'FLAVOUR BASE' and 'JELLIES'. The clash of childhood and institution is strongly felt in a simple label reading 'CANDLES BIRTHDAY'. This reversal of usual word order is noted elsewhere, 'SAUCE TOMATO', and has an almost militaristic ring.

Play was also a part of life at the home. A plastic slippery slide was found in a storage space below one building and cricket stumps were painted on an exterior brick wall (Figure 8.1). These artefacts suggest that outdoor and collective play were encouraged. A box containing small bags of beans, many burst, and a number of wooden beads were also found by Antony Catrice. It is possible that the beads were used as counters or for other games. Bean bags have been a popular choice for a range of games as part of physical education, including bean bag tossing and relays, at primary schools across Australia for generations. Along with the child-sized plastic chair, the bean bags add to the school-related elements in the collection of artefacts.

The artefacts for play described above were clearly provisions made to the children collectively, not individually. The only items that may have been personal toys were two plastic teddy bears, one slightly larger than the other but clearly a pair (Figure 8.13). The aesthetic suggests that they were made in the 1960s. Were these the personal possessions of one of the children? Did they bring the bears with them from home? Or were they, in fact, a provision in a shared toy box? It is difficult to say, but they may well have brought some comfort.

A smaller proportion of the collection speaks to the responses or experiences of children at the home. First, there were two other graffiti found in addition to the 'GOOD BY // LAUNDRY' example discussed above. The first read 'CASSIA HEATH' and was written in chalk on the red brick exterior of one of the buildings (Figure 8.14). The second was a collection of handprints on the exterior wall of Sunnyside Cottage/Nursery, made by multiple children of different ages using blue paint.

8. PLACE AS ARCHIVE

Figure 8.13. Plastic teddy bears.
Photograph: A Catrice.

Figure 8.14. 'CASSIA HEATH' graffito.
Photograph: A Catrice.

189

MEMORY IN PLACE

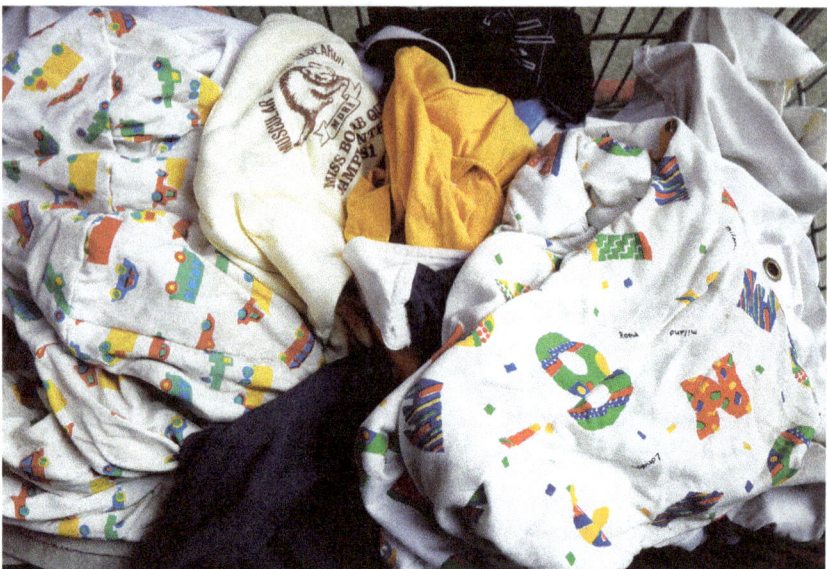

Figure 8.15. Bundle of children's pyjamas.
Photograph: A Catrice.

When Deakin University took over the Allambie buildings, a considerable amount of cheap, poor-quality clothing was found, including a bundle of seven or eight sets of pyjamas printed with brightly coloured cars and trucks (Figure 8.15). Two distinctively 1980s sweatshirts in the same style were also found (Figure 8.16). The fact that the clothing was in multiples of the same design suggests donations of clothing to the home. Items donated were possibly unwanted, unsold stock donated by stores, or, in the case of the sweatshirt, excess promotional merchandise. While this was practical for meeting the needs of clothing the children, it was potentially depersonalising and dehumanising. Being kitted out identically to other children at the home would have compounded the experience of institutionalisation.

The plastic teddy bears and handprints are, in our view, the most affective objects in the collection. There is something intimate in their personal nature: they are deeply humanising. It is easy to see your childhood self, or your own children, reflected in these items. Together with the other items discussed above, they create an enduring sense of the vulnerability of children in care, and of the conflicted and varied experiences that children had in places like Kildonan/Allambie. This is particularly the case when understood in the context of material related to the Allambie Reception Centre in the *Bringing Them Home Report* (Human Rights and Equal Opportunity Commission, 1997) and Find & Connect (2011).

8. PLACE AS ARCHIVE

Figure 8.16. Child's sweatshirt.
Photograph: A Catrice.

The ambivalence of play at Allambie is illustrated through it being an opportunity to see siblings from whom the children had been separated:

> I clearly remember trying to see [my younger brother] in the play area for younger children, an area I was not allowed in because I was too old … [T]he staff [had] no understanding of how upset I was about this when I got caught in the playground because it was the only way I could see him. (cited in O'Neill, 2017)

Another former resident recalled: 'When we did get to play together, we were on leads all the time … I hated that place' (cited in O'Neill, 2017). The traces that remain of these experiences are part of the testimonial inheritance of the Deakin site. As a 'terrible gift' (Simon, 2005), they ask us to bear witness, in the case of the Stolen Generations, to the apparatus of colonial genocide of which Deakin University is a custodian. As Libby Porter has argued:

> It is a deliberate, even required, feature of the settler-colonial dynamic to systematically and publicly forget. Behind this forgetting is a structure of denial: the strategy that settler (non-Indigenous) Australia mobilises to keep hiding from the intolerable injustice of unchecked settler-colonialism. (Porter, 2018, pp. 239–240)

Approaching the seemingly benign buildings that currently serve university functions at Deakin's Burwood campus as an archive suggests an empathic and nuanced understanding of the past. The buildings, fittings and artefacts comprise a rich archive that provides insight into the daily life and experiences of children in care, as well as institutional operations. Drawing together archival, heritage and archaeological methodologies enabled us to treat the place as an archive – one that addresses silences in the archival record regarding the experiences of children in care. Further engagement with this archive might serve two functions: 1) better provide an opening for redress for people with traumatic experiences of care, and 2) raise greater awareness and empathy around the experiences of children in care. We hope that the merging of disciplines utilised here will help not only to make the most of this archive, which deals with a very difficult aspect of Australia's history, but also to give full recognition to the contested and variable experiences of such places.

Conclusion

The practical realities of a place like Kildonan/Allambie meant that, regardless of efforts to create a homely environment or to provide play for the children, the place remained an institution. Children had little control over their lives in such a place, but, equally, there was no straightforward solution for accommodating children who were orphaned or removed from their parents. Society is still grappling with this issue, as is reflected in ongoing controversies around contemporary foster care and group care. The archival traces of Kildonan/Allambie allow us to glimpse both institutional biographies and the biographies of children in out-of-home care. They also reveal the multiplicity of mediated experiences of children, both the production and regulation of carceral spaces and the opportunities for resistance. A focus on archival traces also allows for the potential of material culture to enhance heritage values through the identification of a more nuanced approach to social value, one that acknowledges the importance of place for care leavers and embraces possibilities for raising awareness of the lived reality and legacy of experiences in children's homes.

However, the affective potential of archival traces raises questions as to how such sites of difficult histories can be interpreted. While the affective potential – the potential *'moment of danger'* (Hall, 2001) – of these traces may call forth recognition by care leavers and by those who have some understanding of the histories and legacies of the site, we argue that for those with no knowledge, such potential is limited. If we are to present objects and interpretations of the site for the purpose of acknowledging and welcoming care leavers, this would be best done within the original Kildonan/Allambie buildings. However, if we wish to raise awareness of the presence of this important part of Australian history within the Deakin University community, including among visitors to the campus, there would be an argument for placing the interpretation in new buildings with high traffic.

How might this support Australians in coming to terms with the legacy of children's homes, child sexual abuse and the Stolen Generation through a greater awareness of the complex history of such places along with empathy for the experiences of care leavers? As we noted at the start of this chapter, Kildonan/Allambie is just one of 800 sites across Australia with connections to Forgotten Australians, and many of these sites also housed the Stolen Generations. Through conserving the buildings and having interpretation at the site, these places can play a role in educating people about this painful part of Australia's history. Places such as Kildonan/Allambie have the potential to make colonial dispossession more concrete – to help people understand the mechanisms of dispossession and realise that colonial violence was not limited to the frontiers but was a process that also took place in twentieth-century suburban Australia.

Acknowledgments

This research was funded by a Research Development and Seeding Fund grant from the Alfred Deakin Institute for Citizenship and Globalisation at Deakin University. It was also informed by a symposium held at Deakin University in 2019, funded by the People, Place and Heritage stream of the Alfred Deakin Institute. We would like to thank all the participants of the symposium for their generosity in sharing their experiences and expertise, along with their contributions to a special issue of *Historic Environment* (see 'Places of trauma and healing', 2020). We particularly acknowledge and thank Leonie Sheedy and the Care Leavers Australasia Network for their participation in the symposium and support of our research. We also thank Binny Paris for permission to reproduce extracts from her interview. Finally, we thank Cameo Dalley, Ashley Barnwell and participants of the 'Memory, Colonial Violence and Spaces of Commemoration in Australia' symposium, held over Zoom on 20–21 August 2020, out of which this volume grew.

References

Ashenden, D. (2019, 15 January). Saving the war memorial from itself. *Inside Story.* insidestory.org.au/saving-the-war-memorial-from-itself/

Atkinson-Phillips, A. (2020). Commemorating childhood loss and trauma: Survivor memorials in Australia. *Historic Environment*, *32*(2), 54–67. australia.icomos.org/publications/historic-environment/he-vol-32-no-2-2020-places-of-trauma-and-healing/

Auld, D., Ireland, T. & Burke, H. (2019). Affective aprons: Object biographies from the ladies' cottage, Royal Derwent Hospital, New Norfolk, Tasmania. *International Journal of Historical Archaeology*, *23*(2), 361–379. doi.org/10.1007/s10761-018-0468-z

Batten, B. (2009). The Myall Creek memorial: History, identity and reconciliation. In W. Logan & K. Reeves (Eds.), *Places of pain and shame: Dealing with 'difficult heritage'* (pp. 82–96). Routledge, Taylor & Francis Group. doi.org/10.4324/9780203885031

Byrne, D. (2013). Love & loss in the 1960s. *International Journal of Heritage Studies*, *19*(6), 596–609. doi.org/10.1080/13527258.2012.686446

Carr, G. (2009). Atopoi of the Modern: Revisiting the place of the Indian Residential School. *English Studies in Canada*, *35*(1), 109–135. doi.org/10.1353/esc.0.0161

Casella, E. C. (2000). 'Doing trade': A sexual economy of nineteenth-century Australian female convict prisons. *World Archaeology*, *32*(2), 209–221. doi.org/10.1080/004382400501311 99

Chynoweth, A. (2014). Forgotten or ignored Australians? The Australian museum sector's marginalisation of Inside – life in children's homes and institutions. *The International Journal of the Inclusive Museum*, *6*(2), 172–182. doi.org/10.18848/1835-2014/CGP/v06i02/44448

Clarke, A., Frederick, U. K. & Hobbins, P. (2017). 'No complaints': Counter-narratives of immigration and detention in graffiti at North Head Immigration Detention Centre, Australia 1973–76. *World Archaeology*, *49*(3), 404–422. doi.org/10.1080/00438243.2017.1334582

Cooke, S., Hayes, S., Kay, E. & Catrice, A. (2020). Managing difficult heritage at Kildonan/Allambie: The heritage values of former orphanages and children's homes. *Historic Environment*, *32*(2), 28–33. australia.icomos.org/publications/historic-environment/he-vol-32-no-2-2020-places-of-trauma-and-healing/

Darian-Smith, K. (2012). Children, colonialism and commemoration. In K. Darian-Smith & C. Pascoe (Eds.), *Children, childhood and cultural heritage* (pp. 159–174). Routledge, Taylor & Francis Group. doi.org/10.4324/9780203080641-19

Davies, P., Crook, P. & Murray, T. (2013). *An archaeology of institutional confinement: The Hyde Park Barracks, 1848–1886*. Sydney University Press.

De Cunzo, L. A. (1995). Reform, respite, ritual: An archaeology of institutions. The Magdalen Society of Philadelphia, 1800–1850. *Historical Archaeology*, *29*(3), 1–168. jstor.org/stable/25616415

Dewar, M. & Fredericksen, C. (2003). Prison heritage, public history and archaeology at Fannie Bay Gaol, Northern Australia. *International Journal of Heritage Studies*, *9*(1), 45–63. doi.org/10.1080/1352725022000056622

Feister, L. M. (2009). The orphanage at Schuyler Mansion. *The Archaeology of Institutional Life*, *20*, 105–116. doi.org/10.22191/neha/vol20/iss1/3

Find & Connect. (2011). *Map of children's homes.* map.findandconnect.gov.au/

Flexner, J. L., Jones, M. J. & Evans, P. D. (2015). 'Because it is a holy house of God': Buildings archaeology, globalization, and community heritage in a Tanna Church. *International Journal of Historical Archaeology, 19*(2), 262–288. doi.org/10.1007/s10761-015-0289-2

Giroux, H. (2014). *The violence of organised forgetting.* City Lights Publishers.

Hall, S. (2001). Constituting an archive. *Third Text, 15*(54), 89–92. doi.org/10.1080/09528820108576903

Hayes, S., Cooke, S., Catrice, A. & Kay, E. (2020). Introduction: Places of trauma and healing? Managing the heritage of orphanages and children's homes. *Historic Environment, 32*(2), 4–7. australia.icomos.org/publications/historic-environment/he-vol-32-no-2-2020-places-of-trauma-and-healing/

Hughes, B. (1992). 'Infant orphan asylum hall' crockery from Eagle Pond, Snaresbrook. *London Archaeologist, 6*(14), 382–387. archaeologydataservice.ac.uk/archiveDS/archiveDownload?t=arch-457-1/dissemination/pdf/vol06/vol06_14/06_14_382_387.pdf

Human Rights and Equal Opportunity Commission. (1997). *Bringing them home report: Report of the national inquiry into the separation of Aboriginal and Torres Strait Islander children from their families.* Canberra: Commonwealth of Australia. humanrights.gov.au/our-work/bringing-them-home-report-1997

Jones, R. (2018). 'Send my love': Defiance and material culture at the Parramatta Industrial School for Girls. *Australasian Historical Archaeology, 36*, 47–58. jstor.org/stable/26775689

Kay, E. (2015). Containment of 'wayward' females: The buildings of Abbotsford Convent, Victoria. *Archaeology in Oceania, 50*(3), 153–161. doi.org/10.1002/arco.5077

Logan, W. & Reeves, K. (Eds.) (2009). *Places of pain and shame. Dealing with 'difficult heritage'.* Routledge, Taylor & Francis Group. doi.org/10.4324/9780203885031

Longhurst, P. (2016). Quarantine matters: Colonial quarantine at North Head, Sydney and its material and ideological ruins. *International Journal of Historical Archaeology, 20*(3), 589–600. doi.org/10.1007/s10761-016-0360-7

Longhurst, P. (2017). Madness and the material environment: An archaeology of reform in and of the asylum. *International Journal of Historical Archaeology, 21*(4), 848–866. doi.org/10.1007/s10761-017-0399-0

Luker, T. (2017). Decolonising archives: Indigenous challenges to record keeping in 'reconciling' settler colonial states. *Australian Feminist Studies, 32*(91–92), 108–125. doi.org/10.1080/08164649.2017.1357011

Lydon, J. (2009). *Fantastic dreaming: The archaeology of an Aboriginal mission.* Altamira Press.

McGeachan, C. (2018). Historical geography II: Traces remain. *Progress in Human Geography, 42*(1), 134–147. doi.org/10.1177/0309132516651762

Moses, A. D. (2004). Genocide and settler society in Australian history. In A. D. Moses (Ed.), *Genocide and settler society: Frontier violence and stolen Indigenous children in Australian history* (pp. 3–48). Berghan Books.

Newman, C. (2013). An archaeology of poverty: Architectural innovation and pauper experience at Madeley Union Workhouse, Shropshire. *Post-Medieval Archaeology, 47*(2), 359–377. doi.org/10.1179/0079423613Z.00000000046

O'Neill, C. (2017, 9 January). *Allambie Reception Centre (1961–1990).* Find & Connect. findandconnect.gov.au/ref/vic/biogs/E000152b.htm

Piddock, S. (2007). *A space of their own: The archaeology of nineteenth century lunatic asylums in Britain, South Australia and Tasmania.* Springer. doi.org/10.1007/978-0-387-73386-9

Piddock, S. (2011). To each a space: Class, classification, and gender in colonial South Australian institutions. *Historical Archaeology, 45*(3), 89–105. doi.org/10.1007/BF03376849

Places of trauma and healing. (2020). [Special issue] *Historic Environment, 32*(2). australia.icomos.org/publications/historic-environment/he-vol-32-no-2-2020-places-of-trauma-and-healing/

Pooley, M. (2013). Will the Australian War Memorial tell the story of colonial conflicts? [Press release]. *Australian War Memorial.* awm.gov.au/media/press-releases/will-australian-war-memorial-tell-story-colonial-conflicts

Porter, L. (2018). 'From an urban country to urban Country: Confronting the cult of denial in Australian cities'. *Australian Geographer, 49*(22), 239–246. doi.org/10.1080/00049182.2018.1456301

Public Record Office Victoria. VPRS 3868/P19 Unit 2995.

Public Record Office Victoria. VPRS 3686/P20 3182.

Public Record Office Victoria. VPRS 10516/P5 Unit 1.

Ryan, L., Debenham, J., Pascoe, B., Smith, R., Owen, C., Richards, J., Gilbert, S., Anders, R. J., Usher, K., Price, D., Newley, J., Brown, M., Le, L. H. & Fairbairn, H. (2018). *Colonial frontiers massacres, Australia, 1788 to 1930* (Vol. 2.1) [Massacres map]. University of Newcastle. c21ch.newcastle.edu.au/colonialmassacres/map.php

Simon, R. (2005). Introduction: Remembering otherwise: Civic life and the pedagogical promise of historical memory. In R. Simon, *The touch of the past: Remembrance, learning and ethics* (pp. 1–13). Palgrave Macmillan. doi.org/10.1007/978-1-137-11524-9

Smith, L. (2006). *Uses of heritage*. Routledge, Taylor & Francis Group. doi.org/10.4324/9780203602263

Starr, F. (2015). An archaeology of improvisation: Convict artefacts from Hyde Park Barracks, Sydney, 1819–1848. *Australasian Historical Archaeology, 33*, 37–54. jstor.org/stable/26350171

Swain, S. (2016). Enshrined in law: Legislative justifications for the removal of Indigenous and non-Indigenous children in colonial and post-colonial Australia. *Australian Historical Studies, 47*(2), 191–208, doi.org/10.1080/1031461X.2016.1153119

Tiwari, R. & Stephens, J. (2020). Virtual reality and Aboriginal heritage: Church missions in Western Australia. *Historic Environment, 32*(2), 76–89. australia.icomos.org/publications/historic-environment/he-vol-32-no-2-2020-places-of-trauma-and-healing/

Victoria says 'no' to changing Anzac Day to include Aboriginal people killed in 'frontier wars'. (2018, 4 February). *ABC News*. abc.net.au/news/2018-02-04/no-plans-to-change-anzac-day-utter-disgrace-opposition/9394356

Wilson, J. Z. (2014). Beyond the walls: Sites of trauma and suffering, Forgotten Australians and institutionalisation via punitive 'welfare'. *Public History Review, 20*, 80–93. doaj.org/article/c4dd657930e34cd1b08b62bc38834b93

Woolford, A., Muller, A. & Sinclair, S. (2019). Risky times and spaces: Settler colonialism and multiplying genocide prevention through a virtual Indian Residential School. *Genocide Studies and Prevention: An International Journal, 13*(3), 79–96. doi.org/10.5038/1911-9933.13.3.1674

9

Engaging communities in archives and museums

Imelda Miller, Olivia Robinson and Cameo Dalley

Imelda Miller is an Australian South Sea Islander and curator, First Nations Cultures, at Queensland Museum. Olivia Robinson, a Bidjara Aboriginal woman, leads collection engagement at the State Library of Queensland. In this interview with Cameo Dalley, recorded in 2021, they discuss their experiences working in major collecting institutions, and issues to do with repatriation, community engagement and representing difficult and traumatic histories. They also reflect on their collaborative practice on a major exhibition at the State Library of Queensland in 2019 titled *Plantation Voices: Contemporary Conversations with Australian South Sea Islanders*, which presented stories of South Sea Islanders working on sugar plantations in Queensland from 1863 to 1904, and acknowledged the determination and resilience of the Australian South Sea Islander community today.

Biographies and coming to institutions

Imelda Miller: I'm Imelda Miller and I work at Queensland Museum and I'm the curator responsible for the Pacific and Torres Strait Islander collections. I've been working as a curator for nearly two decades now, and I really enjoy the work – but my main interest is around Australian South Sea Islander history and heritage and creating an awareness about that. My passion also is about not just working in museums, but how I can do this work outside of the museum borders, looking at different ways of working in communities, with communities and for communities to tell the stories that they want to tell.

Olivia Robinson: My name is Olivia Robinson and I lead collection engagement in Queensland Memory at the State Library of Queensland. I have been working in cultural heritage with collections and with communities – telling stories about collections, for probably a couple of decades as well, and I love the opportunity to sit down with people and for people to tell me their stories – about family, experience and about communities and history. There is lots of laughter often times when people talk about things, and sometimes lots of tears as well. So when people are so willing to share their stories, I've been really blessed to hear them. For the last 20 years or so, I have been able to work with a lot of people, particularly a lot of Aboriginal people and Torres Strait Islanders and more recently often times with Imelda working with Australian South Sea Islanders as well.

Cameo Dalley: You come from communities yourselves, and I wonder if you can talk a bit about how you came to be working in the institutions that you're in?

Imelda Miller: So I am a third-generation Australian-born Australian South Sea Islander and I came to museums really just through earning some part-time work and needing to make my way in the world, and during that time I learnt about collections. That's actually where we all met. I really enjoyed the community of the work and working together and learning from one another. I then discovered objects and how objects can actually tell stories about people's experiences, people's lived experiences especially. I learnt how objects they have these lives of their own and how that evolves over time. During my earlier years at Queensland Museum, I discovered the collections from the Pacific Island nations of Vanuatu and the Solomon Islands. They were from the islands where my ancestors come from, and I was really sort of taken back at the time and sort of thought, I really want to know more about this.

It was a time when I was exploring that side of my story, and it was through these collections that I was able to explore my identity and better understand the story of my ancestors. This experience or connection was something I wanted to share with other people, and not just with my Australian South Sea Islander side, but with the many communities who are represented in these collections. I could see it was important to bring people and objects together to help better understand the stories the objects told, but for people, for communities, as I felt like there was just this one side being told within museum walls. I wanted to explore what communities wanted, how they connected to these objects and see what that meant to them when they're in their presence, because I believed that objects come alive and that they're just waiting for people to come along and activate them. I've just always been interested in going into archives and recognising familiar names and familiar places and connecting those things with people who will connect with it. For me that's what the work's all about.

Olivia Robinson: I'm Bidjara and my traditional Country is in south-west Queensland. Despite growing up in Brisbane I've always had quite a strong connection to Bidjara Country. I often visit. I went to university and I did a Bachelor of Arts degree with a double major in history and nearing the end thought 'What am I going to do now? I wonder what they do at a Museum?' So I contacted Queensland Museum and I think they were very excited at the fact that I was a young Aboriginal woman who was coming to the end of my history degree, who was wanting to volunteer just to find out what was going on, and they said, 'Yep, you'll be right. Come in here'.

I volunteered at that museum for a while before working in community organisations. I eventually came back as assistant curator in the Aboriginal studies area at Queensland Museum and then I became senior curator soon after that.

I was quite young at the time, and it was an incredible experience. I learned so much about myself as well as about the collection and about how people interact with it, and the importance of people's cultural heritage, their moveable cultural heritage, that sense of identity that people have and, of course, I had the opportunity to work with communities on the repatriation of ancestral remains and secret sacred objects. It was a big responsibility, challenging, moving and very rewarding. It educated me about all the responsibility that community often take on today to try and fix the problems of the past, those questionable deeds that people did so many years ago. It's good to be part of addressing it and asking, 'Well, what can we do now to allow people to rest or to return those sacred objects that shouldn't have been taken?' It's a healing process and big responsibility that Elders take on to work with places like a museum or cultural and collecting institutions around their cultural heritage and its care.

I extended my interest in collections and moved to the State Library eventually working in 'Queensland Memory', the part of the library that works with building and promoting documentary heritage such as photos, objects, books, documents and digital stories. Like Imelda, I really believe that these tangible objects are nothing by themselves. What brings them alive are the stories that people have about them, and so the great stuff and the stuff that I love is actually getting to that story and seeing the value that people bring to it – it's often the community that brings that understanding and value to objects.

Cameo Dalley: It's interesting hearing you both talk about the kind of potency of objects and of archives and of photographs in terms of people coming into the institution that you're working in and how powerful that can be as an experience. As you say, those spaces historically haven't always been hospitable to communities, to Aboriginal and Torres Strait Islander people or South Sea Islander people. They've not necessarily been seen as places that those communities feel comfortable in or that are accessible. I wonder how you see your role, in sort of managing that or trying to change that for people when it might be quite difficult or confronting for people to come into those spaces?

Imelda Miller: Yeah, good question, Cameo, I think we, staff working in these organisations, talk about this constantly because community is a big part of our jobs. Well, working with community, and I think for me or from my experiences and working with my colleagues over the years, I have seen how people relate to seeing their own working in these institutions and that instant kind of rapport that our community visitors get when they visit. I think having your own people greeting you is really integral to people being comfortable, especially with some of the emotions people experience during a visit. It can be enjoyable, creative, traumatic and/or upsetting, then other times it can be healing. Everyone is different. I think having people who are Indigenous or First Nations or from that community, that no matter what community, that people see themselves there in that institution and see that 'Okay, so there's, you know, a possibility that I'm going to be understood here'. It's integral for cultural safety and the wellbeing of community when they're coming into these historical institutions. It's watching, listening, supporting and caring for your visitor while they're in this space that could bring up histories or lived experiences that might have been traumatic or emotional for them. For example, finding a photo of their ancestor, or their grandmother for the first time, and creating space and time for people to be able to take in new information, but also to be able to give support to people with information at the times when they require it, so they're able to process their way through it.

Olivia Robinson: The other thing that I thought of too, Imelda, when you were talking about it, is that, as collecting and cultural institutions, state-owned institutions, we have a remit to collect the history and cultural heritage of Queensland, and for a lot of Australian South Sea Islander history, Aboriginal history, Torres Strait Islander history, often times those types of histories have been marginalised.

In many cases, our collections are donated by families or we've acquired them from the mainstream of the community, sometimes often wealthier members of the community, going back 100–150 years. What was amazing about the times that I've worked with Imelda, particularly around the Australian South Sea Islander community, when we marked the 150 years of the first South Sea Islanders to come to Queensland in 2013, and then some other work we've done, including *Plantation Voices*, is that it is about agency. We were able to acknowledge the fact that a lot of the material that we had in the collection, in the State Library collection, about Australian South Sea Islanders, was through the lens of Europeans and the way they saw the world around them. There wasn't anything in the collection that was by Australian South Sea Islanders, reflecting on their own history and culture.

So Imelda, as a curator of *Plantation Voices*, went through that journey of going, 'Well, this is our opportunity to do that'. Imelda, you're right in the sense that the collections that we have as state institutions really need to reflect the diverse community. There's a lot of work that we still need to do around that to even out the collection and perspectives in storytelling.

The acquisition of objects and repatriation

Cameo Dalley: As you say, there's a lot of objects and archives and photographic materials that are held both where we are today, at the State Library of Queensland, and also Queensland Museum – some of those objects were acquired in ways that's really … well objects were stolen.

Imelda Miller: Questionable, yeah.

Cameo Dalley: How does that history fit in with the relationship with communities? Do you get a sense of people still feeling that sense of kind of mistrust or distrust in the institutions given some of that history?

Olivia Robinson: Yes, I think so. I mean, it's generational, isn't it? It's been going on for a long time, and so there's been an acknowledgement of that, say, in the last 20 to 30 years, but there's still a long road to go down that path of understanding and the healing process because it seems like a long time ago, I suppose, when you talk about it, but it really isn't. It's only, maybe, one generation from where we are now.

Cameo Dalley: How important do you think repatriation processes and those sorts of things are as part of that journey, that healing journey that you talked about?

Olivia Robinson: Repatriation is very important. Unfortunately, though, it's a complex situation. A lot of communities, they really want material returned to them, but they also acknowledge that they don't have land for a keeping place or secure access to land to put artefacts back on Country or to reinter their ancestors; somewhere safe where it isn't taken again, ending up in a collecting institution or in someone's private home.

In saying that, institutions have become more open and are increasing access. Many communities also know that their heritage is going to be looked after there and accessible. I think that gives people some comfort in the absence of having keeping places or safe spaces where they can bring material back to Country.

The repatriation of ancestral remains, however, is quite different and there's definitely a lot of healing that happens as part of that process. I've been involved in, over the years, a few repatriation ceremonies and there's really nothing like it in that sense of spiritual connection that people have, and it transcends sort of everything, the reality of our day-to-day work. To take a person who has been sitting in a museum storeroom or something like that, for 100 years or so, and take them back home and then lay them to rest on Country – how good is that? It's a privilege to be a part of it.

Imelda Miller: Yeah, I'll leave that with Olivia because she has more experience of working in repatriation. I think it – that word 'repatriation' is really interesting as it starts to then sneak into looking at objects and what is the definition of 'repatriation' when it comes to collections. How do museums or cultural institutions deal with repatriation of objects and deal with Aboriginal and Torres Strait Islander peoples or Pacific Peoples being the owner of the cultural heritage, and I think there's a bigger conversation to be had around that in coming years, and I think that it's going to be a big topic. I think how we deal with that moving forward, there's going to be a lot of conversations with communities at the table to actually work out what does that mean and how does that take place, and what is suitable for everybody.

And I think, Olivia, you touched on something really good, which was just around access, and I think that's access and agency, and representation, and we've been talking about that for a little while. The R words.

We also, in talking over many years, talk about reclamation and that word 'repatriation' was one of the first words that we talked about when we talked about *Plantation Voices*. You know when we were sort of thinking about what that exhibition could be about. It sort of started with repatriation. The repatriation or deportation of South Sea Islander people.

Collaborative curation and *Plantation Voices* exhibition, State Library of Queensland, 2019

Imelda Miller: *Plantation Voices*, that was an exhibition Olivia and I worked on here at the State Library in 2019. The full title was *Plantation Voices: Contemporary Conversations with Australian South Sea Islanders*. I was lucky enough to be brought over to the State Library of Queensland, and really acknowledge and thank the State Library for that opportunity to work here, to do that exhibition. It came at a time when I was looking for a new challenge as a curator, and to explore your own community stories is always an honour, and it is a privilege to be able to do that.

When Olivia and I first met and we sort of thought, 'Oh, well, what is this about?' We talked about repatriation of South Sea Islanders, the deportation of islanders, this mass deportation of islanders out of this country, one of the biggest mass deportations in this country's history, yet nobody knows about it. As part of the exhibition we thought, 'What are our themes going to be for this?'

And we thought about how one is recognising that path, then it was about the repatriation of islanders, and then we thought, the next big thing about reclaiming our own histories, you know, is through a recognition statement, through being nationally recognised and then, finally, the end part was about our – the next generation, like, the resilience that they now stand very confident in who they are, where they come from, where their ancestors come from and how they live. Today they're now telling that story through – and in this case – through their contemporary artworks. I think that was a really powerful moment, and then, you know, we're talking about repatriation, and I think that all that – it all kind of goes in together, and I think it comes also as a part of that recognition and how – and what – are the actions that we do as part of repatriation of stories or objects, what is the action that we're actually going to do to make that happen.

Cameo Dalley: The exhibition ran from February to September 2019, but there was a whole process of developing that exhibition that came before it, but before we kind of get to that collaborative process, for someone who didn't get to see the exhibition, can you give me a sense of what it was like as a physical space or as an experience moving through the exhibition?

Olivia Robinson: It was bright. Imelda worked with the designer who was appointed to the exhibition. When Imelda thought of the exhibition, there was lots of orange, bright colours, reflective, I suppose, of mangos, islands and flowers like frangipanis.

Imelda Miller: I suppose it was the idea of memory as well that when you're thinking of those who are dearest, it is usually around a sunrise or a sunset and you get that orange, and because we were presenting our ancestors in that case, through photographs and objects, it was about evoking a sunset where you think about those memories and those dearest to you.

Olivia Robinson: Listening to Imelda talking about her vision for the exhibition, it was also around how people would sit and talk. Imelda spoke about how Australian South Sea Islanders would plant mango trees and then sit under them and use them for shade and talk. So mango trees were a big part of people's stories across Queensland.

Cameo Dalley: It sounds like it was a rich kind of visual experience, very colourful and bright and attractive. In some of the images that I've seen online [of the exhibition] there were also some historical photographs, black-and-white photographs, taken of South Sea Islanders working in the cane fields. Some of that imagery is also quite difficult or challenging for people. I wonder if you can talk a little bit about how you balance between what we might think of on the one hand as these kinds of bright attractive, seductive aesthetic with also this quite difficult and traumatic history, those two things sitting alongside each other?

Imelda Miller: I think we are very happy people and I wanted people to feel that and, yes, we do have this dark history. It is important to understand that this exhibition built on a project from 2013. I was at the museum, Olivia was here at the State Library, and Ruth McDougall was curator Pacific Art at the Queensland Art Gallery, Gallery of Modern Art, and we joined together for a project called *Memories from a Forgotten People* during the 150th commemoration of South Sea Islanders coming into south-east Queensland. We digitised the collections and we engaged the community with the collections and the institutions. There were many stories and perspectives as well as many mixed emotions. However, for me I saw how resilient the community is and how we have come out the other side.

Going into *Plantation Voices* was about celebrating that, so it was about acknowledging it and then it was about celebrating who we are and how resilient we are as people. Our history is safe, with our young people going forward, I didn't want it to be emotionally dark because it is a dark history, the lightness or brightness of the orange background was about seeing us as well, so in contrast to the black-and-white photographs. We did some life-sized photographs to say to our audiences, 'Don't walk around our history anymore, look at us'.

We started off working through a bit of a timeline, but then what we realised is that this history, these historical photos, are not just about something that happened in the past, it is intrinsically connected to who we are today as part of our identity. I think using that bright colour to connect everything together, the past and the present and the future, I think was powerful.

Olivia Robinson: I would watch Imelda as she was curating the exhibition because we had so much material in the collection, photographs, and how do you distinguish what should go in an exhibition and what shouldn't? Imelda was quite savvy because I think with each selection, Imelda wanted to make a point with it. You [Imelda] wanted it to be meaningful and for it to say something to a person that was viewing it. So, I remember this one photo that you [Imelda] were particularly keen on including, and it was of the mother in the field with her child.

Figure 9.1. South Sea Islander woman planting sugar cane in a field.
Source: State Library of Queensland Collection, negative number: 142325.

Imelda Miller: Yes, I remember that photo. That photograph has been with me since I started in my museum days it was probably one of the first images I saw – and it started to ignite that kind of drive in me to find out more. Like, seeing her picture, and I remember standing in front of it one day. It was a large-scale photograph (Figure 9.1). I probably first saw it in the 1990s and I remember standing there with my parents, she had this little baby in the field at her feet and she was smiling in that photo, and I remember us saying, 'I wonder if she was really smiling?', and because there is another photo and she is not smiling, but when you look at that photo, you see this mother with her child at her feet in a sugar plantation and half the field has been ploughed and there's still half the field to be done. I wondered about her story, what happened to them and where did they go.

I remember sitting in the office trying to write the first words about the exhibition. I sat for four days, and I didn't write a thing, but then I really had to confront in myself, well, why can't I put pen to paper here. I looked at this photo of the woman and child; people on boats and cane fields. What I ended up writing actually became a quote in the exhibition, and it was about seeing those photos for the first time and that I wondered who they were and who were their families and where did they go and what happened to them, and for me it was just, like, I get emotional now talking about it.

Cameo Dalley: I can see some tears there.

Imelda Miller: For me it was, like, 'Oh my, I've been looking at these photos for 20 years and I've finally seen them', they're really real, and they're part of who I am, and I think the line was – I'm trying not to cry – but I think the line was that 'I exist because they did and they now they exist because I do, 150 years on', and I thought that was kind of a magical moment for me, yeah.

South Sea Islanders and Australian history

Cameo Dalley: Memory is very potent for a lot of people, but particularly in this history, which is a history of South Sea Islander people being, in a lot of situations, forcibly kidnapped and brought to Australia to work as slaves. This history is not a benign history. It's one of violence and of the forced movement of people, the kidnapping of people.

Imelda Miller: In a nutshell, between 1863 and 1904, some 60,000 South Sea Islanders … predominantly from Vanuatu and the Solomons, but also from New Caledonia, Fiji, Kiribati and some parts of Papua New Guinea, were brought to Australia to develop – to be the backbone of – the Australian sugar industry. Some were 'blackbirded'; some came by choice. They were brought over here to clear the land. The work was hard, the land was tough. People were coming to strange new places without their families.

So 'blackbirding' is people [South Sea Islanders] being tricked or coerced into getting on board these ships that brought them over here to Australia, and there are many stories in the community about this history. This happened mainly early in the history and then legislation was brought about to try and control this behaviour of movement of human labour across the Pacific.

Some were young, men, women and children coming over here, and the weather conditions that they were working in were not very different to their home island ways, their clothing was different that they had, they were exposed to diseases that they've never been exposed to before, and some of the conditions that they worked under. They faced many levels of discrimination and exploitation.

You try to imagine what would it be like, being young on an island and then coming out here to a place where you don't speak the language, you now talk with a whole heap of people who speak other languages and now expected to work together and get along. In the exhibition you try to put people in that place to think about how you cope in that situation as a human or your child or your son or daughter to go and do that. The other part of this history is about that deportation and then what happened to the community after that deportation.

1901 bought about the White Australia Policy and the implementation of the *Pacific Island Labourers Act*, which bought about legislation to deport South Sea Islanders back to their home islands and, at that time, in the early 1900s, there's probably about 10,000 South Sea Islanders living here in Australia. South Sea Islanders fought for people to stay here because they had families, they had made lives here, some had been here for 40 years, some were elderly, some could no longer go back to their islands, and other people were exempt from going. Some 1,500 people remained here in Australia and my family and many others like my family, who are now called Australian South Sea Islanders, are descendants of those 1,500 who remained here (Figure 9.2).

Figure 9.2. Australian South Sea Islander community looking at the petition of 1904, when South Sea Islanders were campaigning for exemptions from the deportation.[1]
Photographer: Joe Ruckli. State Library of Queensland.

---

1   This petition is currently held at the National Archives of Australia, NAA: A1, 1906/6324, recordsearch.naa.gov.au/SearchNRetrieve/Interface/ViewImage.aspx?B=7379.

Cameo Dalley: That's a great precis. I wonder if there was an intersection, through this history, between Aboriginal and Torres Strait Islander people and South Sea Islander people.

Olivia Robinson: Absolutely. They lived nearby and intermarried basically all up the coast of Queensland. Unlike a lot of the other states, we had quite a large population of Australian South Sea Islanders, and, like Imelda said, they were the backbone of the sugar industry in Queensland, and Australia really, so it was really important. For us at the State Library of Queensland to be able to help to expose that part of the history – to support Australian South Sea Islanders to tell that history – which was very much about a forgotten history. There were and still are lots of people who didn't know anything about Australian South Sea Islanders and their history in Queensland. It's an ongoing story – the fight for recognition continues.

Imelda Miller: So Australian South Sea Islanders were recognised by the federal government in 1994 and then the Queensland Government acknowledged Australian South Sea Islanders' contribution to Queensland's history in – officially in 2000, and I think that today even people, you know, the community, still go, 'Well, but what's happened, you know, from 2000, which was 21 years ago, what actions have actually happened to the – for the betterment of our community?', and so I think still having being recognised is still a big part of that story, but I think the other part which I think we were just talking about a moment ago was the relationship between – with Aboriginal peoples and Torres Strait Islanders as Olivia said, we're all interconnected, and, you know, through marriage, and I think that there is a shared experience there.

But I know that in 2013 we worked hard with the program for *Memories from a Forgotten People*, to sort of create awareness about the history, but also then try and make it okay for our children who have got many identities to be okay to be those many identities. I think that was the great thing when we did *Plantation Voices* is that we did have the likes of people like artist Dylan Mooney and photographer the late LaVonne Bobongie who all have this mixed heritage and who could all be a part of the exhibition.

Community engagement and exhibition development

Cameo Dalley: I wonder if we can switch a bit to talk a little bit about sort of the community engagement side of the project, and there were some crowd sourcing as part of the exhibition in terms of the use of Historypin and Flickr in terms of images. I'm interested to know how you used these technologies to place these memories and photos in there, in the context in the geographies, the places that they came from.

Olivia Robinson: At the outset can I say we couldn't have done it without Imelda curating *Plantation Voices*, but we started in 2013 when Imelda worked with us on the 150th anniversary program, *Memories from a Forgotten People*. We had some amazing content in the collection, everything from publications and rare books to photographs and documentation, diaries, manuscripts, everything like that.

We went on a journey in 2013 of digitising content, putting it on our catalogue and online on the website Flickr Commons. Anywhere we could, we wanted to get the content out there. We used every platform at our disposal like Historypin, and we also did things like creating an Australian South Sea Islander blog at the State Library with Imelda as the guest editor. It was a great way for Australian South Sea Islanders to share their history, stories and our collections and activities. Imelda wrote lots of posts about the 150th anniversary year and what was happening in community at the time.

Imelda Miller: We had guest bloggers as well, from the community – writing about what was happening in their communities at that time, talking about their community projects that they were curating and developing to acknowledge that event. This blog was reactivated again in 2019 as part of *Plantation Voices* to continue that legacy of documenting what was happening out in the community.

Olivia Robinson: During that time in 2013 we did a talk series, we had a large public forum, full-day symposium, and there were exhibitions. It was a big precinct collaboration in Brisbane between the State Library of Queensland, the Queensland Museum and the Queensland Art Gallery and Gallery of Modern Art. The Queensland Performing Arts Complex (QPAC) got involved at one stage too.

Imelda Miller: They sure did.

Olivia Robinson: We took over part of the QPAC building, basically, the outside, and we had lots of different exhibition panels in there as well … It really was an activation of the whole precinct coming together to mark this important milestone. Fast forward to *Plantation Voices*, it was really a matter of let's bring all those resources together, put them in one spot, sort of add to them as well. That's what you see when you go on to the State Library of Queensland website, on the *Plantation Voices* page – you can access all this content. It was about getting the content out there, let's get it digitised and get people being able to access it.

We wanted to let Australian South Sea Islanders in our community know that in this place, in this building, we have all this stuff about their history, all this documentation, all these photos that maybe they had never seen before. Queensland is a big place, so we were trying to get people involved no matter where they were located. We wanted people to know that they could interact with this content and map out their connection to Queensland and its landscape, and bring meaning to it – what does that start to look like in connection to the documentation that's available.

We held a 'White Gloves Experience' for the Australian South Sea Islander community in the lead-up to the exhibition. We sometimes have these events at the State Library where we put the white gloves on, get all this material out of the repository, lay it all out, and people can look through it and interact with it. We did it in 2013 and it was a huge success, and then again in the lead-up to *Plantation Voices*. I remember just before the White Gloves Experience started, I said, 'Imelda, it's only, quarter past 10 and there's a line-up of people waiting to get into the room'. That's quite rare. The community were just so keen to come in and to spend the time with the historical material. I think sometimes these big collecting institutions can be quite daunting to people but having it all laid out for you to see was great. There were so many discoveries made that day, people found their relatives or made those connections, seen things that they had never seen before (Figure 9.3).

Figure 9.3. 'White Gloves Experience' at the opening of *Plantation Voices: Contemporary Conversations with Australian South Sea Islanders*, State Library of Queensland, 16 February 2019.
Photographer: Joe Ruckli. State Library of Queensland.

Imelda Miller: Yeah, it was pretty special. This event was only supposed to go for two hours, and it ended up going for four because a storm came, and nobody could go anywhere. Also, I think a big part of the day was actually watching everybody interact with one another, and you could see people making connections with one another and going, 'I met your cousin'. I think that's the power of this kind of event. Creating spaces for people to come together and talk about the past. As a community we don't get time to spend talking about our history, as we're too busy trying to live our lives and survive. This leaves little time for learning about our own story and our own history. These kinds of times are so precious because it's a couple of hours where you sit down and everyone could actually come together and share their stories. I think the same could be said for bringing community to do digital stories or creating spaces to invite artists with Australian South Sea Islander heritage to tell their perspectives through their work. Bringing the community voice to the forefront was critical to this exhibition. It helps to connect the historical with the present.

I think even after 2020 last year (COVID-19), you know, connecting with people, we can see how important that is to our wellbeing, and our healing. And that action of creating spaces was definitely a big push in developing a community engagement plan for the exhibition.

Olivia Robinson: I think you realise, too, through community engagement just how generous people are. There is this real positive sense of wanting to share and wanting to be better informed or to be part of that education of other people about their history as well. What you think is going to take an hour, it takes all day, and because people just want to sit down and have a yarn and talk about memories and talk about their history.

Imelda Miller: People want to be heard and people want to be recognised and they want to be acknowledged. In the work we did back in 2013, I went out with Ruth McDougall from the Queensland Art Gallery who did some digital stories for an exhibition called *Sugar*, and during that time one of the last questions I'd always ask is about 'Do you have anything else to contribute?' Some of the people were, like, 'Oh, you know, thank you for asking me about my story', you know, 'In my 63 years no one has ever asked me what my story is'. It's such a privilege to do what we do. I'm a true believer in everybody has a story to tell, and we can acknowledge people's stories. As professionals in these institutions, we have the privilege to spend time with people and listen to their stories, this can be very healing. They give their time to us, but that's something that we can give back, and I think that these are the relationships that we're developing. They're not just about taking, that we're also giving back, and that it's a relationship in the way that community sees relationship, and that there's actually an exchange, but it's not a transaction. We need to be givers as well when we're in big institutions, and this action needs to be seriously considered in the development of these kind of projects.

Olivia Robinson: Some of the communities we worked with know what an exhibition is all about, know what a digital story is all about and how you can go about doing it. In fact, one of the communities that we work with – that we worked with for many years now, on the Sunshine Coast in Queensland – they are now developing their own digital stories with a filmmaker. They can see the value in that, and recording their history and Elders and sharing that with people. It's about strengthening those historical and contemporary memories for their own community. They are right into it, which is great.

Cameo Dalley: Well, that seems like a really lovely point to finish up on. Unless, of course, do you have anything else you'd like to contribute?

Imelda Miller: No, well, you know, I suppose the next step on from that work is the Australian Research Council (ARC) grant that I am currently am working on, which is about archaeology and collections and Australian South Sea Islander lived identities. I think that's going to be really exciting, because I think that's stepping the work that we've done and taking it out into those locations and working with communities.

I suppose what I'm sort of trying to do now, next step on, is about – I suppose because with *Plantation Voices* we went from people taking photos of us, to people taking photos with us, to us taking our own photographs and telling our own stories in our own ways. I think now, stepping into the ARC project, it's about us participating in our research as researchers and as equals, and that that knowledge that we carry be acknowledged, and finding ways within that research framework to actually think about, okay, how can this be done, and trying not to settle too early, that we try and have that respected.

Olivia Robinson: *Plantation Voices* I think reminded me about how powerful someone like Imelda can be. Someone who is Australian South Sea Islander, who is a curator, who comes from community, but at the same time knows about cultural heritage and about these institutions. How powerful that combination can be in telling stories and sharing stories. Like we said earlier, *Plantation Voices* is the gift that keeps giving, and it does. It was this exhibition, like you said, that went from February to September [2019], and so many things have happened around that, so many interactions. We've had visitors from Vanuatu come including the foreign minister for Vanuatu. We've had countless community people come through. We've had so many people now better informed about the history of Queensland, about Australian South Sea Islander history. It goes from strength to strength. I think the key part of it is about community, because they own it as well and they're proud of it, and they can see themselves in it and they can see themselves in the collections that we have too.

Figure 9.4. Olivia Robinson, Cameo Dalley and Imelda Miller at the State Library of Queensland, 2021.
Photograph: Imelda Miller.

Imelda Miller: It's just been an absolute pleasure and privilege to be able to do this work. I see the community is proud of what has been done. But it is a privilege to work with the community and to honour these stories and to tell it how they like it to be told, but sometimes it can't be done on your own and you need great colleagues to work with. Part of being great colleagues is about all having the same agenda and being on the same page, and I've been very lucky to have that. Going forward, we've built this great relationship and who knows what might happen next, but it's been an absolutely great ride to be on.

10

History by committee: Representing the 'facts' of settler colonialism in a local historical society museum

Cameo Dalley and Ashley Barnwell

In his critical review of the National Gallery of Victoria's 2018 exhibition *Colony*, Bain Attwood (2019) suggests that the curators' aim of representing colonisation from both settler and Indigenous perspectives reflects the recent boom in exhibitions that seek to address what is termed 'difficult history' (see also Macdonald, 2008). Internationally, museums are displaying confronting histories and challenging nationalist erasures; for example, the International Slavery Museum in Liverpool and the Indian Residential School History and Dialogue Centre in Vancouver. In Australia, Indigenous artists such as Fiona Foley (2018) have pointed out that practices of historiographic critique and memorialisation have taken place in moveable Indigenous art, outside of national and academic institutions, in creative and community spaces (see also Foley & Howell, 2017; Grieves & Spiers, 2020; Konishi, 2019). Magdalena H Gross and Luke Terra (2018, p. 52) define 'difficult history' as 'periods that reverberate in the present and surface fundamental disagreements over who we are and what values we hold'. They note that some schoolteachers are reluctant to teach these periods of history, which include civil wars and colonisation, because they are too 'controversial' and 'divisive'. 'What makes difficult history difficult', they explain, 'is … the degree to which it challenges or undermines the dominant societal narratives' (Gross & Terra, 2018, p. 55). Yet blanket avoidance or assumed sensitivity can overlook the fact that not all history is difficult for specific students in the same way or at the same time. Telling difficult histories can feel relieving for particular audiences; it can open up space for different responses or be valued precisely for its challenge. While the word 'difficult' is perhaps too rigid, what we draw from this discussion is the challenge of storytelling in the museum, especially what is at stake in curatorial decisions about how to narrativise the past. Here, we consider: Do history-workers too readily pre-empt what histories will be 'difficult' and for whom? And how do perceptions about what counts as evidence influence history-making?

We also reopen these questions at a different scale – the local. Attwood (2019) points to a range of intimacies that *Colony* avoided, between past and present, history and memory, settler and Indigenous agencies, and so on. In a local museum – where the descendants of those whose lives hang on the walls often still live in the town – these questions of what is too close or too divisive or too confronting can be exacerbated. The local brings into view the concrete detail of biography and place, which can also sometimes refuse the generalising effects of grand narratives and moral arcs (Buckhorn, 2002; Eklund, 1997). As such, the local offers us new ways to think through how responsibilities, both to history and to contemporary relationships, are negotiated. In this chapter, we explore what we are terming the 'history-work' undertaken by volunteer staff at a museum in the East Kimberley town of Wyndham, which is operated by a local historical society. 'History-work' is a take on the long-established concept of 'memory work' (Darian-Smith & Hamilton, 2013; Kuhn, 1995; Radstone, 2000), and focuses on those who manage the material remnants of history (as one form of memory) in formal institutional settings. We attend to the relationships and sense of belonging that local history-workers develop to a place, and how this informs their feelings of responsibility in interpreting and presenting history. We also document the specific set of questions and limitations the museum faces in its efforts to revise exhibits that are about Aboriginal history or Indigenous–settler relations in the region, especially given that the museum's volunteers mostly identify as non-Indigenous. This knowledge about the working model of a local history society could inform decisions about how such forums might be advised and supported as important places for sharing and learning local history. Our chapter provides a glimpse into the experiences of one local history society museum, but many Australian towns have these museums, and many are run by non-Indigenous volunteers (Furniss, 2001;

Prowse, 2015). While there has been change in these spaces, and we must be careful not to dismiss the unique and sometimes also collaborative or consultative initiatives in place, commonly these museums retain aspects of a 'pioneer mythology' of settlement, with a focus on industry and early settler families. As Cameo Dalley has written elsewhere, these kinds of discussions about 'history by committee' also raise key questions around the reflexive and educational 'pre-decolonial' groundwork that settler individuals and groups can engage in before usefully contributing to decolonial activities, specifically in the realm of narrating local histories (Dalley, 2021; see also Land, 2015).

Local history in focus

Attention to local history spaces is of renewed importance following the 2018 delivery of the *Final Report of the Joint Select Committee on Constitutional Recognition Relating to Aboriginal and Torres Strait Islander Peoples*. The recommendations for truth-telling within the report state that it is 'best implemented at local and regional levels' (Section 6.54). Legal scholars Gabrielle Appleby and Megan Davis (2018) noted in their submission that 'truth-telling must come from local communities, led by Aboriginal and Torres Strait Islander peoples working with non-Aboriginal people in that community'. 'Local history societies' are one of the partners they list (Section 6.56). If such societies are to play a role, it is important to understand more about their current remit, how they are run, and their interest in, and capacity to educate visitors about, histories that may be seen as sensitive, confronting or divisive. This is of particular importance given that, in most Australian towns, local museums are often central venues for learning about history for locals and tourists, making them pivotal in the transmission of information and education.

As noted, local history societies have been primarily run by non-Indigenous volunteers and have tended to display settler histories that centre around pioneering, pastoral and colonial lives – though this is changing (Furniss, 2001; Prowse, 2015; Triolo et al., 2017). According to Frank Bongiorno, local history is often associated with the early reminiscence of pioneers. Such studies present:

> the history of a locality as a series of firsts: the first explorers, the first white settler, the first white child born in the district, the first pastoral run ... [and are] concerned with the business of exploration and settlement, a story presented within a teleology of imperial progress. (Bongiorno, 2009, p. 5)

However, there is also the potential for new local histories that:

> seek to explore rather than discipline memory, to investigate what the remembered past might mean for the communities doing that remembering, as well as tracing the reasons for, and effects of, forgetting on the people whose histories have been erased in conventional local histories. (Bongiorno, 2009, p. 13)

During the 'memory studies' boom of the 1990s and 2000s, Tom Griffiths (1996, 2007), Chris Healy (1997), and Paul Ashton and Paula Hamilton (2010) argued for an end to a pejorative view of local historians as amateur and dismissible. These scholars drew attention to the influential contribution of what Griffiths called 'the antiquarian imagination' and the role of local historians and historical societies in shaping cultural memory in Australia. Existing literature marks local and family historians as long-time contributors to Indigenous–settler histories, including aspects that have been omitted at national levels. Robert Foster and Amanda Nettelbeck argue that memories of frontier violence are cited more openly at the local level, with WEH Stanner's (1968/2009) 'great Australian silence' playing out as more of what they refer to as a 'great Australian whispering' (Foster & Nettelbeck, 2012, p. 142). Frontier conflict is candidly described in memoirs and local histories, albeit amid mythological narratives of pioneer stoicism. Indeed, contemporary surveys of colonial violence with a national scope, including Bruce Elder's (1988) *Blood on the Wattle* and Lyndall Ryan et al.'s (2018) 'Massacres Map', draw on local sources that are often written, recorded, transmitted and preserved by non-professional historians.

Louise Prowse (2015) and Elizabeth Furniss (2001) have both done work on how local historical societies or events address and include Aboriginal history: Furniss in Mount Isa (Queensland) and Prowse in Gilgandra, Gundagai, Mudgee, Uralla and Young (New South Wales). According to Prowse, academic historians have understood local historical societies' publications as contributing to the marginalisation of Aboriginal history, and rightly so in many cases. Local historical societies are seen to 'revere the male pioneer/settler narrative over other non-white local histories', emphasise settlers' hard work in tough conditions as a way to validate white land ownership, and celebrate local enterprise and progress as part of a nation-building story (Prowse, 2015, p. 56). John Hirst (1978) and Mark McKenna (2002) have been critical of local historical societies' failure to address evidence of frontier conflict and violence, in particular. However, looking at the minutes, programs, photographs, correspondence, written histories and newspaper articles of local historical societies in the 1960s and 1970s, Prowse found that their 'activities … reveal a more complex interest in Aboriginal history than their written histories suggest' (Prowse, 2015, p. 56). Her study raises questions about how and why a clear interest in Aboriginal history, while prominent in the societies' records, was not reflected in their public exhibits and publications. Prowse also noted that while a 'desire to learn more about the Aboriginal past' was evident, this rarely resulted in historical societies engaging Aboriginal people as educators (Prowse, 2015, p. 74).

Drawing on three months of fieldwork in Mount Isa in 1998, Furniss, like Prowse, surveyed whether and how Aboriginal history had been incorporated into local history within the town. She also explored whether local histories – as presented in monuments and memorials, tourist sites, festivals and local history books – 'bear the same concerns as academic histories with recognising Aboriginal people in history, with acknowledging the plurality of historical perspectives' (Furniss, 2001, p. 281). Furniss argued that repeated use of language such as 'first', 'discovery' and 'pioneer' across public sites and printed materials erased pre-settlement history and the history of Indigenous–settler relations within the region (p. 285). Where these were included, they were largely subsumed into nation-building mythologies, such as the framing of 'the Kalkadoon's last stand' on Battle Mountain within the Anzac legend – a narrative of sacrificial masculinity that Furniss noted has also been stretched to describe the deaths of early miners (p. 289). Creating space for Aboriginal history in Mount Isa had largely been at the initiative of the Kalkadoon Tribal Council, whose Memorial Keeping Place had garnered council support as a popular tourist destination, museum and meeting place. Furniss observed that the historical narrative at the exhibit of the Memorial Keeping Place reproduced the well-known story of the Kalkadoon's last stand but juxtaposed this with a photo-collage of living descendants to create a story of survival. Prowse's and Furniss's studies, both of which point to negotiations occurring in local history spaces, inform our analysis of the Wyndham Historical Society Museum, and the 'history-work' of its volunteers.

MEMORY IN PLACE

Defining the local: Wyndham Historical Society Museum

Wyndham is situated in the East Kimberley region. It was one of the first port towns established in the north-east of Western Australia, initially to service a gold rush at Halls Creek, inland to the south. Since the closure of a local meatworks in 1985, the town has gone into socioeconomic contraction, the population dwindling to 800 people, about half of whom are Aboriginal people from the Balangarra, Ngarinyin, Gija and Jaru groups. Aside from government jobs servicing the local population, and the port facilities that remain operational, tourism is one of the few industries that employs local people. A combination of Australian and international tourists visit the Kimberley each year in the dry season, generally on self-drive holidays in four-wheel-drive vehicles. Most are attracted to the region's spectacular landscape, including waterfalls, rocky mountain outcrops, and unusual plants and animals. As Ruth Lane and Gordon R Waitt (2007, p. 111) found in a series of interviews they conducted in the nearby town of Kununurra, most tourists experience the Kimberley as 'wild' or a 'wilderness' and are drawn to what they perceive as its 'frontier' qualities. Such is the settler imaginary of travel in the region that many tourists describe their experiences in terms of how they 'did' or have 'done' the Kimberley, framing their travel there as a challenge or quest to be conquered. This frontier status reflects its remote geographic location, scant infrastructure development and the relatively recent history of interaction between Aboriginal people and settlers.

One of the locations that tourists visit to learn more of this history is the Wyndham Historical Society Museum, situated near the port facility at the foothills of the picturesque Mount Bastion (see Figure 10.1). During the day, a meagre stream of tourists come through the museum, wandering through the small rooms, pointing out noteworthy items and flipping through books of photographs and records. Tourists are greeted by one of several volunteers who operate the museum. They pay a small donation for their entry. Among the volunteers are 'Brolga', one of few men still living in Wyndham who once worked at the meatworks; Judy from New Zealand, who lives with her husband on a yacht in the nearby river; and Maxine, who works at the local police station. Another volunteer, Phil, preserves historical pieces of pastoral infrastructure and works at the local port, assisting with the docking and unloading of ships. As in many small towns in Australia, the operational costs of the museum are funded by the entry fee paid by tourists, while specific projects are funded by small, one-off government grants. Objects contained in the collection are donated by the public, among them current and former residents of Wyndham and the surrounding area, including the volunteers who manage the day-to-day operations. Nonetheless, a significant aspect of the museum's operation is that all members of the committee moved to live in the town as adults and did not grow up there.

In this chapter we conceptualise the pivotal work that local volunteers play in interpreting and telling history in this region, focusing particularly on interviews with the secretary of the Wyndham Historical Society Museum conducted in 2016 and 2019. Christine moved to the town in 2007 to live with her partner Phil, whom she met at a wedding in South Australia. Christine had worked for many years as a high school economics teacher, and, upon moving to Wyndham, took up a role working for the local Shire Council as a community liaison officer. In addition to her paid work, which has changed over time to include cleaning at the local school and various short-term contracts at the council, Christine has taken on a number of volunteer roles in various community organisations. These include editing a local newsletter, *The Bastion Bulletin*, and serving on the local tourist committee. It was her partner Phil's pre-existing relationship to the museum as a volunteer, someone who 'goes along [to committee meetings] and … fixes things', in Christine's words, that led her to join their organising committee.

Figure 10.1. Wyndham Historical Society Museum.
Photograph: Cameo Dalley.

MEMORY IN PLACE

Valorising working-class masculinities

A plaque at the front gate of the Wyndham Historical Society Museum reads:

> This memorial recognises the contribution to East Kimberley by William O'Donnell who (with William Carr-Boyd) surveyed the Lower Ord River in 1883. O'Donnell Street adjacent to this memorial was named in his honour. Erected by Wyndham Historical Society.

The plaque is the first indication of the dominant content of the material contained in the museum – material that details and explores the early settler-colonial history of the East Kimberley region. In the museum grounds are various pieces of machinery and equipment, most of them salvaged from the meatworks that operated nearby and from ancillary businesses and operations.

The museum building was once a police station and government courthouse. It was built in 1954 and became the Wyndham Historical Society Museum in 1995. A note on the flyscreen door announces an entry fee of $5. The front door opens onto brown carpet, on which stands a glass cabinet containing black-and-white photographs, skulls of crocodiles and small Aboriginal artefacts, including examples of the famous 'Kimberley points', made of intricately flaked stone and glass (see Figure 10.2). There is a familiar, musty smell of old books and the dull, repetitive 'whurr' of a ceiling fan overhead. Even during the dry season daily temperatures reach over 35 degrees Celsius and, as they step over the threshold, visitors routinely exclaim at the welcome respite from the heat.

The museum building consists of two large and three smaller rooms, each containing combinations of wall-mounted photographic and archival displays, and glass cabinets containing small items. Larger items, including horseriding saddles and machinery, stand freely on the floor. The front room details Indigenous and natural history, while a large middle room describes life on Kimberley cattle stations, the Wyndham meatworks, aviation and shipping from the port (see Figure 10.3). At the rear are two smaller rooms: the back room on the left contains material on the Wyndham Port area and post office, including a few stores operated by Chinese families; the back room on the right features displays on the hospital, Royal Flying Doctor Service and Bluey Lloyd, who was one of the museum's original benefactors.

Figure 10.2. Displays in the front room at the Wyndham Historical Society Museum.
Photograph: Christine McLachlan.

The exhibits tell of the settler history of the region and into the mid-twentieth century, following World War II, when the town reached a social and economic peak generated by the boom of the local meatworks, which employed a predominantly non-Indigenous, male workforce. This mirrors other industries in the postwar period in Australia and is typified by a celebration of white working-class masculinities that remains pervasive in contemporary remembrances of this time. Nonetheless, Indigenous men and women and ethnic migrants, particularly those with a family background in butchery and smallgoods production, also made up a key part of the workforce, including the packing room. Recorded oral histories of meatworkers describe the lifestyle of the period from the 1960s to the 1980s as one of hard work and hard drinking that accompanied long shifts of manual labour in oppressive heat and poor conditions (Dalley, 2018). During this period, the meatworks was heavily unionised, ensuring high wages for workers, most of whom travelled from southern Western Australia for a six-month annual season. In an interview in 2016, Christine, secretary of the museum committee, described the average visitor to the museum as an Australian couple, aged in their 50s or 60s, usually retired

MEMORY IN PLACE

and on an extended self-drive trip through northern Australia. She noted that many visitors to the museum had either worked in the meatworks themselves or had connections to the town through family members who had worked there.

Figure 10.3. Objects on display in the middle room at the Wyndham Historical Society Museum.
Photograph: Christine McLachlan.

10. HISTORY BY COMMITTEE

Along with mid-century history, a portion of the museum's history relates to the town's service during WWII, when the state ship *Koolama* was attacked by a Japanese long-range bomber and later sank off the Wyndham jetty. Despite the town's small size, wartime history was also significant to one of the museum committee members, Dick. In addition to his active role on the museum committee, Dick has also been chairperson of the local Returned Servicemen's League (RSL) for over 10 years. As he explained in an interview in 2019, he took up the position partly as a sense of responsibility to wartime remembrance:

> I heard that they weren't going to have an Anzac Day service. So, I was at home watering my garden at the time and, ah, I remember thinking about it and the thought that came into mind at the time was Wyndham should not be branded as a town that forgot and – and I didn't want that to happen, that Wyndham was to be called the town that forgot Anzac Day.

At the time of the Vietnam War, Dick had completed what was known as National Service – about six months of military training that did not involve active service. Rather than active service, it was his personal history as a small business owner in Wyndham that led him to feel as though he needed to 'give something back' to the community:

> That was my feeling – that I had to give something back. That was I think another reason why I was crooked on other people and other business people who made money out of the town and gave nothing back.

This sense of obligation was a strong motivator for many involved in the museum's organising committee. The committee's six volunteers meet periodically during the dry season to discuss new displays, donations and various procedures associated with the daily running of the museum. About half the volunteers moved to the town as adults, most to work in various industries associated with the meatworks.

'Brolga' was a meat worker during the 1970s and described the cyclical nature of his own history as a volunteer:

> I volunteer at the museum on Mondays, because the museum, years ago, used to be the courthouse. I used to go there Mondays to pay me fines [for drunk and disorderly conduct], because that stinking town pub used to get me into trouble, and [I] used to have to go to

229

the museum, which is the courthouse, to pay me fines on Mondays, which is the museum. I still just go there now and volunteer on the Mondays.

Most of the objects held by the museum have been donated by current and former volunteers, including Bluey Lloyd, who was a cook at the local hospital and donated her house to the Wyndham Historical Society when she died in the 1990s. As heritage scholar Joanna Sassoon (2003) observes, the politics around donations and acquisitions can be silent players in museums' decisions about access and display. This is especially true in this part of the Kimberley, where the museum has accepted some donations, including from current members of the committee, on the proviso that they do not pass these items onto a nearby historical society museum in the neighbouring town of Kununurra. The Wyndham–Kununurra rivalry is legendary in this part of the Kimberley. Wyndham is the older, smaller, more established port town, while Kununurra is a much newer, brash metropolis – a town constructed entirely to service the Ord River development of the 1960s. Part of this rivalry relates to which town and residents are seen as the legitimate holders of history and knowledge in the region, a reflection of the significance of longevity in expressions of settler-colonial belonging.

As this description of the museum and some of the volunteers indicates, the constitution of the museum's contents is not based on a carefully curated and well-financed blueprint. Displays have been put together over time and are, by necessity, driven by happenstance – by what people happen to donate based on what they see as formative stories about the town. Similarly, close attention to who is involved in running the museum shows the personal motives for volunteering, and gestures to the role that volunteers' interests and aptitudes – be these from previous family, professional or life experiences (or weekly routines in Brolga's case) – can play in shaping the focus of the museum's activities. Importantly, the motivating factor may not necessarily be a specific expertise in history, but rather in contributing to the community activities, culture and face of the town. To underscore this intimacy, it is worth noting that, as well as serving on the museum committee, Dick served on the RSL committee and Christine served on the tourism committee, both of which have an interest in how history is commemorated in the museum.

10. HISTORY BY COMMITTEE

Settler belonging and questions of authority in narrating histories

As a key aspect in interpreting and understanding the history-work done at the museum, we draw attention to the relationship between the life experiences of history-workers and how these impact on the kinds of stories that are told. Contextualising Christine's role has been a difficult task because of the richness of her reflections and her astute, matter-of-fact accounting of the limitations on her as a history-maker within the town. However, we have delineated some of the contextual factors that Christine suggests influence her work and how these shape the history-work that she does at the museum. They include her own biography; her sense of belonging and authority within the town as a local, but not a 'true-blue local', and a settler woman; the scale and audience for the museum; the committee and volunteer structure on which the museum runs; the economic and cultural context for the museum; and the perceived rules around what makes an exhibit 'historical'. A close reading of Christine's experiences helps us to understand the potential challenges involved in documenting Indigenous–settler relations, including frontier violence, in a local museum.

In 2016, Christine talked about what it meant to her to belong in the town as someone who had moved there relatively recently, a question she reflected on with reference to her role at the museum. 'I suppose being a part of the museum has made it a lot easier for me,' she said, 'because I know a lot about the history of the place, but I'm aware that I wasn't a part of that history.' In this sense, she differentiated herself from those people who had grown up in the town and gone to school there. Schooling was one of the indicators that Christine considered seminal in a person's belonging: the commencement into the socialisation of knowledge and history about the place. Her positionality was something she was regularly questioned about during volunteer shifts at the museum:

> Probably the first thing people [tourists] ask when they come in the door is, 'Were you born here?' or 'Are you from here?' or 'How long have you been here?' One of these three questions is what they'll ask you as they come in the door, so I'm constantly basically apologising to people that I'm not the 'real deal', you know?

Christine contrasted her feelings of belonging at Wyndham with South Australia, where she grew up and lived most of her life:

> I had had experience of the country towns in South Australia, and in all of those places there was much more of a feeling that you're not from here if you're not born here. I don't get that feeling here. Basically, if you're willing to stay, I find that people are very accepting of you.

These experiences attest to what we understand more generally to be settler anxieties about social belonging that are pervasive in rural and outback Australia.

During the conversation, it became clear that Christine's sense of authority to tell stories in the museum was directly tied to her sense of belonging in the town and to her sensitivity to the politics of claiming particular identities. This includes a fine-grained understanding of what makes you a proper 'local' in the settler community, as well as how settler belonging is determined in relation to the Indigenous community, whom she recognised as having a different experience of connection to place. Christine recognised that, as a settler descendant, 'it's not our Country, and I feel that all the time. All the time'.

In 2016, when discussing what kinds of material visitors to the museum were interested in, Christine paused and hesitated before answering:

> In terms of what people are looking for … Sorry, yeah … quite often they're looking for … I don't even know how to put this. They're looking for information about Aboriginal people, but they're not really looking for … they're looking for current … This will sound terrible, but people come here and go, 'So what's it like living with Aboriginal people?' or 'How do you find it here?' People will make quite racist sort of … even the way they say the statement: 'How do you cope?' Stuff like that.

In this sense, what tourists were interested in discussing was, in many cases, not the (past) history of the town but its current racial dynamics, as well as ventilating pejorative assumptions about Aboriginal people in the contemporary community. However, even if local history was not what tourists were initially seeking, the museum nevertheless played a role in engaging and educating them about the history of colonisation and racism in the region. In describing what stood out to museum visitors, both Dick and Christine noted that many were unfamiliar with the realities of colonial history. In separate interviews, both commented on the profound impact on visitors of the small selection of historical photographs that show Aboriginal people in chains. For example, Christine remarked:

> They're surprised at the amount of stuff that's gone on here, or something to that effect … Then you get various comments within that. You get comments from people who say, 'I didn't realise the Aboriginal people were put in neck chains.' That's a really common one.

As we explain below, this photographic display stood out to volunteers as marking the place where visitors' knowledge of Aboriginal history changed. It was also one of the places where the volunteers' different ideas about their responsibilities in narrating history came to the surface.

One of Australia's most iconic historical photographs depicting Aboriginal people in chains was taken at the Wyndham Port in the late nineteenth or early twentieth century. It was first published in the *Western Mail* on 18 February 1905 (Christine McLachlan, personal communication; see also Lydon, 2010; Owen, 2016). As is extensively detailed in Chris Owen's (2016) history of the region, Aboriginal people in the East Kimberley were imprisoned, often for very minor crimes, and used as penal labour throughout the early to mid-twentieth century (see also Dalley, 2022). The identity of the photographer remains unknown; however, visual cross-referencing from other historical photographs taken at a similar time has enabled Christine to determine that the photograph was taken less than 100 metres from the museum. Reckoning with this history, its evidence in the local topography and its resonance in the contemporary community is an ongoing process. Moreover, there are differing opinions about how to do this, as Dick explained:

> So they [Aboriginal people] were treated like second-class citizens, absolutely bloody shocking, but that's the way things operated in those days, you know? I can't condemn people. You go back in history, which we don't want to do now talking about it, but go back in history … the humankind has – have … done that for years. Look at the early days in England when they sent eight-year-old kids down the coal mines, that's when the union movement started.

This perspective is reminiscent of the political distancing of the Howard era when the 'History Wars' were in full swing (Macintyre & Clark, 2003). In a now infamous speech in May 1997, Prime Minister John Howard, speaking at the Australian Reconciliation Convention, expressed his personal position of 'deep sorrow' regarding past injustices, but located responsibility firmly with past actors, encouraging acceptance of the 'blemishes of history' and a model of reconciliation achieved by 'focusing on the future' (Howard,

1997). Similar perspectives are embedded in the volunteers' differing understandings as to whether and how the museum should go about interpreting or 'commenting on' historical materials, a question that is doubly fraught due to the volunteers' differing politics.

As a result, the volunteers have collectively developed an approach where they only include materials that have appeared in secondary sources and can be confirmed to be what they refer to as 'facts'. Part of the concern about describing this history is that, as Christine explained, the committee did not feel that they had the authority or legitimacy to discuss Aboriginal history. When asked if the museum represents Aboriginal history, she responded:

> Before you ask the question, no. Absolutely, no. Shockingly, no. We have a real dilemma. We have a real dilemma, because we have the dilemma that it's not our story to tell, and so what we do tell is very much sort of third person – you know how you tell things that are already published.

To avoid 'telling the story', the museum only includes material from secondary sources in its displays rather than writing its own interpretation. These sources are mostly written by non-Indigenous authors, including authors of local histories and historical newspaper articles. The underlying assumption is that the history-worker can reserve their claim to authorship by making a clear distinction between 'history' and 'memory' (Hodgkin & Radstone, 2017), or 'fact' and 'story'.

However, Christine understands that primary sources and different perspectives would improve the current displays and she has made some efforts to pursue this. Since commencing as a volunteer, Christine has had conversations with members of the local Aboriginal community to try to get feedback on the kinds of history that the museum tells about Aboriginal people. In 2009, the Western Australian Government, through their Royalties for Regions scheme, made grants available to local community groups. The museum committee applied for a large grant, as Christine explained in 2016:

> The museum committee put in sort of an ambit claim to … I think it was for a new museum. It was to include a whole cultural centre, so to speak. At the same time, Ngnowar Aerwah [a Wyndham-based Aboriginal corporation] was putting a funding proposal for an Indigenous cultural centre. It wasn't as though there was a war or anything, but they [the Aboriginal corporation] specifically said that they did not want to be part of [the proposed museum] … they wanted it as their own thing.

Christine explained that, at the time, the logic behind preserving a division of history – between what was ostensibly coded as non-Indigenous on the one hand and Aboriginal history on the other – was part of a strategic approach to maintain the necessity for an Indigenous cultural centre. This division made sense to Christine, who noted that she could 'really sort of understand their point of view, a bit of that fear of being subsumed by whitefella history, so to speak'.

In any case, both applications for funding were unsuccessful. Adapting to the reality that an Indigenous cultural centre was unlikely, the museum began to adjust its presentation of content to include more Aboriginal history. While government support for an Indigenous cultural centre would have been the preferable outcome, resulting in the kind of dialogue that Furniss describes between the local history museum and Memorial Keeping Home at Mt Isa, Christine was all too aware that the museum was the main place where tourists came to learn the history of the town, and that their exhibits required revision.

Sticking to 'facts'

In their general approach to the display of material, the museum committee was focused on providing assemblages of fact – what they thought of as historically verifiable information. This covered only those aspects of history that could be accounted for through written historical documents. In response to a question about matters that are deliberately kept out of documented history, or that are misrepresented in either primary or secondary documents, Christine acknowledged this was a problem. Elaborating on their rationale, she explained:

> So um, so of course oral history is important but if the oral history is lost or it is very fragmented or three different people have three completely different versions of the oral history, that makes it really, really fraught for someone like me. Do you know what I mean? Because no matter how much ah – you know, we can talk about all the different sorts of narratives and they all – you know, they've all got their point of view and everything. In the end, I have some sort of duty to try and show it as clearly as I can. I can show all the differences but um, sometimes exposing the differences makes more harm than good, do you know what I mean?

In this response we can hear echoes of what Gross and Terra (2018, p. 52) describe as the difficulty within 'difficult history' – the concern that representing a perspective that differs from the known record (or rather, the known reading of the record) may cause harm and division – 'expose the differences' – in the present.

To build on Gross and Terra's conclusions, here we see that it is not only topics but also *types* of history-making that are perceived to open spaces of 'difficulty'. Oral sources and memoir were considered more 'difficult' than, for example, published histories or historical newspaper articles. However, it is worth noting that oral history projects have been common within local history societies since the 1980s (Eklund, 1997; Hodge, 1995; Horne, 1987; White-McColl & Dean, 2002; Wyatt, 1981). Writing in 1987, Gail Griffith surveyed local oral history projects in Victoria, seeing oral history as a potential way to remedy the fact that 'written local histories tend to be characterised by an absence of conflict, to be Anglo-centric in their approach and are seemingly unaware of distinctive social classes, sectarianism, and racism' (Griffith, 1987, p. 50). But Griffith was also wary of emerging oral history projects that continued these biases, were 'nostalgic' and were 'strangely depopulated of all except for local councillors, clergy and the odd eccentric or successful businessman' (p. 50). She saw the potential for settler mythologies to inflect both forms of history-making. Thus, the inflection of racist attitudes about Aboriginal people as inaccurate narrators of oral history, compared with the superiority of 'documented' settler history, perpetuates.

Oral history's vulnerability to the vicissitudes of memory was a concern held by others on the Wyndham museum committee; they saw oral history as more like memory and written history as more like history, making the latter ostensibly more reliable than the former. Some held this view more strongly than others. For example, when discussing colonial violence in the East Kimberley region, Dick referred to the book *Massacre Myth* by Rod Moran (1999), which challenges accounts of the massacre of Aboriginal people at nearby Forrest River Mission (Oombulgurri) in 1926. The massacre was well documented at the time by the then mission superintendent, Reverend Gribble, and a Royal Commission Inquiry in 1927, and thoroughly researched in Neville Green's (1995) *The Forrest River Massacres*. Dick noted that although he had not read *Massacre Myth*, its title alone had led him to question other accounts of colonial violence:

10. HISTORY BY COMMITTEE

> So it makes you wonder about some of these other massacres you hear about, you know, did they actually happen or are they just a figment of imagination, you know?

It was these potentially conflicting accounts that Christine felt she needed to weigh up in her telling of stories at the museum:

> Well, my best reading of all the information I've been able to read, it's really, really difficult to be able to say factually what happened, and so what do you do with that? Especially seeing that it's a highly sensitive topic because I can guarantee that 101 per cent of Aboriginal people absolutely know that that happened. Absolutely know it happened. But from a whitefella museum point of view, what do I do with that? Because from a secondary resources point of view, there are two sides to that story, and so I'm in a real dilemma.

What is telling about Dick's and Christine's views about the massacre at Forrest River is that the event is clear in Aboriginal oral history *and* was also thoroughly accounted for by non-Indigenous people *at the time*. Yet, committee members remained concerned about how to represent the event, highlighting the significant influence that the membership of local history committees can have on what is and is not displayed.

The hesitation and conservatism of this approach reflected both the pre-emptive understanding of the museum's visitors as tending towards racist ideas about Aboriginal people (as previously mentioned), and the reality of the museum committee, which was composed of members with differing views about colonial history. In this sense, as the main writer of exhibition content for the museum, Christine explained that there were, in fact, two audiences she had to appease:

> I'm not just selling it to the public. I'm selling it to the other members of the committee, and … so it has to stand up. It has to stand up to sort of like … rigorous [questioning]: 'Where did you get that from?' and 'What about this?' and 'What about that?' and I have to not only know about what I'm putting on the wall, I have to know about what I'm not putting on the wall, too, you know.

While Christine noted several times that the museum committee felt they had to 'fairly rigidly stick to historically accurate events' and 'have fairly deliberately shied away from controversial stories', it was clear that they did include stories that depicted the violent treatment of Aboriginal people and also attempted to include countering perspectives, albeit using only published records. Christine noted this with reference to the display about Aboriginal prisoners in chains:

> So the ones – the stories we do – that we do tell we do try and at a minimum allude to the fact that there's different points of view. So say the display on um, Aboriginal prisoners. I mean, you can't say that that was a display saying that that was in any way a good thing to do. Um, so um, you know, the best that I could do was put up testimony of Aboriginal prisoners when they went to court or when they were interviewed and things they have said about what had gone on. Um, ah, but it is still on the record, do you know what I mean? It is still on the record. It is still something that they told to somebody who was in – to someone in authority.

As Christine and Dick both mentioned, this display was often reported as the most affecting for visitors.

Dick understood the significance of the museum as a place for visitors to access stories, not only assemblages of fact:

> The thing I've noticed that – with the museum that people are most interested in, or like about the museum, is the fact that they come and there's stories here in the museum … they'd much rather go into the museum and see a story about something rather than just go and see an object with a label on it.

Thus, while the volunteers were reluctant to include commentary beyond the materials or records on display, they also acknowledged that it was the exhibits that were narrativised and contained different voices and perspectives that most engaged visitors. This raises the question of whether the pre-empting of viewers' responses to 'difficult' histories, as well as the perceived need of visitors to see verified accounts from authoritative sources, is borne out in their actual responses. While Christine was tentative in her approach and aware that the museum needed to consult the Aboriginal community to expand their displays, responses to the existing exhibits demonstrated the museum's capacity to engage visitors on Wyndham's history beyond a tale of settler stoicism and industry, and to include potentially confronting materials using a range of historical sources.

A collaborative future?

Christine wanted to pursue a collaborative approach to curating Aboriginal history within the museum, to reach beyond the expertise of the committee and 'to have a conversation about what would be the important stories that we should be telling as a town'. In 2019, she submitted an application for funding to expand the museum's display area, which has been one of the limiting factors in determining the museum's scope. In response to the themes prioritised in the grant application process, a foundational part of the application was to include Aboriginal history in the new displays. Christine had in mind a set of engagements with the local Aboriginal community to collaboratively generate text and input. This proposal met with some nervousness from the museum committee, as Dick explained:

> I think that's a prerequisite with the – getting a grant from the Lotteries Commission … that the Aboriginal population be involved to a certain extent. I – that was brought up at our committee meeting the other night. I did say to – at the time at the meeting, I said 'Yeah, I'm in agreeance with that as long as they don't want to take over the whole lot' … but Chris[tine] said 'No, no, they won't be taking over the whole lot', that's what she said.

Here, again, it is clear that the committee structure of a local history museum, the negotiation of relationships, and differing views and investments, informs the aims and progress of the museum's activities and remit. This chimes with Prowse's finding that, while the minutes of meetings held by local historical societies were often full of discussions about representing Aboriginal history and community collaboration, such discussions rarely bore fruit. Directions from beyond the committee – in this case, the rules of the grant funding – may be useful in convincing or overruling otherwise reluctant committee members to reach a collaborative approach.

Christine predicted that the more likely outcome would be, as had been the case in the past, that few local Aboriginal people would be available to engage with the process of updating the museum, usually because of already limited resources and more pressing priorities. She hoped they would get at least some evaluation from the Aboriginal community of what the museum put together:

> I don't feel as though um, there's a huge amount of negativity but I'm expecting that there'd probably be a huge amount of ambivalence really you know. It is like – I mean, I'm assuming that there will be a lot of people who will say 'well … you know what you do is your own business but don't stuff it up.'

Within the museum committee, there was an acknowledgement of the need and desire (at least from Christine) to collaborate with Aboriginal community members on the displays. But Christine also demonstrated a commitment to persevere with the museum's aim to include more Aboriginal history even without such collaboration – that is, a pragmatism to work with what was available even if it meant the story was incomplete. She reflected:

> So yeah, it bothers me a lot, because the history we have at the museum isn't the whole history, but it's all we've got. What do you do? Pack up shop and go home and say, 'We can't do it properly so don't do it all', or do we just go with ... ?

Here, Christine made it clear that, even without the desired consultation or funding needed to realise what she and the rest of the museum committee acknowledged would be the better approach, the museum sought to include more Aboriginal history in its displays.

This context and outcome, which, of course, does not reflect all local historical societies but may well accord with some, raises questions about how best to support local history spaces run by non-Indigenous 'history-workers' (usually untrained volunteers) to shift away from reifying the pioneer myth and reproducing silences about Aboriginal history and Indigenous–settler relations in their displays. Even in cases where, as Furniss (2001) found, keeping places and other Indigenous-led history spaces are providing Indigenous perspectives, it is still desirable for non-Indigenous-led local history societies and museums to provide a less whitewashed account of local history within their existing themes and displays. As Mark McKenna has written:

> The difficulty today for the local historian is to build a sense of pride in the community's past and at the same time acknowledge that their town was founded on the violent theft of Aboriginal land ... The local dilemma is the national dilemma. (McKenna, 2002, p. 95)

Indeed, while we cannot assume that such committee-run spaces are unanimous in their aims, our case study demonstrates that moves to change and revise can come from within local history societies themselves. The hesitancy in the case of the Wyndham Historical Society Museum centred more on questions about *how* this history-work should be done with regard to the validity of historical evidence, the ethics of representation – including what is and is not settler history-workers' 'story to tell' – and whether, and how, shared histories could be told without community consultation, if not without recorded Indigenous perspectives.

Conclusion

Through discussing some of the history-work being done at the Wyndham Historical Society Museum, we gain insight into how volunteers negotiate their positions and make compromises in their efforts to engage visitors in the history of the area. Biography underscores the volunteers' sense of belonging and authority in the town, and their historical and political interests play into their roles at the museum. In addition, the volunteers pre-empt the responses of each other, and of their visitors, when deciding what to pursue or display, as well as deciding on the guidelines that inform their history-work, such as only including 'facts' that appear in secondary sources. There are obvious historiographic concerns here, including a less critical view of conflict between written documents than between written and oral sources. But we are also interested in how this compromise has been arrived at, how it is managed, and how it comes to shape what is and is not shown at the museum at Wyndham. This tells us a lot about how museums can be supported in making change.

As a case study, the Wyndham Historical Society Museum shows how history is curated from within a committee with conflicting political and historical views. This is part of the 'history-work' that is done in the local setting, as Dick's reference to his dialogue with Christine about potential Aboriginal collaboration indicates. While the volunteers are reluctant to include their own historiographic or interpretive voices on the walls, the iterative nature of actually doing history is at the forefront of their conversations. There is a frankness about the difficulty of establishing effective collaborations both within the committee and between the museum and the Aboriginal community. Noting the society's humble scale and capacities, Christine observed:

> We are a small little society of people that vaguely think that telling the history of the town is important and that is, you know, that's the bare bones of it. It's not like, you know, they – you know, we don't have university degrees in how to tell a story even.

In many ways, the scale of the museum – volunteer-led and funded by small grants – requires measures of pragmatism and compromise, but it is also important to carefully consider how these measures can serve multiple purposes, sometimes perhaps unnecessarily limiting the kinds of history-work that could be done in the space, even within their means. Understanding the behind-the-scenes considerations that play into the production of history in local spaces is vital, because these spaces can be significant in educating people about specific, localised experiences of colonisation. They can also direct people to sources that offer Aboriginal perspectives on history and history-making.

In considering this case study, we are interested in further exploring how history-work at the local level can speak to questions around how we address 'difficult history'. To return to questions we raised in our introduction: Do history-workers too readily pre-empt which histories will be 'difficult' and for whom? What counts as evidence in history-making, and why? The responses from Christine and Dick offer rich insights into how local history-workers approach these concerns, as well as how their strategies come to shape the histories that are eventually exhibited and shared with visitors. As with Prowse's (2015) work on local historical societies in New South Wales, there is much more to the activities and discussions of the Wyndham Historical Society than what is on display in the museum. Often, history-workers are aware of the limitations of the collections and expertise they have, and they know what is needed to redress this. The process is iterative. Taking this into account, we are interested in the way certain constraints can be affirmed even as they are being worked through, particularly when tied to assumptions about the needs, tenor and consequences of presenting historical knowledge from within a specific local context. This is an important conversation as we turn to the potential participation of local history societies as non-Indigenous partners in truth-telling processes, and as we consider the different curatorial and collaborative strategies that may be needed in the unique settings of local (rather than state or national) history spaces.

Acknowledgements

Our sincere thanks to Christine McLachlan for correcting errors of fact in an earlier draft of the chapter and, more importantly, for her willingness to participate in our research. Vale Mr Dick Daniels who was an active volunteer in Wyndham civic and social life for many years.

References

Appleby, G. & Davis, M. (2018). [Submission number 480.1]. In *Final report of the Joint Select Committee on constitutional recognition relating to Aboriginal and Torres Strait Islander peoples*. Canberra. aph.gov.au/Parliamentary_Business/Committees/Joint/Former_Committees/Constitutional_Recognition_2018/ConstRecognition/Submissions

Ashton, P. & Hamilton, P. (2010). *History at the crossroads: Australians and the past*. Halstead Press.

Attwood, B. (2019). The National Gallery of Victoria's *Colony* and difficult history. *Australian Historical Studies*, *50*(1), 99–116. doi.org/10.1080/1031461X.2018.1557225

Bongiorno, F. (2009). *From local history to the history of place: A brief history of local history in Australia*. Symposium of the Victoria County History – Institute of Historical Research, 6–8 July 2009.

Buckhorn, R. (2002). Breaking the silence. *Teaching History*, *36*(3), 4–10.

Dalley, C. (2018). Death Knells. *Meanjin*, Spring. meanjin.com.au/essays/death-knells/

Dalley, C. (2021). Becoming a settler descendant: Critical engagements with inherited family narratives of indigeneity, agriculture and land in a (post)colonial context. *Life Writing*, *18*(3), 355–370. doi.org/10.1080/14484528.2021.1927493

Dalley, C. (2022). Pastoralism's distributive ruse: Extractivism, financialization, Indigenous labour and a rightful share in Northern Australia. *History & Anthropology*, [online 15 Feb 2022], 1–19. doi.org/10.1080/02757206.2022.2034622

Darian-Smith, K. & Hamilton, P. (2013). Memory and history in twenty-first century Australia: A survey of the field. *Memory Studies*, *6*(3), 370–383. doi.org/10.1177/1750698013482868

Eklund, E. (1997). Memories of place: Local history and oral evidence. *Oral History Association of Australia Journal*, *19*, 73–77.

Elder, B. (1998). *Blood on the wattle: Massacres and maltreatment of Aboriginal Australians since 1788*. New Holland Publishers.

Foley, F. (2018, 6 July). *The spectacle of Aboriginal Frontier War memorial research*. ArtsHub. artshub.com.au/2018/07/06/the-spectacle-of-aboriginal-frontier-war-memorial-research-256020/

Foster, R. & Nettelbeck, A. (2012). *Out of the silence: The history and memory of South Australia's frontier wars*. Wakefield Press.

Furniss, E. (2001). Timeline history and the Anzac myth: Settler narratives of local history in a North Australian town. *Oceania, 71*(4), 279–297. doi.org/10.1002/j.1834-4461.2001.tb02754.x

Green, N. (1995). *The Forrest River massacres*. Fremantle Arts Centre Press.

Griffith, G. (1987). Oral history or nostalgia? Oral history and local historical societies. *Oral History Association of Australia Journal, 9*, 47–51.

Griffiths, T. (1996). *Hunters and collectors: The antiquarian imagination in Australia*. Cambridge University Press.

Griffiths, T. (2007). *Hunters and collectors: The antiquarian imagination in Australia*. Cambridge University Press.

Grieves, G. & Spiers, A. (2020). Counter-monuments. Session one [Seminar presentation]. In *Counter-monuments: Indigenous settler relations in Australian contemporary art and memorial practices*. Symposium conducted at the Australian Centre for Contemporary Art, Melbourne, Victoria, 17–19 March 2020. acca.melbourne/counter-monuments-indigenous-settler-relations-in-australian-contemporary-art-and-memorial-practices/

Gross, M. H. & Terra, L. (2018). What makes difficult history difficult? *Phi Delta Kappan, 99*(8), 51–56. doi.org/10.1177/0031721718775680

Healy, C. (1997). *From the ruins of colonialism: History as social memory*. Cambridge University Press.

Hirst, J. (1978). The pioneer legend. *Historical Studies, 18*(71), 316–337. doi.org/10.1080/10314617808595595

Hodge, D. (1995). Malagasy at work: Aspects of a Northern Territory oral history project. *Oral History Association of Australia Journal, 17*, 20–25.

Hodgkin, K. & Radstone, S. (2017). Introduction: Contested pasts. In K. Hodgkin & S. Radstone (Eds.), *Memory, history, nation: Contested pasts* (pp. 1–21). Routledge, Taylor & Francis Group. doi.org/10.4324/9780203785751

Horne, J. (1987). Some expectations of local history and the relevance of oral history to these expectations. *Oral History Australia, 9*, 52–57.

Howard, J. (1997, 26 May). *Prime Minister the Hon John Howard MP, opening address to the Australian Reconciliation Convention* [Speech transcript]. pmtranscripts.pmc.gov.au/sites/default/files/original/00010361.pdf

Howell, E. & Foley, G. (2017). *Performing political history: An interview with Gary Foley* [Interview transcript]. The Commons: Social Change Library. commonslibrary.org/performing-political-history-an-interview-with-actor-academic-and-activist-gary-foley/

Joint Select Committee. (2018). *Final report – Joint Select Committee on Constitutional Recognition relating to Aboriginal and Torres Strait Islander peoples*. Parliament of the Commonwealth of Australia.

Konishi, S. (2019). First Nations scholars, settler colonial studies, and Indigenous history. *Australian Historical Studies, 50*(3), 285–304. doi.org/10.1080/1031461X.2019.1620300

Kuhn, A. (1995). *Family secrets: Acts of memory and imagination*. Virago.

Land, C. (2015). *Decolonising solidarity: Dilemmas and directions for supporters of Indigenous struggles*. Zed Books.

Lydon, J. (2010). 'Behold the tears': Photography as colonial witness. *History of Photography, 34*(3), 234–250. doi.org/10.1080/03087291003765836

Macdonald, S. (2008). *Difficult heritage: Negotiating the Nazi past in Nuremberg and beyond*. Routledge, Taylor & Francis Group.

MacIntyre, S. & Clark, A. (2003). *The history wars*. Melbourne University Press.

McKenna, M. (2002). *Looking for Blackfellas' point: An Australian history of place*. University of New South Wales Press.

Moran, R. (1999). *Massacre myth: An investigation into allegations concerning the mass murder of Aborigines at Forrest River*. Access Press.

Owen, C. (2016). *'Every mother's son is guilty': Policing the Kimberley frontier of Western Australia 1882–1905*. UWA Press.

Prowse, L. (2015). Parallels on the periphery: The exploration of Aboriginal history by local historical societies in New South Wales, 1960s–1970s. *History Australia, 12*(3), 55–75. doi.org/10.1080/14490854.2015.11668586

Radstone, S. (Ed.). (2000). *Memory and methodology*. Bloomsbury Academic.

Ryan, L., Debenham, J., Pascoe, B., Smith, R., Owen, C., Richards, J., Gilbert, S., Anders, R. J., Usher, K., Price, D., Newley, J., Brown, M., Le, L. H. & Fairbairn, H. (2018). *Colonial frontiers massacres, Australia, 1788 to 1930* (Vol. 2.1) [Massacres map]. University of Newcastle. c21ch.newcastle.edu.au/colonialmassacres/map.php

Sassoon, J. (2003). Phantoms of remembrance: Libraries and archives as 'the collective memory'. *Public History Review, 10*, 40–60.

Stanner, W. H. (2009). *The Dreaming and other essays*. Black Inc. (Originally published 1968).

Triolo, R., Doyle, H. & Johanson, K. (2017). *Writing and publishing local history: A guide for first-time authors and historical societies*. Royal Historical Society of Victoria, Federation of Australian Historical Societies Inc.

Waitt, G. & Lane, R. (2007). Four-wheel drivescapes: Embodied understandings of the Kimberley. *Journal of Rural Studies, 23*(2), 156–169. doi.org/10.1016/j.jrurstud.2006.07.001

White-McColl, M. & Dean, J. (2002). Kingborough Oral History Project, Tasmania. *Oral History Association of Australia Journal, 24*, 103–104.

Wyatt, M. (1981). Oral history: An analysis in the context of a local area study of North Turramurra. *Oral History Association of Australia Journal, 4*, 58–61.

11

Displaying frontier violence at the Australian War Memorial

Thomas J. Rogers

Introduction

In this chapter, I want to add to a discussion about how stories of frontier violence have been told in the galleries of the Australian War Memorial (AWM) in Canberra. I wrote this from the perspective of a settler-descended Australian inside the institution, having worked as a historian at the memorial from June 2017 to February 2023. After a brief overview of the historiography of frontier violence, the discussion turns to the AWM's position on displaying frontier violence. The chapter then briefly traces the memorial's position on the question of gallery displays of frontier violence since the 1970s. In greater depth, I consider how this position is reflected in the activity of collecting and in the galleries themselves. I use as a case study the refurbishing of the colonial gallery in February 2019 to highlight some of the difficulties faced by historians and curators in telling frontier stories in a national museum. I conclude by speculating about where future research might take this debate.

It is not only through its galleries that the AWM tells Australian histories. Publications are another significant avenue by which historians and curators at the memorial fulfil the institution's charter to disseminate Australian military history. Taking myself as an example, I note that while working at the AWM, I wrote about frontier violence in a monograph, book chapters and media articles (e.g. Rogers, 2018a, 2018b, 2019a, 2019b). In this chapter, however, I focus on the memorial's galleries, as the content of publications fits into a different analytical field.

Frontier violence: An overview

The frontier period, and frontier violence, have been variously defined and described (e.g. Broome, 1988, p. 120; Reynolds, 2013, pp. 49–50). In this chapter, I use the term 'frontier violence' to describe the violent clashes between settlers and Indigenous peoples across Australia between 1788 and 1928. In the Australian colonial context, the broad term 'violence' encompasses a variety of acts, including war, massacre, poisoning, spearing, rape, shooting, pitched battle, skirmish and arson. On the British side, the main actors were convicts, free settlers, government officials, British Army regulars and colonial police. Across Australia, Indigenous peoples fought as individual clans, language groups and sometimes larger alliances to retain their land, their law and lore, their sacred sites and their economies (Broome, 2010, pp. 36–56; Connor, 2008; Rogers, 2018b, p. 30). This is the broad picture – the details varied across different locations and during more than a century of tactical and technological development. As I have argued elsewhere, violence was not incidental to British settlement in Australia – it was not an unfortunate side effect. Rather, violence was the means by which British settlers dispossessed Indigenous peoples across the continent (Rogers, 2018a, pp. 10–14, 222–224, 2018b, p. 30).

Settler pursuit of profit on the grasslands of south-eastern Australia was the initial impetus for conflict between Aboriginal people and British settlers. Early settler and explorer accounts of the Australian landscape emphasise grasslands (Batman, 1835; Boyce, 2013, p. 5; Mitchell, 1839, p. 171). Grasslands represented a potentially huge profit to be gained from sheep grazing. It is becoming more widely understood among non-Indigenous Australians that these grasslands were formed by generations of carefully coordinated Aboriginal burning regimes (Gammage, 2011, p. 3). This gradual realisation has come after more than two centuries of Aboriginal and Torres Strait Islander testimony to the importance of custodianship and care for Country.

For much of the twentieth century, the violence of the British invasion of Australia was ignored by Australian historians and the Australian public. In 1968, the anthropologist WEH Stanner posited that non-Indigenous

Australians practised a 'cult of disremembering' of Aboriginal people and their shared histories, which he termed 'the Great Australian Silence' (Stanner, 2009, p. 189). Against this trend, Amanda Nettelbeck (2011, p. 1118) reminds us that frontier violence was often remembered by local historians and local museums, sometimes even 'cemented in social memory as foundational moments'. At the national level, academic historians began to ask questions about Australian colonial encounters from the 1970s onwards, and, in particular, the violence that facilitated the British settlement of Australia (e.g. Reynolds, 1982; Rowley, 1970). This work followed a rising interest in Australian history among archaeologists and art historians, and heralded a growing recognition of frontier violence in Australian society (Attwood & Foster, 2003). Since the late 1970s, the AWM has considered whether frontier violence should be part of its displays (McKernan, 1991, pp. 293–294).

The Australian War Memorial

The AWM was conceived as a place to remember and understand the experience of Australian forces during World War I. The institution traces its history to that war, and to its founder, Charles Bean, Australia's first official war historian (McKernan, 1991, pp. xi–xiii). Australian families suffered through WWI, with the deaths of more than 60,000 members of the Australian Imperial Force and the return to Australia of more than 150,000 wounded personnel (Pedersen, 2010, p. 454). For some families, the end of the war marked the beginning of life with a physically or mentally scarred veteran (Larsson, 2009, pp. 16–17). Despite these losses, Bean and the others working to establish the AWM were concerned that Australians could not understand the realities of a distant war. The memorial's approach since that time has been, in historian Michael McKernan's (1991, p. xii) phrase, 'commemoration through understanding'.

In pursuit of this aim, the AWM has three distinct but interlinked purposes: it is a shrine, an archive and a museum (AWM, 2021; Inglis, 2008, p. 316; McKernan, 1991, p. xiii). The shrine comprises the Pool of Reflection, the cloisters that house the Roll of Honour (bronze panels that list the names of more than 103,000 Australians who have died in conflict or on operations while serving in the Australian Defence Force and its predecessors), and the Hall of Memory, in which is entombed the Unknown Australian Soldier. In its expansive collection of the records and relics of war, the AWM functions as a central archival repository of the experiences of Australians during wartime. The memorial's third function, the museum, is the focus of this chapter.

Although founded to commemorate WWI, the AWM building in Canberra did not open until 1941, at a time when Australia was involved in an even larger world war, one that would strike much closer to home. As McKernan (1991, p. 178) observes: 'This was a different war, in scale, in Australian involvement, and, above all, in mood.' Some returned men of WWI were concerned that their experiences might be subsumed by WWII (McKernan, 1991, pp. 159–191). Some simply assumed that a new memorial would need to be built for WWII (McKernan, 1991, p. 178). From the time of its opening, therefore, Australians have debated the precise contours of the AWM's role. As with all museums, the question of whose stories are to be told and how they are to be told have always been subject to negotiation.

A few words on the AWM's governing legislation are in order. The AWM is an Australian federal agency, with its charter defined by the *Australian War Memorial Act 1980*. The AWM was initially established by the *Australian War Memorial Act 1925* as the national memorial for those who had died in the war beginning on 4 August 1914, the day Britain declared war on Germany (Section 2). Later Acts, however, have not listed eligible wars but rather used a formula first developed in a 1952 amendment: 'any war or war-like operations in which Australians have been on active service' (Section 3[b]). This formulation was not without difficulties of its own. Then director John Treloar was concerned that this iteration left out non-combatants such as Australians who had served as official photographers, as war correspondents, in the Merchant Navy or in non-government organisations such as the Red Cross (McKernan, 1991, pp. 227–228). It was not until a 1975 amendment to the Act that the AWM could commemorate these Australians left out of the 1952 Act (McKernan, 1991, pp. 261–262). The 1980 Act, which is the current legislation, made the AWM a statutory authority, no longer with a board but a council, bringing it in line with the National Library of Australia and the National Gallery of Australia (McKernan, 1991, pp. 287, 289). The 1980 Act (Part I, Section 3) is most significant for history-telling because it added to the AWM's remit, for the first time, the causes and aftermath of the wars in which Australians have fought (see also McKernan, 1991, p. 287).

The AWM's position

The AWM publicly stated its position on frontier violence in a media release in 2014. Acknowledging that 'the protracted conflict that occurred during the colonial dispossession of Indigenous Australians is a tragic fact of Australia's history', the statement drew on the memorial's charter to define the role of the institution:

> As defined in the *Australian War Memorial Act 1980*, the Memorial's official role is to develop a memorial for Australians who have died on, or as a result of, active service, or as a result of any war or warlike operation in which Australians have been on active service. The definition does not include internal conflicts between the Indigenous populations and the colonial powers of the day. (AWM, 2014)

The AWM's statement notes that the colonial militia units that were raised from the middle of the nineteenth century – which are sometimes seen as the precursors to the modern Australian Defence Force – were not involved in frontier violence. The story of these units is told in the memorial's colonial galleries. The statement adds that because the British combatants in frontier violence were settlers, police or British soldiers the story falls outside the remit of the AWM.

Such, then, is the bald statement of policy. Yet there is a seeming tension between words and deeds. The AWM's galleries do mention violence between Aboriginal people and British settlers. My research suggests that this has been the case since the late 1980s, with the opening of Soldiers of the Queen, the permanent colonial gallery. At some point in the late 1980s, the lithograph *Mounted Police and Blacks*, drawn by Godfrey Charles Mundy (1852), was displayed in that gallery. Like many of the photographs and artworks in Soldiers of the Queen, it did not have a caption. This lithograph will be studied in detail in the next section, including its seeming contradiction of the AWM's statement – the colonial force in question having 'police' in its title.

The AWM has not denied the historical fact of frontier violence, but some have interpreted its policy to be a denial of the importance of frontier conflict in understanding Australian history. The memorial has argued that the story of frontier violence does not belong in the memorial, but rather at the National Museum of Australia or another national institution (AWM, 2014). The memorial did, however, go through a period in the 1980s when it advanced the view that frontier violence did not amount to 'war', and thus did not belong in a war memorial. This line of thinking continues to be raised from time to time by commentators, but it has been roundly rejected by various historians, including military historians (e.g. Coates, 2006, p. 6; Grey, 2008, pp. 28–29; Reynolds, 1982, pp. 198–202). Because AWM historians keep up to date with historiography, this old debate around the definition of war is no longer relevant to their thinking.

In the late 1970s, the AWM commissioned historian Geoffrey Blainey to write a report on improving the gallery displays. Among other recommendations, Blainey (1979) observed:

> Within the next decade, I imagine that the Memorial will have to include a section on Aboriginal–European warfare, including the Black War in Tasmania in the 1830s, the guerrilla attacks on white settlers etc.

This recommendation was one of several ideas for exhibition renewal and building works that appear to have been too radical for the director, Noel Flanagan, and the board of the time (McKernan, 1991, pp. 292–294). In the 1980s, Blainey was not alone in highlighting frontier conflict. At the memorial's 1981 history conference, one of its historians presented a paper on the 1838 Slaughterhouse Creek massacre (Stanley, 1981). In 1984, the AWM's council approved a chapter on frontier conflict to be written for its bicentennial publication, *Australia: Two Centuries of War and Peace* (Macintyre & Clark, 2003, p. 205). Written by the historian Richard Broome (1988), the chapter remains one of the best overviews of frontier conflict in Australia. The inclusion of this chapter did not elicit the kind of superheated outrage that would come to define the 'History Wars' some 15 years later. As Stuart Macintyre and Anna Clark (2003, p. 205) noted nearly 20 years ago: 'Back in the 1980s it was still possible to call for a more inclusive commemoration of war without attracting accusations of betrayal.'

Macintyre and Clark's words remind us that perceptions of frontier violence form part of a broader public debate about Australia's colonial past. For its part, the AWM's responses to queries on frontier violence disclose a theme of avoiding the repudiation of past practices while answering to public expectations. Public opinion is notoriously hard to pin down, but historical and curatorial research is one avenue by which it is inferred. In the course of their research, the AWM's curators and historians remain in touch with (and contribute to) the changing contours of historiography. This is as true for the aspects of Australia's history that are obviously within the memorial's remit, such as Australia's involvement in WWI, as it is for more wideranging elements of Australian experiences of war and conflict. Curators and historians are citizens of Australia too and, as such, are aware of the thrust of debates in the public sphere, especially those that impact directly on work carried out at the memorial.

There is also a practical consideration: the AWM holds very few objects relating to the frontier period. This has affected the other colonial-era conflicts too, as the case of the South African (Boer) War reveals. As noted above, the original 1925 Act had established a national memorial for those who had died in the war beginning 4 August 1914. When the legislation was amended in 1952, the memorial's task was changed to cover 'any war or war-like operations in which Australians have been on active service' (Section 3[b]). It was only at this point, 50 years after the signing of the Treaty of Vereeniging, that the AWM began actively collecting objects and manuscripts from the South African War. As former AWM historian Peter Stanley (2007, p. 30) notes, 'the process of collecting (or not collecting), of deciding what should be kept or displayed or emphasised, is an act of historical interpretation'. Common to all stories told at the memorial, the existing collection feeds into decisions about what to display, but there are also processes by which exhibition curators can seek out and acquire new collection material with which to tell stories. Gradual change is evident with regard to frontier violence, with the memorial's most recent *Collection Development Plan* listing 'material related to frontier violence' among collecting priorities (AWM, 2019, Section 14).

Colonial refurbishment

The AWM purchased two significant works of art by noted Aboriginal painters in 2016, both of which relate explicitly to frontier violence. These artworks, Queenie McKenzie's (1996) *Horso Creek Killings* and *Ruby Plains Massacre I* (1985) by Rover Thomas (Joolama) depict events that occurred from the late nineteenth into the early twentieth century in the East Kimberley region of Western Australia. The paintings were first displayed at the entrance to *For Country, for Nation*, a temporary exhibition that related histories of Aboriginal and Torres Strait Islander military service. *For Country, for Nation* was on display at the AWM in 2016 and 2017 and later toured nationally. Because they were painted with traditional pigments on canvas, the artworks were too fragile to go on the exhibition's national tour, and a print of *Ruby Plains Massacre I* joined the travelling exhibition instead. In late 2018, plans were made to put one or both paintings on permanent display in the memorial's galleries. These plans led to a modest refurbishing of the Soldiers of the Queen gallery, which dated from the late 1980s, making it the oldest in the memorial until its dismantling in June 2020. The gallery itself was a museum piece, reminiscent of an older way of presenting history. An example, noted above, was that many of the images in the gallery were uncaptioned; such an approach would be unthinkable now.

A team that included an art historian, curators, exhibition officers and others assembled to refit the selected wall of the gallery. I was the historian on the team, and my role was to research and help write text relating to the objects. *Ruby Plains Massacre I* is based on histories that Gija Elders told Thomas. The painting depicts the aftermath of a massacre of Aboriginal people by white stockmen on Ruby Plains cattle station, probably around the turn of the twentieth century. The bodies were discovered by Aboriginal stockmen, who walked off the station in protest (Thomas, 1985). The text label for *Ruby Plains Massacre I* was carried over, with minor tweaks, from its earlier display. One of my main tasks, therefore, was to write a text label for *Mounted Police and Blacks*, the lithograph noted above that had long been in the gallery but was uncaptioned. Even the relatively straightforward story behind this little lithograph presented challenges for our team.

The attack depicted in the lithograph is the Waterloo Creek (or Slaughterhouse Creek) massacre, which was carried out by British soldiers in a colonial police unit, the New South Wales Mounted Police, on or about 26 January 1838 (see Rogers, 2018b, pp. 30–31). This 'collision', as contemporary British sources called it, occurred when mounted police under Major James Nunn battled with Gomeroi warriors near the Gwydir River in northern New South Wales. One mounted policeman was wounded, and one soldier estimated that 40–50 Gomeroi were killed, although, as always, the exact death toll is impossible to know with certainty (Connor, 2002, pp. 102–113; Ryan, 2003). The New South Wales Mounted Police was originally formed in 1825 to deal with Aboriginal resistance and bushrangers. Its members were British soldiers from the New South Wales garrison, and for this reason the unit has sometimes been referred to as the 'Military Mounted Police' (Milliss, 1992, pp. 15–16; O'Sullivan, 1979, pp. 1–34). The dress-uniform shoulder scales of this unit, dating from the 1840s, were also on display beneath the lithograph. These scales are the earliest known Australian military uniform items to feature Australian native fauna – the kangaroo and emu. *Mounted Police and Blacks* was first published in the memoir of its creator Mundy, a professional officer in the British Army. Mundy was in Sydney from 1846 to 1851 as deputy adjutant-general of British military forces in Australia (Macnab & Ward, 1967).

On display in a history museum, *Mounted Police and Blacks* presents three significant problems. First, Mundy's sketch is not that of an eyewitness – he was not even in the colony when the event occurred. It is believed that he heard about the event from soldiers in the Sydney garrison during his time there (Katz, 2017, pp. 47–49). Second, piecing together the actual timeline of the killings is challenging. There appear to have been two 'firings' or periods of shooting: the first in response to a mounted policeman, Corporal Hannan, being speared in the calf; and the second a short time later that lasted some hours (Ryan, 2003; Watson, 1924, pp. 243–259). The third issue is the perennial problem of numbers killed. This is a particularly acute problem at an institution that is centred on the Roll of Honour, on which the names of all Australians who have died in uniform are listed without rank or decoration (McKernan, 1991, p. 226). In any case, a military history museum would be expected to give an estimate of the number of deaths. Yet none of these problems was insuperable. Much is lost in the fog of war, and many displays in the AWM can only present what is known, or alert visitors to that which cannot be known using surviving records. Three soldiers gave testimony to the inquiry into the 1838 killings at Waterloo Creek, and each gave a different version of events. The commanding officer, Major Nunn, did not go on the second firing, and saw four or five bodies (Watson, 1924, p. 251). Lieutenant Cobban saw four or five bodies as a result of the first firing, so his account matches Major Nunn's. He then saw three or four bodies as a result of the second firing. However, he was not with the main body of men at the second firing, being on the other side of the river from them (Watson, 1924, pp. 255–256). Sergeant John Lee estimated that 40–50 people were killed in the second firing (Watson, 1924, p. 251). He was in the thick of the fighting, and his account provides insight into the nature of the event: 'The confusion was so great and the scrub so thick, that I had enough to do to take care of myself and my horse.' Seeking to explain why the shooting had gone on for so long, he testified: 'It was impossible for the party to act in a body; every man had in fact to act for himself' (Watson, 1924, p. 251). These men gave sworn evidence nearly 18 months after the event took place, in April 1839, after the Myall Creek executions, which could possibly have tempered their evidence.

An AWM exhibition is developed by a team. Our team included an art curator, who was Aboriginal; the Indigenous liaison officer; an exhibitions officer, who, among other things, coordinated the production of display cases and text labels; an objects curator; and a historian. After the text was written, an editor copyedited it to ensure that it conformed to the memorial's style guide. As is usual for work on a permanent display, all the team members were memorial staff. When captioning *Mounted Police and Blacks*, our team was faced with the challenge of transmitting all the relevant, nuanced information via a caption card of perhaps 150 words. The final text label read as follows:

> The Slaughterhouse Creek massacre of 26 January 1838 occurred when the New South Wales Military Mounted Police, under the command of Major James Nunn, set out in response to violence on the Liverpool Plains. At Slaughterhouse Creek, also known as Waterloo Creek, the Mounted Police battled with Gomeroi warriors. A trooper was wounded, and one soldier estimated that 40 or 50 Gomeroi were killed.
>
> This image originally appeared in the 1852 memoirs of Lieutenant Colonel Godfrey Mundy. A professional officer in the British Army, Mundy was in Sydney from 1846 to 1851 as deputy adjutant-general of British military forces in Australia. The Mounted Police at that time was made up of British soldiers, and when he arrived in Sydney Mundy heard about the incident from soldiers in the garrison. He completed this print from his imagination. (AWM, 2020)

Our team hoped that a useful tension could be developed through the juxtaposition of *Ruby Plains Massacre I*, which was based on oral tradition handed down to Thomas, and *Mounted Police and Blacks*, an artwork that was likewise created on the basis of received oral testimony, but for which official documentary evidence also existed. The juxtaposition of two forms of storytelling, one Aboriginal and one British colonial, might generate audience contemplation of the different ways frontier stories might be remembered and told.

The challenges our team faced at a national institution were similar to those faced by the curators at the Wyndham Historical Society Museum, described by Dalley and Barnwell elsewhere in this collection. In preparatory discussions, our team identified the same tension between oral history and written historical records, for example. A major difference between the AWM and the Wyndham museum, however, is that a national museum must appeal to a national audience. To answer this need, we included an overview text panel relating the two frontier incidents to the broader story of frontier conflict across Australia.

Future movement

The AWM's public stance on frontier violence has been a topic of analysis by historians, journalists and other commentators. Some have viewed the memorial's position as indicative of a broader reticence about, or denial of, frontier conflict in Australian public discourse (e.g. Ashenden, 2019; Chun, 2018; Daley, 2021; Inglis, 2008, pp. 423–427, 501–504). Critics have asked why the memorial's stance has not shifted with changing understandings of Australia's history in scholarship. Peter Stanley has speculated that the AWM's council is concerned that acknowledging the frontier wars 'will somehow bring Anzac into disrepute' (quoted in Green, 2014). Others have argued that the memorial has traditionally encouraged a type of white Australian nationalism. In addition to more inclusive forms of commemoration, such as *For Country, for Nation*, these commentators argue, gallery exhibitions on the topic of the frontier wars would be an important step in national reconciliation (Reynolds, 2013; Stephens, 2014).

Whether Australia's frontier conflicts 'belong' in the AWM's galleries remains a live question. Past decisions of the Council of the Australian War Memorial have been guided by interpretation of the Act. The Act defines 'Australian military history' as the history of 'wars and warlike operations in which Australians have been on active service', including in the lead-up to them and the aftermath of them. The Act includes in its definition of the Defence Force 'any naval or military force of the Crown raised in Australia before the establishment of the Commonwealth' (Part I, Section 3). Questions asked in 2008 by the late Ken Inglis, historian of Australia's war memorials, are still relevant. Were British soldiers who were deployed against Aboriginal people on the orders of a colonial governor to be considered 'Australian forces'? Should colonial police or private citizens mustered by the colonial government under martial law be considered 'military' (Inglis, 2008, p. 426)?

The uniform shoulder scales and the artwork *Mounted Police and Blacks* went on display in Soldiers of the Queen at some point in the late 1980s. This fact suggests that the AWM's curators at the time deemed the New South Wales Mounted Police to be a 'military force of the Crown raised in Australia'. These objects met the terms of the Act because the unit was raised by a colonial authority, and the men of the unit were British regular soldiers, led by an officer of the British garrison. In the years since Inglis's book was published, work on frontier histories around Australia has raised other moments in colonial Australian history that might also need to be considered in this light.

Stephen Gapps's 2018 book, *The Sydney Wars* (which, incidentally, won the AWM's inaugural Les Carlyon Literary Prize in 2020), drew attention to the establishment of 'loyal associations' in New South Wales by Governor Hunter in 1800. Raised in response to the threat of an uprising by Irish republicans among recent convicts, these associations comprised property-owning free men in Sydney and Parramatta. They were armed and drilled by garrison soldiers. In 1816, Governor Macquarie ordered more associations to be raised in response to Aboriginal warriors committing 'atrocious Acts of Barbarity on the unoffending Settlers and their Families' in the Nepean and Hawkesbury River districts (Gapps, 2018, pp. 144–146, 247–248; Macquarie, 1816). Among other things, Gapps (2018, p. 9) argues that historians have overlooked the militarisation of early New South Welsh society. Recent work on Australian frontiers shows that other colonies can be similarly characterised. In the Port Phillip District (Victoria), some authorities understood their role to be one of military occupation. They established the first native police force and based its structure on the sepoy armies of British India (Rogers, 2018a, pp. 147–185, 192). In Queensland, the Native Police Corps has been described by its historians as a military force (Bottoms, 2013, pp. 5–6; Ørsted-Jensen, 2011, p. 43; Richards, 2008, pp. 7–9). In Van Diemen's Land (Tasmania) and at the Swan River (Western Australia), colonial authorities put British regular soldiers in charge of armed settlers in pursuit of Aboriginal people (Brodie, 2017, pp. 231–235; Owen, 2016, pp. 72–75). The question for the AWM is whether these varied colonial forces fit the definition of colonial-raised military units, as stipulated by the Act.

Conclusion: The frontier at the AWM

Violence was an important means by which the British dispossessed Aboriginal and Torres Strait Islander peoples across Australia. Histories of frontier warfare, however, were largely ignored by Australian historians for much of the twentieth century. In stark contrast, the remembrance of twentieth-century warfare in Australia has been marked by ritual and tradition, both grassroots and state-sponsored. The AWM was conceived in the shocking industrial warfare of WWI, and it serves as a shrine, a museum and an archive of the wartime experiences of Australians. Its role has been debated since it opened, with questions being asked about whose stories were to be told and the manner in which they should be told.

As the case study of *Mounted Police and Blacks* shows, frontier violence is a very different conflict from the overseas, twentieth-century conflicts that have formed the mainstay of the memorial's permanent exhibitions. The familiar hallmarks are absent: clearly defined combatants, an accurate estimate of casualties, and a great distance between the physical fighting and the mainstream of Australian society. Mundy's artwork instead refers to a sporadic conflict that took place here, where we live, and involved armed and unarmed civilians as well as military, police and warriors. Casualties were not always recorded, and colonial authorities and settlers often deliberately understated Aboriginal losses. A code of silence reigned. For the AWM, questions of classification also arise. Do ad hoc and mixed military–civilian colonial forces equate to military forces raised by the Crown? Where do colonial police sit in this?

The AWM's Act informs the council's position on frontier violence. In 1952, colonial armed forces entered the memorial's remit, as did the causes and consequences of war in 1980. Collecting activity belies the seeming hard line of the memorial's public statements, with acquisitions relating to frontier warfare dating back to at least the mid-1980s. The placing of some of these objects on permanent display suggests an evolution in the memorial's approach to the frontier wars, but the direction the memorial will take in the future remains to be seen.

Acknowledgements

I am grateful for the constructive questions posed by the other panellists. I also thank my colleagues at the Australian War Memorial: Michael Bell, Margaret Farmer, Lachlan Grant, Karl James and Andrew McDonald, who read earlier drafts and with whom I have had productive discussions on this topic.

References

Ashenden, D. (2019, 15 January). Saving the war memorial from itself. *Inside Story*. insidestory.org.au/saving-the-war-memorial-from-itself/

Attwood, B. & Foster, S. G. (2003). Introduction. In B. Attwood & S. G. Foster (Eds.), *Frontier conflict: The Australian experience* (pp. 1–26). National Museum of Australia.

Australian War Memorial. (2014, 27 January). *Will the Australian War Memorial tell the story of colonial conflicts?* awm.gov.au/media/press-releases/will-australian-war-memorial-tell-story-colonial-conflicts

Australian War Memorial. (2019). National *Collection Development Plan, 2019–2022*. awm.gov.au/about/organisation/corporate/national-collection-development-plan

Australian War Memorial. (2020). [Museum label for Godfrey Mundy, *Mounted police and blacks*]. awm.gov.au/collection/C174087

Australian War Memorial. (2021). *About the Australian War Memorial*. awm.gov.au/about

Australian War Memorial Act 1925 (Commonwealth, No. 18, 1925). classic.austlii.edu.au/au/legis/cth/num_act/awma1925181925271/

Australian War Memorial Act 1952 (Commonwealth, No. 12, 1952). legislation.gov.au/Details/C1952A00012

Australian War Memorial Act 1980 (Commonwealth, No. 104, 1980). legislation.gov.au/Details/C2016C01079

Batman, J. (1835). *Journal, 10 May – 11 June 1835*. State Library of Victoria, MS 13181. handle.slv.vic.gov.au/10381/249297

Blainey, Geoffrey. (1979). Letter to Robin Wade, 2 April. In *Proposed alterations to the AWM building – 1978*. Australian War Memorial, AWM315 234/003/007, part 2.

Bottoms, T. (2013). *Conspiracy of silence: Queensland's frontier killing times*. Allen & Unwin.

Boyce, J. (2013). *1835: The founding of Melbourne and the conquest of Australia*. Black Inc.

Brodie, N. (2017). *The Vandemonian war: The secret history of Britain's Tasmanian invasion*. Hardie Grant.

Broome, R. (1988). The struggle for Australia: Aboriginal–European warfare, 1770–1930. In M. McKernan & M. Browne (Eds.), *Australia: Two centuries of war & peace* (pp. 92–120). Australian War Memorial.

Broome, R. (2010). *Aboriginal Australians: A history since 1788* (4th ed.). Allen & Unwin.

Chun, M. (2018, 3 May). Enduring silence: Anzac Day and the Frontier Wars. *Overland*. overland.org.au/2018/05/enduring-silence-anzac-day-and-the-frontier-wars/

Coates, J. (2006). *An atlas of Australia's wars* (2nd ed.). Oxford University Press.

Connor, J. (2002). *The Australian frontier wars, 1788–1838*. University of New South Wales Press.

Connor, J. (2008). Frontier wars. In P. Dennis, J. Grey, E. Morris, R. Prior & J. Bou (Eds.), *The Oxford companion to Australian military history* (2nd ed., pp. 216–221). Oxford University Press. doi.org/10.1093/acref/9780195517842.001.0001

Daley, P. (2021, Autumn). Fault lines at the Australian War Memorial. *Meanjin*. meanjin.com.au/essays/fault-lines/

Gammage, B. (2011). *The biggest estate on Earth: How Aborigines made Australia*. Allen & Unwin.

Gapps, S. (2018). *The Sydney wars: Conflict in the early colony, 1788–1817*. University of New South Wales Press.

Green, M. (2014, 25 February). Lest we remember: The Australian War Memorial and the frontier wars. michaelbgreen.com.au/lest-we-remember/

Grey, J. (2008). *A military history of Australia* (3rd ed.). Cambridge University Press. doi.org/10.1017/CBO9780511481345

Inglis, K. S. (2008). *Sacred places: War memorials in the Australian landscape* (3rd ed.). Melbourne University Press.

Katz, M. (2017). *Not as the songs of other lands: Nineteenth-century Australian and American landscape painting*. Ian Potter Museum of Art, University of Melbourne. art-museum.unimelb.edu.au/exhibitions/not-as-the-songs-of-other-lands-19th-century-australian-and-american-landscape-painting/

Larsson, M. (2009). *Shattered Anzacs: Living with the scars of war*. University of New South Wales Press.

Macintyre, S. & Clark, A. (2003). *The history wars*. Melbourne University Press.

Macnab, K. & Ward, R. (1967). Mundy, Godfrey Charles (1804–1860). In *Australian Dictionary of Biography*. Melbourne University Press. adb.anu.edu.au/biography/mundy-godfrey-charles-2490/text3351

Macquarie, Governor Lachlan. (1816, 20 July). [Proclamation]. *Sydney Gazette and NSW Advertiser* (p. 1). nla.gov.au/nla.news-article2176728

McKenzie, Q. (1996). *Horso Creek killings* [natural earth pigments on canvas]. Australian War Memorial, AWM2017.665.1. awm.gov.au/collection/C2584648

McKernan, M. (1991). *Here is their spirit: A history of the Australian War Memorial, 1917–1990*. University of Queensland Press.

Milliss, R. (1992). *Waterloo Creek: The Australia Day massacre of 1838, George Gipps and the British conquest of New South Wales*. University of New South Wales Press.

Mitchell, T. (1839). *Three expeditions into the interior of eastern Australia* (Vol. 2). T. & W. Boone.

Mundy, G. C. (1852). *Mounted police and blacks* [lithograph]. Australian War Memorial, ART50023. awm.gov.au/collection/C174087

Nettelbeck, A. (2011). The Australian frontier in the museum. *Journal of Social History 44*(4), 1115–1128. doi.org/10.1353/jsh.2011.0047

Ørsted-Jensen, R. (2011). *Frontier history revisited: Colonial Queensland and the 'History War'*. Lux Mundi Publishing.

O'Sullivan, J. (1979). *Mounted police in NSW*. Rigby Ltd.

Owen, C. (2016). *'Every mother's son is guilty': Policing the Kimberley frontier of Western Australia, 1882–1905*. UWA Press.

Pedersen, P. (2010). *The Anzacs: Gallipoli to the Western Front*. Penguin Books.

Reynolds, H. (1982). *The other side of the frontier: Aboriginal resistance to the European invasion of Australia*. Penguin.

Reynolds, H. (2013). *Forgotten war*. University of New South Wales Press.

Richards, J. (2008). *The secret war: A true history of Queensland's native police*. University of Queensland Press.

Rogers, T. J. (2018a). *The civilisation of Port Phillip: Settler ideology, violence, and rhetorical possession*. Melbourne University Press.

Rogers, T. J. (2018b). From the frontier to the veldt: Indigenous Australian service, 1788–1902. In L. Grant & M. Bell (Eds.), *For Country, for nation: An illustrated history of Aboriginal and Torres Strait Islander military service* (pp. 29–39). Australian War Memorial.

Rogers, T. J. (2019a). Anzac trauma and frontier violence? Re-examining the Coniston Massacre. In K. Reeves and C. Holbrook (Eds.), *The Great War: Aftermath and commemoration* (pp. 124–134). University of New South Wales Press.

Rogers, T. J. (2019b). William Murray and the Coniston massacre: A returned soldier's frontier crimes were probably not a result of his war service. *Wartime 85*, 36–40.

Rowley, C. D. (1970). *The destruction of Aboriginal society*. Australian National University Press.

Ryan, L. (2003). Waterloo Creek, northern New South Wales, 1838. In B. Attwood & S. G. Foster (Eds.), *Frontier conflict: The Australian experience* (pp. 33–43). National Museum of Australia.

Stanley, P. (1981). 'While acting under orders': The Slaughterhouse Creek massacre of 1838. Unpublished paper. *Australian War Memorial Military History Conference*, Australian War Memorial, Canberra.

Stanley, P. (2007). In the 'street of the historians': Practising history at the Australian War Memorial. *Dialogue, 26*(2), 30–38.

Stanner, W. E. H. (2009). *The Dreaming & other essays*. Black Inc. Agenda.

Stephens, Alan. (2014, 7 July). Reconciliation means recognising the Frontier Wars. *ABC News: The Drum*. abc.net.au/news/2014-07-07/stephens-reconciliation-means-recognising-the-frontier-wars/5577436

Thomas, R. (1985). *Ruby Plains Massacre I* [natural earth pigments on canvas]. Australian War Memorial, AWM2016.718.1. awm.gov.au/collection/C2148046

Watson, F. (Ed.). (1924). *Historical records of Australia*, Series I, Vol. XX. Library Committee of the Commonwealth Parliament.

12

Blue sky mining and *Sweet Country*: Is it too soon to commemorate colonial violence?[1]

Chris Healy

Galk dhelk
djuwima
djalpunda
ngurari guli
ngurari gurrk

Manna Gum Avenue shows respect and remembers our ancestors
Frontier Wars

In July 2021, north of Melbourne, in Dja Dja Wurrung Country just outside of Daylesford, a stand of manna gum trees (*Eucalyptus viminalis*) marked with a bilingual roadside sign (Figure 12.1) joined the small corpus of memorials to colonial violence in Australia. As is so often the case with memorialisation, there were plural invocations of temporality at the opening of the memorial: future present, future past, present past. Mayor of Hepburn Shire Council Lesley Hewitt claimed that 'acts of reconciliation such as this change attitudes to settlement and show a willingness to work together for a better future'. Rodney Carter, Dja Dja Wurrung Clans

---

1 Since completing this essay an important book on commemoration has appeared that would have informed my work here. See Carlson and Farrelly (2023)

Aboriginal Corporation CEO, said: 'The Frontier Wars Memorial Avenue affords a greater recognition to our fallen Ancestors and helps us all heal.' The shire newsletter claimed: 'The establishment of this Avenue of Honour is a public acknowledgement, the first of its kind in our country' ('Manna gums memorial', 2021).[2]

Figure 12.1. Hepburn Memorial.
Photograph: Chris Healy.

---

2   A videorecording of the opening is available at youtu.be/NADNki7sy0Q.

While that avenue of honour might well be 'the first of its kind', and while I have no interest in condemning moderate municipal boasting, it is important to be clear that in 2021 'public acknowledgement' of 'colonial violence' was neither new nor transparently elementary. This essay contributes to conceptualising some complex configurations of remembrance by proceeding from specific starting points. I can borrow the first starting point from the language of the Hepburn Shire newsletter and state simply that from the very beginning – when Lieutenant James Cook's crew confronted Gweagal men on the shore of Kamay – the colonisation of Australia has been violent in ways that have been publicly, if not always and not fully, acknowledged. Hence, to imagine commemoration – a form of remembering after the fact – as compensatory, or as an antidote to 'Indigenous absence' or 'silence' is neither accurate nor useful. Indeed, there are substantial histories of remembering in the domain of Aboriginality and Australian Indigenous presence, including work by both First Nations intellectuals and others, like me, who want to insist that Australian Indigenous peoples never 'disappeared', were never historically absent and, importantly for my purposes here, have certainly never forgotten colonial violence. Rather, if there has been forgetting, it has been non-Indigenous people forgetting the history of colonising and its multiple acts of dispossession and, in some cases, attempts to annihilate First Nations people. In other words, memorials to colonial violence exist within the temporally, spatially and culturally differential ebbs and flows of remembrance.

This leads to my second point: that much of Australia can be thought of as a landscape of organised forgetting embedded in forms of nationalism that are themselves celebrations of colonisation. These range from transplanted practices of naming and the establishment of 'Old Colonists' associations to the mourning of the 'passing of the Aborigine' and the memorialisation of the 'the last of' this or that 'tribe', from the physical removal of Australian Indigenous peoples from their lands to the legislation of so many kinds of 'special treatment', and from 'recognising Aborigines' on the basis of non-Indigenous criteria to the selective inclusion of respectable 'Aborigines'. With these and so many other gestures, the settler-colonial state imagines whitefellas as becoming Indigenous in a narrative of succession (Thomas, 1999). It is in this imaginative landscape that I ask whether the commemoration of colonial violence is, like 'Aboriginal art', a 'white thing' (Bell, 2002). Of course, I mean this provocatively, as does Richard Bell in the formulation that I am borrowing. I am certainly not posing the question as offering a fair or exhaustive motif, but it does enable me to think about how the vitality of such commemoration is distributed. My purpose in adopting this characterisation is not to go hunting for commemorations of colonial violence that disclose their whiteness and, hence, their inadequacy. Bell's 'theorem' forces me, as a non-Indigenous writer, to examine my own investment in settler-colonial forms of memorialisation, and to assess more broadly the energies unleashed and constrained by the commemoration of colonial violence, as these energies can be mapped across settler-colonial and Australian Indigenous communities of practice.

Here I consider two contemporary instances of Australian Indigenous engagement with the violence of colonisation. The first focuses on mining at Wittenoom, the site of a blue asbestos mine in the north-west of Western Australia between 1942 and 1966, and where in the decades since its closure local Traditional Owners have been campaigning to have their Country rehabilitated. In this case, I am trying to understand how it is that an 'industrial disaster' that led to so many deaths from asbestos-related disease has been memorialised, while the deaths of Traditional Owners and the damage to Country has been phlegmatically tolerated by the state as unremarkable – as business as usual.

The second instance considers Australian Indigenous deaths in custody. I contrast a memorial to colonial-era 'freedom fighters' with the way in which *Sweet Country*, a film set in the Northern Territory in the early part of the twentieth century, evokes colonialism's violence (Thornton, 2017). I argue that *Sweet Country* sets up a continuity between the extrajudicial killing of Sam and the ongoing catastrophe of Australian Indigenous deaths in custody. At first blush, these two very disparate instances of Australian Indigenous engagement with the damage wrought by mining and incarceration do not seem to be in the least commemorative. However, I will argue that in their attention to the ways in which colonisation has brought destruction to Country and death to Australian Indigenous people, these instances are deeply memorial, not in commemorating the dead but in mobilising the forces of memory as an urgent call to end such violence and seek reparative justice. What whitefellas might learn from these forms of First Nations 'commemoration' is that unless and until there is full respect and legal recognition of the multiple forms of First Nations sovereignty – to Country, narratives, languages, cultural property and so on – commemoration in this settler colony will too often have to be a demand on the future rather than a lament, a mourning or a history lesson.

Wittenoom

> A breach of our values
>
> We apologise unreservedly to the Puutu Kunti Kurrama and Pinikura (PKKP) people, and to people across Australia and beyond, for the destruction of Juukan Gorge.
>
> In allowing the destruction of Juukan Gorge to occur, we fell far short of our values as a company and breached the trust placed in us by the Traditional Owners of the lands on which we operate. It is our collective responsibility to ensure that the destruction of a site of such exceptional cultural significance never happens again, to earn back the trust that has been lost and to re-establish our leadership in communities and social performance. (Rio Tinto, n.d.)

On 24 May 2020, as part of the expansion of their Brockman 4 mine in the Hamersley Range in the Pilbara, and with the aim of stripping high-grade iron ore worth approximately A$135 million, RioTinto workers blew up an area of their leasehold and, in the process, destroyed two ancient shelters. The company knew these shelters were both sacred to the Puutu Kunti Kurrama and Pinikura peoples and of considerable archaeological significance, having been continuously occupied for around 40,000 years. What was extraordinary about this destruction of sacred places is not that it happened, nor that it happened legally and with all the appropriate approvals, but that it had remarkable consequences (Allam & Wahlquist, 2021). In Australia, mining and other extractive industries have routinely destroyed Country and desecrated sites of major significance to Indigenous peoples. Near where I live, Dja Dja Wurrung recall the destruction of their Country wrought by mid-nineteenth-century gold mining with the term 'upside down Country'. This damage visibly and prolifically still marks the land around towns such as Castlemaine (Dja Dja Wurrung Clans Aboriginal Corporation, n.d.).

Today, most intensive, large-scale mining occurs hundreds of kilometres away from major population centres. High degrees of mechanisation and automation mean that mining depends on a relatively small workforce, who are often visible outside of regional and remote Australia only in queues of high-vis-attired, fly-in-fly-out workers in airport terminals waiting for connecting flights. Of course, mining is publicly legible in the presence of purpose-built communities, and in national account data and company balance sheets. It is a matter of concern when the price of minerals fluctuates on international exchange markets or when a major shareholder like Andrew Forrest receives (another) multibillion-dollar dividend payment.

Mining has been the focus of some of the most important struggles for Indigenous rights in Australian history, including the Yirrkala bark petitions opposing the development of a bauxite mine and alumina smelter at Gove (1963), the fight by Mirarr peoples against the Ranger uranium mine in the Northern Territory (1970s), the blockade against drilling for oil at Noonkanbah, Western Australia (1980s), contemporary opposition to a gas process plant at James Price Point in Western Australia, led by the Goolarabooloo people, and the ongoing Wangan and Jagalingou fight against the Carmichael coal mine in central Queensland (Scambary, 2013). In a major historical shift, most mining ventures today involve negotiations and agreement-making with Australian Indigenous people as Traditional Owners under native title and other provisions.

The extent to which Traditional Owners are enabled to enter into, or refuse to enter into, genuine agreements is an area of significant disputation. Marcia Langton (2015), for one, is upbeat on the matter, while other scholars who have surveyed and assessed a significant number of extant agreements are less enthusiastic. However, two things about contemporary mining are clear: first, the various state-based and federal regulatory regimes pertaining to mining are designed and operated primarily to enable mining; second, the demolition of the Juukan Gorge shelters is but a recent example of a regime of colonial violence in which the devastation of Country, including sites of heritage significance to Traditional Owners, is business as usual (Allam & Wahlquist, 2020).[3] This should not be surprising, given that Indigenous heritage protection is subordinate to resource extraction, and that, in the absence of a right of refusal, Traditional Owners are required to negotiate and are often poorly matched in negotiations over compensation (see Cleary, 2021).

***

---

3   Currently, BHP has 'approval to destroy at least 40 – and possibly as many as 86 – significant Aboriginal sites in the central Pilbara to expand its A$4.5bn South Flank iron ore mining operation, even though its own reports show the Traditional Owners are opposed to the move' (Allam & Wahlquist, 2020).

Figure 12.2. Plaque commemorating Western Australians who have died from asbestos-related diseases.
Source: Produced by the Asbestos Diseases Society and Unions WA. Father Ted Doncaster. Monuments Australia.

> THEY SHALL NEVER BE FORGOTTEN
>
> While the devastation of the lives of Wittenoom workers and their families continues unabated, WE VOW never to forget and [to] keep fighting for justice and to save lives. Rest in peace dear friends.
>
> August 18, 2018
> Asbestos Diseases Society of Australia Inc. (ADSA) (See Figure 12.2)

This inscription, along with some shockingly ordinary photographs of non-Indigenous men, women and children playing and working at Wittenoom, appears on a memorial plaque dedicated to those whose lives have been devastated by asbestos-related diseases caused by living and working at Wittenoom, the site of what is sometimes called Australia's worst industrial disaster.[4] The significance of Wittenoom is well known, so I will rehearse it only briefly here (see Layman & Phillips, 2019; Soeberg et al., 2018).

---

4   I have not visited the memorial, so my comments about the photographs are based on my assessment of images online. See asbestosdiseases.org.au/perthbiz_home_slider/wittenoom-unveiling-of-a-lasting-memorial/

Around 100 kilometres north-west of Juukan Gorge, the traditional lands of the Banjima, Kurrama and Innawonga people were taken up as pastoral leases by the early part of the twentieth century. Following a short-lived, minor asbestos rush in the 1920s, Lang Hancock and his business partner Peter Wright built an asbestos crushing mill at Wittenoom in 1939, which was bought by CSR four years later when mining began in Wittenoom Gorge. In 1947, a company town was built, and by the 1950s it was the Pilbara's largest town. During the 1950s and early 1960s, Wittenoom was Australia's only supplier of blue asbestos. The mine was shut down in 1966 due to unprofitability. In the decades since, Wittenoom has lived on in three major forms. There have been hard-fought campaigns by workers injured by asbestos exposure to receive recognition and compensation (see Hills, 1989). Second, there have been protracted efforts to 'close' – to prohibit public access to – the site of the former town – efforts that, quite bizarrely, are ongoing (Government of Western Australia, 2021). Third, Banjima and other Australian Indigenous people have sought to have damage to their people recognised and the devastated Country rehabilitated.

The effects of asbestos mining on Australian Indigenous people were first brought to widespread public attention through the impact of James Hardie's mine on Bundjalung people and Country in New South Wales. This was followed by a significant report that recommended, among other things, 'complete rehabilitation' of the Baryulgil mine and mill (Haigh, 2006; McCulloch, 2007; Parliament of the Commonwealth of Australia, 1984; Peacock, 1978, 2009). Aboriginal workers were more heavily involved in the production process at the Baryulgil mine than at Wittenoom, where they tended to work in bagging and transport rather than mining. At Wittenoom, they were marginalised, living with their families in fringe camps rather than in the town proper. Despite this, a 2016 study found that '67 per cent of mesothelioma cases affecting Indigenous West Australians could be linked directly to asbestos mining at the Wittenoom Gorge in the Pilbara' and concluded that 'Indigenous West Australians have the highest death rate for malignant mesothelioma in the world' (Franklin et al., 2016, cited in Sargent, 2016). The danger posed by the Wittenoom mine was radically reduced for most people when the mine closed in 1966, although asbestos-related diseases often take decades to manifest, and products containing Wittenoom's blue asbestos continue to pose a risk to health. However, for Banjima people and Country, the afterlife of the mine continues to pose grave risks. There has been minimal rehabilitation of the mine site and processing facilities, with the result that 'the declared contaminated site comprises 50,000 hectares (120,000 acres), making it the "largest contaminated site in the southern hemisphere"', covering approximately 3 million cubic metres of tailings in the Wittenoom Gorge, and areas where contamination has washed into neighbouring waterways (Macmath, 2019).[5] The Western Australian Department of Planning, Lands and Heritage, which is responsible for the site, has explicitly identified Banjima people as the 'highest risk user group'. In the same presentation, they claimed that a two-year study had concluded that remediation was 'cost prohibitive'; hence, they have focused on 'restricting access and risk management'. As far as I can determine, there have been no publicly available costings for remediation, nor any consideration of how remediation might be funded from mining company profit or state government mining-excise funds.[6]

***

> The NAIDOC 2021 theme – Heal Country! – calls for all of us to continue to seek greater protections for our lands, our waters, our sacred sites and our cultural heritage from exploitation, desecration, and destruction …
>
> For generations we have been calling for stronger measures to recognise, protect, and maintain all aspects of our culture and heritage.
>
> We are still waiting for those robust protections …
>
> Healing Country means finally resolving many of the outstanding injustices which impact on the lives of our people. (NAIDOC, 2021)

---

5   There is a low level of awareness of risks among the highest risk user group. Work is underway to quantify current exposure and develop management strategies.
6   In May 2023, the Western Australian Government brought down a State Budget with a $4.73 billion surplus, largely thanks to revenue from record iron ore prices.

Figure 12.3. Mine tailings, Wittenoom, Western Australia.
Source: Creative Commons.

Banjima people have long sought reparative justice in relation to the despoilment of Wittenoom. The departmental report referred to above came on the back of a 2019 award-winning ABC *Earshot* documentary examining the impact of Wittenoom on Australian Indigenous peoples. That radio documentary and the online reporting made clear both the scale of the devastation of Country and the desire of Banjima to have their Country rehabilitated. Yet, more than two years later, the only government action in relation to Wittenoom has concerned the final chapter in the long-running saga to 'close' the town. This is basically an attempt to restrict tourist access to the area, incidents of which are periodically noted in newspaper articles such as 'Ignorant Influencers Slammed for Risking Their Lives to Holiday in Asbestos-Riddled Wittenoom' (Ryan, 2020). Consequently, in 2021, the call to attend to the tailings at Wittenoom came in NAIDOC (National Aborigines and Islanders Day Observance Committee) week in the form of another ABC Radio documentary. Again, the public face of the campaign was Banjima Elder Maitland Parker:

> The tailings dumps have been blown by wind and rained on for decades, causing asbestos pollution to move down into the Fortescue River valley and catchment from Wittenoom Gorge after rains flush through the deep gorges of the Karijini National Park ... Mr Parker is concerned the country all the way to Millstream may be polluted, making it unsafe for Aboriginal people to do their cultural business while fishing, swimming, camping and visiting the affected areas ... 'The RIOs, the BHPs, the FMGs, Hancock, they all need to step up and take responsibility for maintaining the heritage of Aboriginal land they access,' Mr Parker said. (Standen, 2021)

The only response thus far from the state government came from lands minister Dr Buti, who said:

> The Wittenoom Steering Committee will reconvene to progress ongoing management options and advise the state government on what actions could be considered to maintain public safety in the area and reduce ongoing impact on Country. (Standen, 2021)

They have been considering those matters for 55 years.

At around the same time, Traditional Owners were again putting the case to 'Heal Country', and the Asbestos Diseases Society of Australia (ADSA) was mounting a campaign to have permanent memorial sculptures erected in Perth and in the Karijini National Park:

> We are proposing permanent memorials be erected in Perth and ... in Karijini National Park, naming the thousands of workers, residents, Traditional Owners and their family members who have lost their lives to asbestos-related diseases. (ADSA, n.d.)

The ADSA is, no doubt, well-intentioned in including a mention of Traditional Owners, and the absence of Indigenous people in the 2018 memorial has been replaced by a commitment to consult: 'We will also be visiting the Shire of Ashburton and the Traditional Owners of the land to discuss the best way forward in the Pilbara.' But it is no secret what Banjima people want, and it is not another memorial. Sincerity aside, it seems the ADSA's proposal is particularly odd, because they already have an artwork in mind and have gained permission from the artist, Jan Senberg, whose work *Blue Angel of Wittenoom* (1988) is the work in question. It is an expressionist painting of the processing plant at the entrance to Wittenoom Gorge. The right-hand third of the painting is taken up by a massive blue figure, clearly recognisable as a copy of a Wandjina figure. Wandjina are sacred to Ngarinyin, Worrorra and Wunambul people in the Kimberley, a long way from Banjima Country. In 1988, Jan Senberg should have known that this image was not his to appropriate and that it had no place in the Karijini National Park (Browning, 2019).

The destruction of the Juukan Gorge shelters and the unremediated catastrophe of Wittenoom are differing cases, but, for at least two reasons, both might give pause to any impulse for commemoration in a straightforward sense. First, in each case, First Nations sovereignty continues to be radically 'forgotten' as it is subordinate to the primacy of extractive industries. Second, these cases represent recent and continuing processes – not some legacy, not past, not over and done with. On the contrary: as I was revising this essay, the ABC reported that a freedom of information action on behalf of Banjima Tradition Owners had disclosed that Hancock Prospecting, a company owned by Lang Hancock's daughter Gina Rinehart, had, in 2008, proposed to mine for iron ore on contaminated Country near Wittenoom (Robinson, 2022). In the case of both the shelters and Wittenoom, what's alive and animating are the actions and determination of First Nations people who continue to remember ongoing dispossession and injustice, and to demand rights and reparation. They hope to make a future that might commemorate their persistence.

Sweet Country

The following inscription can be found on a public artwork commemorating the resistance to colonial settlement mounted by two Aboriginal men in Victoria in the early 1840s. Their struggle is commemorated annually in Melbourne (Figure 12.4):

> [Right side inscription]
>
> This artwork was initiated by the Tunnerminnerwait and Maulboyheenner Commemoration Committee, which holds a gathering here annually to honour the two men who were executed by public hanging on this location at midday, 20 January 1842.
>
> Commissioned by the City of Melbourne

12. BLUE SKY MINING AND *SWEET COUNTRY*

Figure 12.4. Invitation to the 2020 Tunnerminnerwait and Maulboyheenner Commemoration Committee.
Source: 3CR.

In 1842, Tunnerminnerwait and Maulboyheenner were the first people killed by public, judicially sanctioned hanging in the Port Philip District. The two Aboriginal men had been brought to the very new outpost of Melbourne from Tasmania by George Augustus Robinson, chief protector of Aborigines in the district of Port Philip (1838–1849). The men were part of a group of five that included Trugernana, Planobeena and Probelattener. They left Melbourne and headed east to the area around Western Port Bay, where, over a period of weeks, they stole from settler colonials, burned their property and attacked them, killing two whale hunters. The artwork that constitutes the memorial, *Standing by Tunnerminnerwait and Maulboyheenner*, is located on Victoria Street between the Old Melbourne Gaol and the cemetery where the men would be buried, now the site of the Queen Victoria Market. The artists, Brook Andrew and Trent Walker, created the work with several elements, including six colourful news-stand boxes each containing commentary on the men, and the oversized frame of a playground swing, its two chains not suspending a swing-seat but anchored to a coffin-like box of bluestone, one for each man whose name is engraved in the stone (Andrew & Walker, 2016). The work is surrounded by bluestone paving and sits among indigenous medicinal plants that are useful for regeneration and native to the landscape of the Parperloihener clan (Cape Grim), Iarapuna (Bay of Fires), and Woiworung and Boonwurrung of the Kulin Nation (Melbourne). Dr Joseph Toscano, convenor of the 'Tunnerminnerwait and Maulboyheenner Commemoration Committee', celebrated the memorial as 'the first significant monument to the frontier wars in any major capital city in this country, 175 years after the execution' (Toscano, 2019; see also Grieves et al., 2014; Land, 2014). It is, in many ways, an impressive commemorative monument, but it is worth noting that it draws no connection to the contemporary catastrophe of Australian

Indigenous imprisonment and deaths in custody. Perhaps it is not fair to ask this of the artwork; perhaps it is useful and evocative to memorialise the two men as executed freedom fighters; and perhaps the annual January ceremony at the artwork has already made connections between these colonial executions and the death in custody of Tanya Day, a 55-year-old Yorta Yorta woman in December 2017 or the death in custody of Frank 'Gud' Coleman, a 43-year-old Ngemba man in July 2021, or any of the nearly 500 Australian Indigenous men and women who have died in prison or police custody in the 30 years since the Royal Commission into Aboriginal Deaths in Custody (Allam, 2021).

Sweet County takes a different approach. The very first scene of the film takes us not to the beginning of this story but, in a leap forward in time, to a scene that perhaps refers to events we see later in the film, while affectively recalling the horrific, institutional violence of places like Don Dale Youth Detention Centre in the Northern Territory, where a young Dylan Voller was assaulted, hooded and 'restrained' in 2015. So uncanny is the evocation of custodial violence that the soundtrack of this screen could have been lifted straight from the 2021 documentary, *Incarceration Nation* (Gibson, 2021). In the opening shot of *Sweet Country*, a billy comes to the boil over an open fire. As tea and then sugar is added, we hear non-diegetic sounds. The dialogue is angry and begins with the voice of a white man:

> 'What are you fuckin' doin' standing around?'
> [subtitled] 'Back to work! Work!'
> 'Eh.'
> 'Oi.'
> 'That's it, walk away. Fuckin' idiot.'
> [subtitled] 'You want to hit me. Come on! Come on!'

The dialogue becomes chaotic as we hear blows raining down on flesh, and cicadas become louder and louder, gradually filling the soundscape – then:

> [subtitled] 'Ok, leave him alone! Ok, that's enough!'

Finally, the relief of silence as the opening credits begin.

Sweet Country was inspired by, and based on, a true story told to David Tranter, the co-writer, by his grandfather, a story handed down through Tranter's family.[7] The film is set in the Northern Territory in 1929 and

---

7   In 2007, the screenwriters David Tranter and Steven McGregor made a documentary called *Wilaberta Jack*, based on this story. See Tranter (2007).

12. BLUE SKY MINING AND *SWEET COUNTRY*

magnificently shot around Alice Springs. Sam (Hamilton Morris) is an Australian Indigenous stockman who kills a deranged white station owner, Harry March (Ewen Leslie) in self-defence. Sam and his wife Lizzie (Natassia Gorey-Furber) head out bush on the run. They are chased by a posse of white men and an Australian Indigenous tracker, Archie (Gibson John), but evade capture until Sam decides to give himself up because of the health of his wife who is pregnant after being raped by Harry March. Sam is put on trial and acquitted, only to be shot and killed as he returns home a free man. The story of *Sweet Country* is a deeply unsettling reflection of settler colonialism. Rather than colonisers becoming in place, this is a film about white men as unhinged, obsessive, violent, drunk failures. Rather than being threatened by 'natives', these men are waging war against those who belong to Country. Rather than triumphing, the settler colonials of *Sweet Country* are doomed to a deracinated life of rape, murder and barbarism. While *Sweet Country* is widely described as a 'Western', it fits much more obviously, as Collins and Davis argue, within a broader landscape tradition, one that is based on Australian Indigenous understandings and experiences of Country. But *Sweet Country* is also a deeply historical film in the ways in which it seeks to dismantle conventions of the Western. Country in *Sweet Country* is agential and at the centre of things. White men do not dominate Country through the omnipotence of the wide shot and a possessive musical score, but are both impotently violent and pathetic behind closed doors, blind to the obvious, blustering on their liminal verandahs or lost in Country. The storytelling of the film is nonlinear but disturbingly nimble in moving us around in time.

For me, the character of Philomac (played by twins Tremayne and Trevon Doolan) is at the centre of *Sweet Country*. Philomac is the son of Pansy, an Australian Indigenous woman, and Mick Kennedy (Thomas M White), the owner of Acacia Downs Station. It is Philomac's actions that precipitate the entire narrative when, after Kennedy loans him out to work for Harry March, March chains him to a boulder because he suspects that Philomac will steal from him. Philomac escapes – using a pocketknife that he stole from Archie when Kennedy (his father), has him beaten for a minor infraction at the station – and heads to Black Hill Station, where Sam and Lizzie live. March and Archie pursue Philomac to the station. March, believing that Sam is 'harbouring a deserter', shapes up to shoot Sam, only to be killed when Sam fires first. After Sam and Lizzie head to the bush, Philomac, who has witnessed the shooting, steals a watch and tobacco pouch from March's corpse.

279

There is a repetitive return to Philomac throughout the film in ways that seem to serve no diegetic purpose, nor are these segments didactically concerned with character development or psychology.[8] Because of this, we could understand Philomac as standing for a number of racist cliches that are deeply entrenched in settler-colonial culture: 'half-caste', thief, troublemaker, treacherous person. Yet Philomac is also on his Country; he will not be enslaved and he is connected to kin. He refuses again and again the option of becoming white that is offered by his father's patrician condescension and by the 'magic' of some of the white objects he acquires, particularly Harry March's watch, which Philomac drops into a waterhole. He is both a young Sam and a future survivor who has learned how to adroitly negotiate two worlds. In this sense, he carries forward the memory of violence of the frontier and the barbarism of carceral colonialism.

As in my discussion of Wittenoom, this account of some aspects of *Sweet Country* might seem to be a riff on Patrick Wolfe's well-known characterisation of 'invasion as a structure not an event' (Wolfe, 2006). Wolfe's characterisation was drawn from, and reiterated, arguments within Western Marxism in which 'structuralism' was cast in opposition to 'historical empiricism'. This characterisation has been widely welcomed as a formulation that locates colonialism as enduringly of the present rather than in the past. However, I have always thought of it as having a specific Australian resonance, in that it refuses the banality of a nationalist history that is deeply enamoured with a story of progress in which First Nations peoples come ever closer to the prosperous egalitarianism of Australia. Patrick Wolfe was much too thoughtful a scholar not to understand the significance of 'events', and just as we can think of structures as constituted by events, so events, as phenomena, are structured by the conditions that enable them. I think Warwick Thornton comes from the same mould. His films recursively chart structures: Country, family, white racism, dispossession, poverty, incarceration, substance dependence, precarity. But his films also revel in events that erupt in the everyday like a tune on the wind, often as unexpected or fortuitous moments of possibility, and Philomac is one such 'event'.

---

8   This aspect of the film is accentuated by the fact that, while the script included several scenes in which Philomac and his mother interact, these scenes were either not filmed or, if they were, did not survive the final edit.

Conclusion

> How, then, do we deal with the Aboriginal dead? … If the Aborigines are to enter our history 'on terms of most perfect equality', as Thomas Mitchell termed it, they will bring their dead with them and expect an honourable burial. Our embarrassment is compounded. Do we give up our cherished ceremonies or do we make room for the Aboriginal dead on our memorials, cenotaphs, boards of honour and even in the pantheon of national heroes? (Reynolds, 2006, p. 202)

The starting point for Henry Reynolds's proposal to include Indigenous names in Australian memorials dedicated to those who died in war is a stark question: 'How, then, do we deal with the Aboriginal dead?' When Reynolds posed that question in 1981, it was, for most white Australians, a puzzling if not challenging question because of the ways in which the (mostly white and male) war dead always died serving Australia in other countries. To talk about those who died in this country defending their Country was, at that time, almost oxymoronic. As the contributions to this volume demonstrate, this is no longer the case, and in fact, there is something of a head of steam, perhaps even a dispersed movement, building in some non-Indigenous communities for colonial violence to be recognised and memorialised. Yet, according to my account, the damage to Country and people associated with Wittenoom, and the continuing disaster of Australian Indigenous people dying in custody, do not evoke much interest in memorials to 'the Aboriginal dead'. There is something in this contrast that invokes the contradictory momentum of reconciliation, something that involves differing investments in truth-telling and particular kinds of history, and differently configured relations between past and present. It brings us back to the question I posed at the beginning of this essay: is the memorialisation of colonial violence a 'white thing'?

Writing in the wake of the murder of George Floyd in the USA, and campaigns in the UK to have the statues of slave traders and others toppled, the journalist and academic Gary Younge (2021) argued that 'every single statue should come down'. Although Younge's case is focused on statues of people and my focus here has been on different forms of memorialisation, some aspects of his arguments are worth considering. He makes the general point that statues are an instantiation of an historical imagination that he associates with a 'Great Men theory of history':

> Statues do not just fail to teach us about the past or give a misleading idea about particular people or particular historical events – they also skew how we understand history itself. (Younge, 2021)

This characterisation joins a substantial body of scholarship concerning the amnesia of statuesque memory that stretches from Proust to James E Young. In his essay, Younge also makes the more specific, empirically based point that most statues are erected long after the death of the person concerned. This is important in relation to the argument that we should not judge the past by the standards of the present. Thus, in the case of the statue of slave trader Edward Colson, Younge observes that it was erected not only more than 150 years after his death in 1721 but a full 60 years after slavery had been abolished in Britain. Younge is, therefore, insisting that those who erected the statue to a slave trader were doing so in a culture in which slavery was understood to be both immoral and illegal. In relation to monuments to the Confederate cause, more than half went up between 1905 and 1912, more than half a century after the end of the American Civil War, when memories of the damage and dishonour of the conflict were less raw. Of course, this allows Younge to make the broader point that statues, like most history-making, 'always tell us more about the values of the period when they were put up than about the story of the person depicted' (Younge, 2021) – or, as Greg Dening was fond of putting it, history-making is about the bound-togetherness of past and present.

I am not suggesting that First Nations peoples in Australia are uninterested in history: that would be an absurd generalisation. Not only is truth-telling central to the program enunciated in the 'Uluru Statement' but also much of the post-1960s cultural renaissance that stretches from Papunya Tula to Boomalli, Blackfella Films and Tony Birch is manifestly invested in historical narratives. However, in the case of the Banjima, and in activism around Australian Indigenous deaths in custody, there seems to be an urgency to deal first and foremost with the ongoing, horrifically present forms of colonial violence. In this impulse, violence to Country and to people does not belong in the past: there is no disconnection between past and present, nothing that needs to be recalled, remembered or uncovered – it is all there to see. When the urge to memorialise colonial violence is a white thing, it is often initiated by a troubling experience – often one involving a younger person: a moment when a sense of their past, their family or local history shifts from having been settled (like the country) to a disturbed or agitated state because of new information or new stories. This presence of the past often calls forth revelations and a desire for that new past to be acknowledged in the present for a reconciliation to take place, for tranquillity to return. However, this is only one interpretation. It may also be that such memorialisation invites the possibility of recognising colonial violence as a part of healing, as Rodney Carter imagines it.

However, there seems to be no easy fit between celebrating freedom fighters, or recalling frontier wars, and the structural violence of mining and incarceration. This dissonance will not be resolved by historians who can adjudicate between truth and justice deferring to the wisdom of 'critical history' (see Attwood, 2019). A better option would be to call forth the kind of Nietzschean 'critical history' being produced by the Banjima and activists around Australian Indigenous incarceration, to 'bring the past to the bar of judgement, interrogate it remorselessly and finally condemn it' (Nietzsche, 1974, p. 28). These efforts might join what has been called the 'here-now' of Australian Indigenous memory, which Collins et al. (2020) describe as:

> [the] undoing of the dead weight of history in a distinctive, postcolonial … configuration of place/time that belongs neither to modernity's 'here and now' nor to what has been variously described as Indigenous Australia's nonlinear, active, continuous or 'deep time'.

Tim Rowse has drawn attention to what he calls the two 'truths' of truth-telling in proposals supporting constitutional recognition: truth-telling in relation to colonisation, and truth-telling about the 'negative effects of colonisation for Aboriginal and Torres Strait Islander peoples *and how that has accumulated across generations*' (Commonwealth of Australia, 2018, in Rowse, 2021, emphasis added). 'Historians are professionally qualified to establish the truths of colonisation', Rowse notes, then asks: 'But who has the authority to generalise about the cumulative malformation of colonised subjectivity?' This is one way to pose the question, but the Victorian Yoorrook Justice Commission, which is less about colonised subjectivity and more about colonial structures, events and systems, frames the question differently. The Commission aims to:

> establish an official record of the impact of colonisation on First Peoples in Victoria using First Peoples' stories. This will be done by inquiring into and reporting on historical systemic injustices perpetrated against First Peoples since colonisation (for example massacres, wars, and genocide) as well as ongoing systemic injustices (for example policing, child protection and welfare matters, health, invasion of privacy and exclusion from economic, social, and political life). (First Peoples – State Relations, 2022)

Time will tell if this produces a monument to colonial violence that is forgotten (again).

References

Allam, L. (2021, 14 July). Family of Aboriginal man who died in custody say Covid restrictions prevented them visiting him. *The Guardian.* theguardian.com/australia-news/2021/jul/14/family-of-aboriginal-man-who-died-in-custody-say-covid-restrictions-prevented-them-visiting-him

Allam, L. & Wahlquist, C. (2020, 13 August). BHP shareholders demand immediate stop to mining that disturbs Aboriginal heritage. *The Guardian.* theguardian.com/australia-news/2020/aug/13/bhp-shareholders-demand-immediate-stop-to-mining-that-disturbs-aboriginal-heritage

Allam, L. & Wahlquist, C. (2021, 24 May). A year on from the Juukan Gorge destruction, Aboriginal sacred sites remain unprotected. *The Guardian.* theguardian.com/australia-news/2021/may/24/a-year-on-from-the-juukan-gorge-destruction-aboriginal-sacred-sites-remain-unprotected

Andrew, B. & Walker, T. (2016). *Standing by Tunnerminnerwait and Maulboyheenner* [Public art installation]. City collection, City of Melbourne.

Asbestos Diseases Society of Australia. (n.d.). *Welcome to the Asbestos Diseases Society of Australia Inc.* asbestosdiseases.org.au/

Attwood, B. (2019). The National Gallery of Victoria's *Colony* and difficult history. *Australian Historical Studies, 50*(1), 99–116. doi.org/10.1080/1031461X.2018.1557225

Bell, R. (2002). Bell's theorem: Aboriginal art – it's a white thing! *Koorie Web.* kooriweb.org/foley/great/art/bell.html

Browning, D. (2019, 20 February). Why it's not OK for just anyone to paint a Wandjina. The Art Show with Daniel Browning. *ABC Radio National.* abc.net.au/radionational/programs/the-art-show/why-its-not-ok-for-just-anyone-to-paint-a-wandjina/10826928

Carlson, B. & Farrelly, T. (2023). *Monumental disruptions: Aboriginal people and colonial commemorations in so-called Australia.* Aboriginal Studies Press.

Cleary, P. (2021). *Title fight: How the Yindjibarndi battled and defeated a mining giant.* Black Inc.

Collins, F. & Davis, T. (2004). *Australian cinema after Mabo*. Cambridge University Press.

Collins, F., Healy, C. & Radstone, S. (2020). Provincializing memory studies: The insistence of the 'here-now'. *Memory Studies, 13*(5), 850. doi.org/10.1177/1750698020946415

Commonwealth of Australia. (2018, November). *Final report of the Joint Select Committee on Constitutional Recognition relating to Aboriginal and Torres Strait Islander Peoples.* aph.gov.au/Parliamentary_Business/Committees/Joint/Former_Committees/Constitutional_Recognition_2018/ConstRecognition/Final_Report

Dja Dja Wurrung Clans Aboriginal Corporation. (n.d.). *Dhelkunya Dja: Dja Dja Wurrung Country Plan 2014–2034.* djadjawurrung.com.au/wp-content/uploads/2015/11/Dja-Dja-Wurrung-Country-Plan.pdf

First Peoples – State Relations. (2022). *Truth and justice in Victoria.* www.firstpeoplesrelations.vic.gov.au/truth-and-justice

Franklin, P., Reid, A., Peters, S., Brims, F., Klerk, N., Olsen, N. & Musk, A. (2016). Malignant mesothelioma in Aboriginal people in Western Australia. *ISEE Conference Abstracts,* 2016(1). doi.org/10.1289/isee.2016.3393

Gibson, D. (Director). (2021). *Incarceration nation.* Bacon Factory Films, Bent 3 Productions, NITV.

Government of Western Australia. (2021, 4 August). *Final closure of Wittenoom nears as Bill returns to Parliament* [Press release]. mediastatements.wa.gov.au/Pages/McGowan/2021/08/Final-closure-of-Wittenoom-nears-as-Bill-returns-to-Parliament.aspx

Grieves, G., Cameron, P., Land, C., Boyce, J. & Loeffler, N. (2014, 31 March). Melbourne conversations: Tunnerminnerwait & Maulboyheenner: Stories & Connections [Panel discussion]. Melbourne Knowledge Week, City of Melbourne. youtube.com/watch?v=fn6s1qF5yDA&ab_channel=MelbourneKnowledgeWeek

Haigh, G. (2006). *Asbestos house: The secret history of James Hardie industries.* Scribe Publications.

Hills, B. (1989). *Blue murder: Two thousand doomed to die, the shocking truth about Wittenoom's deadly dust.* Sun Books.

Land, C. (2014). *Tunnerminnerwait and Maulboyheenner: The involvement of Aboriginal people from Tasmania in key events of early Melbourne.* City of Melbourne. melbourne.vic.gov.au/SiteCollectionDocuments/tunnerminnerwait-and-maulboyheenner.pdf

Langton, M. (2015). *From conflict to cooperation: Transformations and challenges in the engagement between the Australian minerals industry and Australian Indigenous peoples*. [MCA Monograph 7]. Minerals Council of Australia. minerals.org.au/sites/default/files/MCA%20Monograph%207%20-%20From%20Conflic-on%20by%20Professor%20Marcia%20Langton.pdf

Layman, L. & Phillips, G. (2019). *Asbestos in Australia: From boom to dust*. Monash University Publishing.

Macmath, A. (2019, 11–13 November). The Wittenoom legacy [Keynote discussion]. *Asbestos safety 2019 conference*, Perth, Western Australia. asbestossafety.gov.au/sites/default/files/documents/2019-11/DAY%202%20PLENARY.pdf

Manna gums memorial first of its kind. (2021, 16 July). *The Wombat Post*. thewombatpost.com.au/2021/07/16/manna-gums-memorial-first-of-its-kind/

McCulloch, J. (2007). The mine at Baryulgil: Work, knowledge, and asbestos disease. *Labour History, 92*, 113–128. doi.org/10.2307/27516191

NAIDOC. (2021, 20 January). *2021 NAIDOC week theme announced: Heal Country* [Press release]. naidoc.org.au/news/2021-naidoc-week-theme-announced-heal-country

Nietzsche, F. (1974). *The use and abuse of history*. Gordon Press.

Parliament of the Commonwealth of Australia. (1984). The effects of asbestos mining on the Baryulgil community. *Report of the House of Representatives Standing Committee on Aboriginal affairs*. aph.gov.au/parliamentary_business/committees/house_of_representatives_committees?url=reports/1984/1984_pp232a.pdf

Peacock, M. (Presenter). (1978). Asbestos: Work as a health hazard. ABC transcripts. Australian Broadcasting Commission in association with Hodder & Stoughton.

Peacock, M. (2009). *Killer company: James Hardie exposed*. Harper Collins Publishers & ABC Books.

Reynolds, H. (2006). *The other side of the frontier: Aboriginal resistance to the European invasion of Australia*. University of New South Wales Press.

Rio Tinto. (n.d.). *Juukan Gorge* [Press release]. riotinto.com/en/news/inquiry-into-juukan-gorge

Robinson, T. (2022, 22 August). FOI documents reveal Hancock's plan to mine iron ore at asbestos-riddled Wittenoom. *ABC News*. abc.net.au/news/2022-08-22/gina-rinehart-hancock-prospecting-considered-mining-at-wittenoom/101353730

Rowse, T. (2021) The opinions of Indigenous Australians as viewed through a population lens: The reconciliation barometer. *Centre for Aboriginal Economic Policy Research Discussion Paper No. 297/2021*. The Australian National University. caepr.cass.anu.edu.au/research/publications/opinions-indigenous-australians-viewed-through-population-lens-reconciliation

Ryan, K. (2020, 10 December). Ignorant influencers slammed for risking their lives to holiday in asbestos-riddled Wittenoom. *Perth Now*. perthnow.com.au/news/wa/ignorant-influencers-slammed-for-risking-their-lives-to-holiday-in-asbestos-riddled-wittenoom-ng-b881744796z

Sargent, A. (2016, 6 July). Indigenous West Australians have highest death rate for asbestos-related disease: Study. *ABC News*. abc.net.au/news/2016-07-06/indigenous-west-australians-highest-mesothelioma-rate-study/7575240

Scambary, B. (2013). *My Country, mine Country: Indigenous people, mining, and development contestation in remote Australia* (CAEPR Monograph 33). Centre for Aboriginal Economic Policy Research, College of Arts and Social Sciences. The Australian National University. doi.org/10.26530/oapen_459939

Soeberg, M., Vallance, D. A., Keena, V., Takahashi, K. & Leigh, J. (2018). Australia's ongoing legacy of asbestos: Significant challenges remain even after the complete banning of asbestos almost fifteen years ago. *International Journal of Environmental Research and Public Health*, *I*(2), 384. doi.org/10.3390/ijerph15020384

Standen, S. (2021, 4 July). Wittenoom's asbestos mining waste continues to lay unresolved after 55 years. *ABC Pilbara*. abc.net.au/news/2021-07-04/healing-of-banjima-country-at-wittenoom/100216504

Thomas, N. (1999). *Possessions: Indigenous art/colonial culture*. Thames & Hudson.

Thornton, W. (Director). (2017). *Sweet Country* [Feature film]. BunyaProductions.

Toscano, J. (Speaker). (2019, 29 January). Part I: 'The Tunnerminnerwait & Maulboyheenner Saga'. [Video file]. *Tunnerminnerwait & Maulboyheenner commemoration committee.* youtube.com/watch?v=W-YthV-uvp0&ab_channel=PublicInterestsBeforeCorporateInterests-PIBCI

Tranter, D. (Director). (2007). *Wilaberta Jack*. CAAMA Productions.

Wolfe, P. (2006). Settler colonialism and the elimination of the native. *Journal of Genocide Research*, 8(4) (Dec. 2006), 388. doi.org/10.1080/14623520601056240

Younge, G. (2021, 1 June). Why every single statue should come down. *The Guardian*. theguardian.com/artanddesign/2021/jun/01/gary-younge-why-every-single-statue-should-come-down-rhodes-colston

Afterword: Re-membering history at our current juncture

Yin Paradies

> Australia is haunted: a vast colonial aftermath. For generations, layers of damage caused by settler colonisation have been buried under buildings, bitumen, untruths and nationalist agendas, but haunting traumas resurface sooner or later. (Waters, 2021, p. 104)

> Hauntings … are not mere subjective rememberings of a past (assumed to be) left behind (in actuality), but rather, hauntings are the ontological re-memberings, a dynamism of ontological indeterminacy of time-being in its materiality. (Barad, 2019, p. 539)

We live in a human-centric world (sustained by the, largely ignored, living Earth) characterised by artificial scarcity and demand, profit and accumulation, hierarchy, individualism, exploitation, competition, commodification, comparison, judgement, condemnation and alienation, cynicism, craving, fear, anxiety, guilt, shame, greed, control, conformity, coercion, compliance, cruelty, purity, protagonism, protest and popularity. A world underpinned by a cisheteropatriarchal-ableist-ageist-fatphobic-colonial-capitalist-white supremacy-financial-military-political-educational-pharmaceutical-industrial-agricultural-complex based on debt, private property, institutions and nation-states. 'Each time history repeats itself, the price goes up' (Wright, 2011, p. 107), with the lacerating cost of this intensifying cycle of modernity over the past 10 millennia now utterly unfathomable.

How did we get stuck in the present configuration of globalised political-economic, third-order societies characterised by violence embedded in relations of care, informational bureaucracies and the spectacle of modern democratic politics? Societies in which we can barely even conceive of, let alone enjoy, the primordial freedoms of movement (welcome elsewhere), disobedience (without coercion, punishment and retribution) or social transformation (of ossified political assemblages) (Graeber & Wengrow, 2021).

Asking such questions brings the hulking colossus of modernity to historical scholarship, an unwelcome and spurned presence. A visceral reluctance and a perceptual void arise when we seek to re-member history other-wise to the inexorable march of progress. Modern history is ineluctably embroiled in differentiating pasts and futures (Simon & Tamm, 2021), while emplacing the much-tortured present, betwixt. Gesturing towards a postcolonial future (Paradies, 2020) necessarily challenges history as we feel and know it. While we cannot change the past that constitutes us, we can digest and metabolise the broader truths about history into our present and future becomings. Doing so entails examining history, which, of course, is not the same as studying the past (Cowlishaw, 2021).

Eruptions of colonial histories in the present-future (e.g. mass-graves of massacred children in Canada, the repeated destruction of sacred sites in Australia) rupture the central tenet of modern historical time that a 'temporal distance separates past and present' (Simon, 2021, p. 498). A definitive break between colonialism and post-, anti-, de- or ex-colonialism is impossible while we remain enamoured by the myth of processual incremental improvement over time and space.

In this collection, Hayes et al. highlight 'the affective potential of … material remains … to reanimate memory in place' and 'make colonial dispossession more concrete'. What if we embrace the layered materiality of place as the loci of memory-histories? Not as a reanimation of zombified remembering but as the life force of our own being and becoming, acknowledging that 'there is no separation from the place where we live, except for the one made by our own forgetting' (Turner, 2017, p. 248). In other words, we are ever-always surrounded by the 'genealogical ghostscapes' (Waters, 2021, p. 104) of our unacknowledged ancestors. What would it mean to embrace discursive materialities, not as remnants or remains, but as the very manifest fabric upon which we weave history-memories etched in our cells, bones and every part of us (Yunkaporta, 2019)?

AFTERWORD

Through an analysis of representation at a local historical society museum, Dalley and Barnwell contend that we are only beginning to be told of the historical violence and the massacres of Aboriginal people on Australia's colonial frontier. They ask how forgetting-remembering constitutes everyday life, whether through the compartmentalising impacts of manufactured doubt or via consolidated wilful ignorance (Mills, 1997). What of the many generations of Indigenous peoples who have (re)told stories of colonial violence? Where does the beginning of such butchered histories of massacre begin? With the ignored and silenced wailing grief of the surviving victims or the first tentative, politically fraught and contentious forays of the 'history-worker' descended from, and continuing as, colonial perpetrators?

In a similar context, Miller et al. surface the tension of working with communities from within curatorial institutions to strengthen memories. This involves giving through non-transactional exchanges as well as the pleasure of honouring stories that Indigenous peoples have pride in. Rogers also analyses a museum context, specifically the Australian War Memorial, demonstrating that, while some changes are slowly emerging, representations of frontier violence are still resisted through deliberations on the classification of civilians, military, police and warriors in legislation and policy, and, ultimately, what counts as a real war.

Beyond the majority of monuments that 'memorialize the dark deeds of unhinged lunatics driven by rampant ego and raving greed' (Ryan, 2019, p. 76), Gibson et al. (this volume) consider counter-monuments of tragedy shaped by orality, patchy archives, memory-reserves, mutual ignorance and misunderstanding, as place-holders for domination and resistance. They highlight the futility of truth-telling when nobody is listening; the meaninglessness of free speech without the concomitant freedom to be heard. Their suggested move from 'narratives of estrangement' to 'stories of entanglement' is prudent only in material conditions that eclipse both the imbroglio of imperialism and the swirling spectre of further colonial bondage.

Focusing on the historical import of an unassuming rock, Roginski's contribution concerns the repatriation of 38 Indigenous peoples' remains from the Melbourne Museum to a burial site within the Royal Botanic Gardens. Repatriation is shown as a 'compelling performance' palatable to those across the whole political spectrum, while nonetheless holding potential for truth-sharing, protest and calls for reparation, among other things, to flow. Roginski (this volume) finds the potential in this monument to 'disorient, disturb and embarrass settler governments'.

Griffiths grapples with the challenges of interpreting places of 'difficult heritage' and the possibilities represented by reading 'the outback archive': histories and stories imprinted in the land that often seem, to the modern gaze, both maddeningly 'grey' and as ephemeral as the shifting sands. Hurst and Maber invite us into a different form of imprinting – the haptics of muscle-memory through painting and shell-making, propelling us towards recuperated future selves through 'ancestral gestures that have … otherwise inaccessible meanings' (Waters, 2021, p. 110). Such poetic offerings entice us to journey beyond the seductive urge to want ever more history ineluctably inflected with toxic settler-invader modalities.

Healy asks us to consider if the increasing number of non-Indigenous people memorialising colonial history is a 'white thing'. A move to settler innocence (Tuck & Yang, 2012) that is both redemptive and conveniently redirects attention away from ongoing manifestations of colonial violence that are at least as horrific. For example, despite ever-always being our kin, memorials to damaged Country are yet to become trendy in the whitewashed hand-wringing grief about how to honour the Aboriginal dead. Beyond a self-referential politics of deferral, placation, regret and guilt, what real potential for transformation is entailed in the latest treaty-based forms of reconciliation? Will the de rigeur of whiteness ever amount to more than decorative baubles adorning the colonial megamachine?

Judd and Ellinghaus explore what can happen outside the metropolis, when scholars relinquish the ease of disconnection, distance and objectivity to instead engage in the messy emergent complexity of time-places. What learnings can spring forth in a dance of cyclically revisited experiential relationships? Can this cultivate dialogic meaning much richer and more textured than abstractions of evidence, commemoration, repatriation or even decolonisation? Similarly, Krichauff highlights the vital importance and fundamental effect of lived experience and personal connection in how we know, sense and shape the past in nuanced, alive, dynamic ways that can sustain us into the future.

Martin and Pascoe remind us that the living links between colonial violence and contemporary communities continue to this day and in perpetuity, through irrevocable losses of kin, Country, language, ceremony, ritual and knowledge. Beyond straightforward forensic accountings of history, what revelations await in the liminal spaces of inconsistency and unindexability? What strength can be drawn from the simple fact that, despite the crushing weight of coloniality, we, as Aboriginal people, still endure?

Given the many ambivalences, contradictions and paradoxes unearthed in the contributions to the volume, perhaps the time is ripe to focus on extra-colonial histories that do not orbit settler-colonial exploitation, expropriation or domination – histories that instead re-present a narrative for emerging generations of peoples both Indigenous (Konishi, 2019) and Indigenous to place. This may entail a praxis of decolonial history that is unintelligible to the contemporary non-Indigenous intellectual (Anderson, 2020).

If we wish to influence the present and prefigure future potentialities we need to seek guidance from the past, not just what mistakes to avoid but how to foster senseful, happier, meaningful, contented, connected lives through a 'return to the … tried and tested ways of the [deep] past' (Jung, 1965, p. 237). I refer here not to a romanticised unchanging conformist monochrome past where we were all simple hunter-gathers, but the reality of our past as a vastly creative tapestry of societies that consciously 'played' with various forms of sustenance, politics, social structure, art, movement, dwellings, sexuality, gender and so forth, over time scales spanning seasons to year, decades and centuries (Graeber & Wengrow, 2021).

Bryant and Knight (2019) articulate the phrase 'a time of crisis' as a temporalising of temporality, producing an uncanny, elongated, oppressively unprecedented present that appears suspended between past and future, unsupported by the teleology of ascent that, intertwined with crisis from the eighteenth century onwards, usually shapes this temporal relation within modernity. This creates a self-preserving 'crisis ordinariness', marked by an en/foreclosing of futures, in which it is easier to imagine the world's end than an end to the delusion of a successful modernity (Scott, 2014).

What is it about our impoverished universalist understanding of history, shackled as it is by our immersion in presentism, that we struggle mightily even to contemplate how we could transform ourselves locally and contingently within an emerging future (Graeber & Wengrow, 2021)? Born of the same hubris as a declared 'end of history' (Fukuyuma, 1992), alongside a failure to grasp that an unsustainable society has, by definition, no future, our current conceptual imprisonment may, in fact, bring about such an end through the self-destruction of the human species.

Perhaps we need to mature beyond debating whether inviting Indigenous peoples or communities into the process of writing histories will distort historical evidence and, instead, reject the 'epistemic violence inherent in conventional histories' (Anderson, 2020, p. 372). Working with the weave, warp, weft and heft of history is not about pursuing objectivity; rather, it is a call to be 'integrated within a sentient system that is observing itself' (Yunkaporta, 2019, p. 170).

Shibboleths of the present entail a deriding of the (colonial) past ritualised by a cult of barren commemoration, in which seeds of decolonial transformation are unable to sprout. What will happen when history comes for us in a reckoning that is nigh? Our home of material conditions and our hearth of social relations cannot be healed until our existing ways of being, knowing, doing, relating and perceiving are abandoned. In search of future wholeness, we are called to the raw vulnerability of becoming generously lost, to the shedding of old skins, and to the ruptured re-membering of our more awkward, capacious historical ourselves in the 'present future and the future present' (Lempert, 2018, p. 210).

References

Anderson, W. (2020). Decolonizing histories in theory and practice: An introduction. *History and Theory, 59*(3), 369–375. doi.org/10.1111/hith.12164

Barad, K. (2019). After the end of the world: Entangled nuclear colonialisms, matters of force, and the material force of justice. *Theory and Event, 22*(3), 524–550.

Bryant, R. & Knight, D. M. (2019). *The anthropology of the future*. Cambridge University Press. doi.org/10.1017/9781108378277

Cowlishaw, G. (2021). Misreading *Dark Emu*. *Pearls and Irritations: John Menadue's Public Policy Journal*, 15 August. johnmenadue.com/misreading-dark-emu/

Fukuyuma, F. (1992). *The end of history and the last man*. Free Press.

Graeber, D. & Wengrow, D. (2021). *The dawn of everything*. Penguin Books.

Jung, C. (1965). *Memories, dreams, reflections*. Vintage Books, Knopf Doubleday Group.

Konishi, S. (2019). First Nations scholars, settler colonial studies, and Indigenous history. *Australian Historical Studies, 50*(3), 285–304. doi.org/10.1080/1031461x.2019.1620300

Lempert, W. (2018). Generative hope in the postapocalyptic present. *Cultural Anthropology, 33*(2), 202–212. doi.org/10.14506/ca33.2.04

Mills, C. (1997). *The racial contract*. Cornell University Press.

Paradies, Y. (2020). Unsettling truths: Modernity, (de-)coloniality and Indigenous futures. *Postcolonial Studies, 23*(4), 438–456. doi.org/10.1080/13688790.2020.1809069

Ryan, C. (2019). *Civilized to death: The price of progress*. Simon & Schuster.

Scott, D. (2014). *Omens of adversity: Tragedy, time, memory, justice*. Duke University Press. doi.org/10.1215/9780822377023

Simon, Z. B. (2021). Domesticating the future through history. *Time and Society, 30*(4), 494–516. doi.org/10.1177/0961463x211014804

Simon, Z. B. & Tamm, M. (2021). Historical futures. *History and Theory, 60*(1), 3–22. doi.org/10.1111/hith.12190

Tuck, E. & Yang, K. W. (2012). Decolonization is not a metaphor. *Decolonization: Indigeneity, Education & Society, 1*(1), 1–40.

Turner, T. (2017). *Belonging: Remembering ourselves home*. Her Own Room Press.

Waters, S. (2021). A care-full re-membering of Australian settler colonial homemaking traditions. In B. Sliwinska (Ed.), *Feminist visual activism and the body* (pp. 104–120). Routledge, Taylor and Francis Group. doi.org/10.4324/9780429298615

Wright, R. (2011). *A short history of progress*. House of Anansi Press.

Yunkaporta, T. (2019). *Sand talk*. The Text Publishing Company.

Index

Note: Page numbers in italics indicate illustrations. Page numbers with 'n' indicate footnotes.

Aboriginal children, *see* Indigenous children
Aboriginal history, *see* Indigenous history; Wyndham Historical Society Museum, Aboriginal history
Aboriginal peoples, *see* Indigenous peoples
Aboriginal population
    census 123, 149
    decline 123
    physical absence 124, 135, 169
Aboriginal protectors 47, 119, 120, 129, 144, 150, 151, 158, 277
    see also Dredge, William; Parker, Edward Stone; Robinson, George Augustus; Sievwright, Charles; Thomas, William
'Aboriginal Reburial Site', Kings Domain, Melbourne 143, *145*, 154, 159, 160, 291
Aboriginal Tent Embassy 155
Aboriginal women, *see* Indigenous women
Aboriginality 32, 38, 267
    see also First Nations identity
Albrecht, FW 12, 35, 37, 40, 42, 43, 44–46
Alice Springs, *see* Mparntwe
Allambie Children's Home, *see* Kildonan Children's Home

Anmatyerr
    Country 56, 58, 59, 70
    language 58, 59
    people 13, 55–57, 60, 61, 63, 66–69, 73, 74, 76, 78
Arrernte 47, 57, 59, 59n.3, 66, 67, 69, 71, 78
Asbestos Diseases Society of Australia 275
    see also disease, asbestos-related; blue asbestos
assimilation 35, 87
Athimpelengkwe (Baxters Well) 63, 64, *64*, 65, 66
Attwood, Bain 108, 219, 220
Australia Day, *see* Invasion Day
Australian War Memorial
    representation of frontier violence 16–17, 247, 249–253, 255–259, 291

Banjima 272, 273, 274, 275, 276, 282, 283
Baxters Well, *see* Athimpelengkwe
Bell, Jack 93, 96, 97, 97n.11, 98, 98n.12
Berg, Jim 14, 152–154, 156, 159, 160
biography 1, 193, 220, 231, 241
Birch, Tony 11, 155, 156, 158, 282
Bird, Tommy, *see* Mpetyan, Tommy Bird

MEMORY IN PLACE

blackbirding 209
blackfellow, label 75n.12
Blackfellows Bones Bore, see Itarlentye
Black GST 155, 156
   see also Camp Sovereignty
blue asbestos 268, 272
boab trees 13, 106–107, 112, 113, 114
   Retribution Camp boab *105, 106*, 113
Bourke, Richard 148
Bringing Them Home Report 169, 190
Brooks, Fred 61, 62, 63, 65
Brooks Soak, see Rrkwer/Yurrkuru
Brusso, Noah 96
Bullfrog, see Kamalyarrpa Japanangka
Bunurong 146, 149, 150
Burns, Tommy 13, 90–91, 93–94, 96–102
   birth 97
   death 95, 96
   grave *95*
Burns, Tommy (white boxer), see Brusso, Noah

Camp Sovereignty 146, 155, 156, 157, 159
Captain Cook stories 86, 87, 88, 89, 98, 100
care leavers 168, 170, 174, 178, 193
Carter, Rodney 265, 283
Carter, William Moore 117, 120, 121, 122, 122n.1
cattle
   industry 93, 94, 102
   stations 42, 45, 90, 99, 107, 109, 113, 226, 254
   stealing 94, 102
child migrants 167, 168, 171
children's homes, see Kildonan Children's home
collaborative history 3, 12, 36, 39–40, 50, 88, 90, 173, 221, 239–242
Colonial Frontier Massacres in Australia, see Massacres Map

colonial violence 13, 50, 76, 85, 89, 98, 118, 194, 222, 236, 291
   commemoration 56, 58, 130, 170, 265, 267–268, 281–284
   current 18, 270, 282, 292
   dispossession 167, 194, 248
   forgotten 60, 66
   legacy/ongoing effects 18, 99, 100, 131, 134, 167, 292
   Myall Creek 3
   oral history 88
   periodisation 100
   politicisation 88
   research methodologies 99
   truth-telling 99, 101
   see also frontier violence
colonisation
   absence of Indigenous people 124
   Indigenous perspectives 86, 88, 89, 90, 99, 100–101, 219
   legacy/ongoing effects 11, 100, 132, 134, 135, 281
Colony (exhibition) 2, 219, 220
commemoration 9, 15, 60, 156, 249, 252, 265n.1, 276, 292, 294
   colonial violence 130, 267–268
   concept 10
   form 56, 158, 257
   remembering after the fact 17, 267
Commonwealth Games (Melbourne) 155
community memory 118, 123, 126, 127
Coniston massacres 7, 60–63, *62, 65*, 66, 75, 77
   monuments 61, 63, 65, 74, 77
   oral history 64
consensus histories 160, 169, 173
cultural misunderstandings 63, 66, 72, 147, 149
Curr, Edward 85

298

Dale-Hallett, Liza 62
dark history 76, 207
dark tourism, *see* memorialisation
Day, Tanya 278
Delta Downs Station 90, 91, *92*
difficult history 168, 174, 178, 193, 219, 220, 236, 238, 242
disease
  asbestos-related 268, *271*, 271, 272, 275
  introduced 85, 123, 151, 209
dispossession, *see* Indigenous dispossession
Dja Dja Wurrung 146, 265, 269
Dorunda (outstation) 91, 93–96, 93n.5, 97n.10, 98–99, 101
Dredge, William 149, 150

encampment 146, 147, 151, 155, 156, 157, 160
entangled history 13, 73, 77, 78, 169n.1, 291

family history 1, 7, 12, 27, 56, 123, 127, 133, 222, 282
Finniss, Boyle Travers 119
First Nations identity 146, 157
  see also Aboriginality
Foley, Fiona 18, 219
Foley, Gary 155
Forgotten Australians 167, 168, 171, 193
frontier violence
  absence of stories 123
  claims of fabrication 111
  commemoration 16–17, 146, 231, 247, 251–259, 291
  culture 13
  focus on physical violence 128–129, 131, 135
  historiography 248–249
  human remains 151
  Indigenous responses 87, 100, 128, 129, 130

justified 61
legacy 7
massacres 108
means of dispossession 248
memories 13, 56, 58, 59, 222
narrow understanding 16, 118, 128, 129
official responses 128–129
placenames 56, 67, 76, 87, 107, 113
truth-telling 131, 144, 159
ubiquitous 112, 128
see also colonial violence; Australian War Memorial
frontier wars 158, 170, 257, 258, 259, 265, 266, 277, 283

genocide 98, 132, 169, 192, 283
Ghan, The 43
Gilbert, Rolly 86, 87, 88, 98, 100
Gomeroi 254, 256
Gough, Julie 17, 18
Great Australian Silence 222, 249
Grieves, Genevieve 7

Hallett, John 117, 119–122, 124, 132, 133
Hancock, Lang 272, 275, 276
historical archives
  built environment/traces 173–174
  limitations 68
  outback 112, 113, 292
  'terrible gift' 174, 192
  traumatising 42
  unreliable witnesses 8, 42
historical consciousness 118, 123, 126, 127
historical evidence
  Aboriginal oral testimony 68, 69, 88, 112
  absence 78, 86, 88, 109, 124, 173
  buildings 169, 172, 174–175, 192
  bullet shells 112, 113
  destruction 11, 109

'facts' 234, 235, 241
limitations 13
living documents 69, 112
longevity 13, 14
photographs 12, 15, 36–40, 42, 47, 49, 50, 172, 233
privileging of non-Indigenous sources 4, 86, 112
validity 8–9, 220, 240, 242
written/conventional 8, 16, 75, 235
history, *see* biography; collaborative history; consensus history; dark history; difficult history; entangled history; family history; Indigenous history; Indigenous-led history; local history; narrating history; revisionist history; South Sea Islander history; traumatic history; violent history
Historypin 212
History Wars 11, 16, 60, 88, 111, 128, 233, 252
history-workers 220, 231, 234, 240, 241, 242, 291
Hokari, Minoru 90
Holocaust 10
Howard, John 155, 157, 233
human remains 14, 15, 67, 143, 144, 151–154, 152n.3, 158
see also repatriation

Incarceration Nation (film) 278
Indigenous agency 77, 129, 132, 203, 205
Indigenous children 17–18, 167, 169, 171, 183
education 42, 43, 46, 148
kidnapping 85
massacre survivors 98
othering 108
see also Stolen Generations
Indigenous deaths in custody 268, 278, 282

Indigenous dispossession 7, 13, 40, 108, 111, 118, 130, 134, 146–147, 158, 160
colonial 76, 194, 251, 267, 290
frontier violence 248
ongoing 134, 276, 280
Indigenous history
denial 2, 11, 108, 124, 132, 134, 192, 251, 257
forgetting 1, 14, 60, 66, 75, 109, 192, 267, 276, 284, 291
Indigenous-led 36, 240
Indigenous practices of 12, 56, 219
Indigenous mobility 44, 50, 107
Indigenous names, importance of 28, 49, 130, 150
Indigenous peoples, *see* Anmatyerr; Arrernte; Banjima; Bunurong; Dja Dja Wurrung; Gomeroi; Kaytetye; Kulin; Kurtjar; Ngadjuri; Ngaliwurru; Ngarinyman; Puutu Kunti Kurrama and Pinikura; Taungurung; Wadawurrung; Warlpiri; Wirrayaraay; Wurundjeri
Indigenous resistance 66, 72, 76, 87, 100, 108, 111, 125, 128, 130, 254, 276
Indigenous–settler relations 1, 9, 220, 223, 231, 240
Indigenous studies 36, 39
Indigenous women 12, 27–33, 61, 62, 93, 108
abduction 85, 110
shell-work 30–31
interdisciplinarity 9, 10
see also multidisciplinarity
Invasion Day
dawn service 144, 158, 159, 160
Itarlentye (Blackfellows Bones Bore) 56, 67, 68, 69, 71, 74, 75, 77, 78
massacre 70–71, 75
oral history 68, 71, 72
ruins 67

INDEX

Juukan Gorge 269, 270, 272, 276

Kamalyarrpa Japanangka (Bullfrog) 61, 63
Kangaroo Jack, *see* Ngaltya, Pinpa
Kangkinang, Big Mick 109, 110, 111
Kanjamala 13, 108–114
Kaytetye 57, 59n.3, 60, 61, 63, 65, 66
keeping places 14, 16, 143, 154, 158, 204, 203, 240
Kemarr, Paddy Willis 61
Kildonan Children's Home 15, 167, 169–194
    architectural plans 175–178
Kngwarraye, Tommy Thompson 64–65, *65*
Konishi, Shino 5
Kudnatya, Pari 121, 122n.1
Kulin
    confederation 146, 149
    Country 15
    Nation 277
    people 144, 146–151
    see also encampment
Kununurra 106, 224, 230
    rivalry with Wyndham 230
Kurtjar 13, 90, 90n.4, 93
    Country 85, 90, 99
    native title claim *91*, 97n.10
    oral history 87, 97n.10, 98
    people 86, 88, 89, 89n.3, 91, *95*, 98–102
Kurtjarra, *see* Kurtjar

landscape
    archive 3, 11, 12, 13, 63, 69, 111, 112, 144, 158, 213
    imaginative 267
Langhorne, George 148
LaPa, *see* La Perouse
La Perouse 29, 31, 32, 33
La Trobe, Charles 150, 156
Leane, Jeanine 5

Lewis, Darrell 13, 107–114
local history 118, 126, 220–221, 223, 232, 235–237, 239, 240, 242, 282
Lonsdale, William 148
Lydon, Jane 37
Lywenge, Tom 71

Massacres Map 4, 75, 88, 111, 112, 113, 126, 126n.5, 128, 222
    criteria for inclusion 4, 126, 128
material culture 14, 16, 17, 152, 169, 171–172, 175, 179, 181, 193
McKenzie, Queenie 253
Melbourne Museum 14, 291
    see also Museums Victoria; National Museum of Victoria
memorialisation 17, 18, 56, 74, 154, 173, 219, 223, 265–268, 278, 292
    forms of 57, 60, 63, 74–75, 268
    roadside 74
    sites of trauma/violence 2, 7, 61, 170, 281–283
Memories from a Forgotten People (exhibition) 207, 211, 212
memory-lines 56, 77, 78
memory studies 1, 5, 9, 10, 11, 222
Mim, Kylie 153, 159
mobility, *see* Indigenous mobility
monuments
    counter-monuments 7, 59, 75, 291
    massacre 61, 63, 65, 74–75, 77
    removal 58
Morton, Nugget 61
Mount Bryan murders 117–135
Mount Denison Station 61
mourning ritual 71
Mparntwe (Alice Springs) 37, 38, 40, 42, 43, 45
Mpetyan, Tommy Bird 68, 71–74, 76, 77
multidirectional memory 143
multidisciplinarity 3, 36
    see also interdisciplinarity
Mundine, Djon 18

301

Mundy, Godfrey Charles 251, 255, 256
Mounted Police and Blacks (lithograph) 251, 254–257, 259
Murray, William George 61, 62, 63
museum studies 3
Museums Victoria 153, 153n.3
see also Melbourne Museum; National Museum of Victoria
Myall Creek massacre 3, 7, 255
myall, definition 73

Napaljarri 62
narrating history 5, 144, 221, 231–233
National Museum of Victoria 151
see also Melbourne Museum; Museums Victoria
Native Mounted Police (Qld) 85, 97, 98n.12, 258
Native Police Corps (Vic.) 150, 258
neck chains 232, 233, 238
Ngadjuri 14, 114, 117, 121, 123–125, 127, 130, 134
Ngaliwurru 13, 108, 109
Ngaltya, Pinpa (Kangaroo Jack) 120, 121
Ngarinyman 106, 109, 113
Nicholson-Brown, Vicki 155, 156
Nunn, James 254, 255, 256

oral history 9, 56, 74, 86–89, 97n.10, 98, 100–101, 109, 118, 135
    criticisms 88–89, 235, 236
    memories of frontier violence 59–60, 64, 68, 69, 71, 72, 77, 237
    relationship to other evidence 75, 88, 112, 113, 127, 172, 175, 236, 241, 256
orphanage, *see* Kildonan Children's Home
Overland Telegraph Line 59

Parker, Edward Stone 149, 150
Parker, Maitland 274–275
Pascoe, Fred 89–91, *91*, 93–95, 97–102
Penangk, Ken Tilmouth 68, *69*, 70, 71, 72, 74, 76, 77
Phelps, PH 12, 27, 29
photography 9, 36–38, 47
see also historical evidence, photographs
phrenology 15, 151
Plantation Voices (exhibition) 15, 199, 203, 205–208, 211–214, 216
poddy-dodging, *see* cattle, stealing
Port Phillip Association 147–148
Puutu Kunti Kurrama and Pinikura 269

Queensland Museum 200, 201, 203, 212

Radke, Olga 40, 42
relationality 12, 36, 39, 40, *48*, 48, 49
repatriation 16, 144, 152–154, 156, 160, 201, 203–206, 291, 292
see also human remains
resilience 13, 77, 199, 206
retribution 107, 108, 110, 113, 290
see also boab trees, Retribution Camp boab
revisionist history 125, 131–132, 134
Robinson, George Augustus 149, 150, 277
Rodinga Siding 43
Rowse, Tim 283
Royal Botanic Gardens (Melbourne) 143, 147, 148, 160, 291
Royal Commission into Aboriginal Deaths in Custody 278
Rrkwer/Yurrkuru (Brooks Soak) 61, 63
Ryan, Lyndall 4, 88, 111, 112, 222
see also Massacres Map

Scullion, Nigel 60
settler colonialism 1, 11, 36, 37, 151, 192, 279
settler descendants 7, 101, 118, 123–124, 126–127, 131–134, 220, 232, 247
Shrine of Remembrance 143, 146, 156
Sievwright, Charles 149, 150
Slaughterhouse Creek massacre, *see* Waterloo Creek massacre; *Ruby Plains Massacre I* (painting)
Slowgrove, Margaret 27
South Sea Islander
  history 199, 203, 216
  people 15, 199, 200, 202, 203, 205–213
sovereignty 144, 154, 160, 268, 276
  see also Camp Sovereignty
Spencer, Walter Baldwin 151
Stolen Generations 17–18, 43, 131, 167, 168, 169, 171, 192, 193
Stolenwealth Games 155
Strehlow, TGH 56n.2, 71
Stuart Highway 57, 58, 60, 63, 71
Stuart, John McDouall 59
subservience, academic researcher 48–49
Sweet Country (film) 268, 276, 278, 279, 280

Taungurung 146, 149
Thomas, Rover (Joolama) 17, 253, 254, 256
  Ruby Plains Massacre I (painting) 253, 254, 256
Thomas, William 149, 150, 151
Thorpe, Lidia 158, 159
Thorpe, Marg 155
Thorpe, Robbie 155, 156
Thwaites, John 155
Tilmouth, Ken, *see* Penangk, Ken Tilmouth
Titjikala 38, 43, 44, 45

trauma 2, 7, 8, 10, 15, 42, 112, 167, 192, 202
  see also traumatic history
traumatic history 2, 69, 199, 207
Truganini 152, 277
Trugernana, *see* Truganini
truth-telling 2, 3, 17, 36, 135, 144, 160, 221, 242, 281, 291
  challenges 90
  colonial violence 99–101, 158–159
  local stories 7, 69
  talking cure 76
  Uluru Statement from the Heart 6, 9, 58, 88–89, 112, 282–283
Tunnerminnerwait *277*, 277

Uluru Statement from the Heart 6, 9, 58, 88, 89, 112, 282–283

Victoria River District 106, 108–110
Victorian Aboriginal Legal Service 152, 153, 156

Wadawurrung 146
Warlpiri 57, 59, 59n.3, 60–63, 65, 66, 75
Waterloo Creek massacre 254, 255, 256
  see also Ruby Plains Massacre I (painting)
Watson, Jack 108, 110
White Gloves Experience 213, *214*
  see also Plantation Voices (exhibition); South Sea Islanders
white guilt 40
Willshire, William 56, 66, 68, 108, 109, 110
  staged photographs 47
Wilson, Lorna 12, 37, 40–49, *41*, *45*
Windschuttle, Keith 60, 111–112
Wirrayaraay 3
Wittenoom 268, 269, 271–276, 281
Wolfe, Patrick 280

Wurundjeri 146, 149, 150
Wyndham 16, 220, 224, 226, 229–231, 233
Wyndham Historical Society Museum 223–226, *225*, *227*, *228*, 230, 236, 240–242, 256
    representing Aboriginal history 233, 234, 235, 239, 240

Yoorrook Justice Commission 88, 158, 283

www.ingramcontent.com/pod-product-compliance
Lightning Source LLC
Chambersburg PA
CBHW052045220426
43663CB00012B/2451